Shandyism

THE CHARACTER OF ROMANTIC IRONY

PETER CONRAD

Shandyism

THE CHARACTER OF ROMANTIC IRONY

BARNES & NOBLE
BOOKS
10 East 53d St., New York 10022
(a division of Harper & Row Publishers, Inc.)

Published in the U.S.A. 1978 by HARPER & ROW PUBLISHERS,
INC., BARNES & NOBLE IMPORT DIVISION

ISBN 0 06 491267 1
Library of Congress Catalog Number 78-52487
Printed in Great Britain

Contents

Preface

This is a book less about than around *Tristram Shandy*. I have set out to find various, interlocking contexts for it in the art of its period, and in relating it to its aesthetic surroundings have attempted to suggest its romantic quality. In the history of the novel it seems fated to remain in exile as a sport, or at best to be allowed the impudent negative status of an "anti-novel", perpetually in opposition. But if considered in relation to the history of romanticism, which extends over many literary forms and beyond literature into painting, architecture and music, *Tristram Shandy* acquires a complicated and central significance which makes it genuinely original, not merely exhibitionistically new, and a source of originality in others, anticipating in comedy the ethics and aesthetics of romantic poetry.

Shandyism refers to a character and a form: to an inspirationally erratic individual and the chaotic structure he inhabits. This book begins by deriving both the character of Tristram and his collapsed, wayward form from a romantic recomposition of Shakespeare. Romanticism discovers its source in Shakespeare, and Sterne's romantic originality consists in his rearrangement of the vexed Shakespearean relation of tragedy and comedy, which for him are no longer literary forms but reflexes of moods, paradoxically interchangeable. From this similitude between tragedy and comedy comes irony, the visionary composite expounded by Sterne's German critics.

Shandyean character and form are equally introverted: the novel becomes an image of mind, and tragedy and comedy its alternate, capricious whims. The subversive character and its antic, associative form are related to a number of aspects of emerging romantic culture. *Tristram Shandy* is implicated in the history of virtuosity and that of libertinism. The two histories are interdependent. The virtuoso is close to the libertine, since he exists by taking liberties with texts and forms, and romanticism subjects both to a Shandyean introversion: they change from collectors – the virtuoso of curios, the libertine of conquests – into explorers, self-involved Shandyean fantasists. *Tristram Shandy* is then aligned with those aesthetic speculations of Sterne's contemporaries which shape the theory of romantic art: Hogarth's serpentine line of beauty, which curls through Tristram's mis-shapen narrative; Burke's sublimity, which Shandyean irony miniaturises; and Fuseli's introversion of pictorial genres, for which he was attacked as a libertine of painting.

Finally, *Tristram Shandy's* metamorphoses in German criticism demonstrate its transformation into a sacred text of romanticism. Jean Paul Richter, Lichtenberg, Heine, Friedrich Schlegel and Schopenhauer describe the fulfilment of its apparently perverse prophecies in the later history of romantic art and the justification of its madness as a method of visionary perception. Gustav Mahler, returning the argument to its beginning in the tragicomic Shakespeare, admires *Tristram Shandy* for its macabre, disproportionate interfusion of tragedy and comedy. But whereas the romantics had found this hybrid form characteristic of a versatile, dexterous, sentimentally agile mind, for Mahler it is an image of mental instability and the obsessive improprieties of consciousness.

1

Mental Space

Change in English literature derives its pattern from the quizzical relations between tragedy and comedy. Shakespeare's fusion of the opposite forms creates an enigma which the writers of each subsequent period fret to understand and to imitate. But whereas Shakespeare holds in balance tragic pain and comic fecklessness even while intertwining them, his successors in attempting such a union find tragedy and comedy blurring into an ambiguous composite: instead of tragicomedy, the seventeenth century produces satire, the eighteenth century sentiment, the nineteenth century irony.

The character of Tristram Shandy and the form of his novel lie between these three variants of tragicomedy. Against the self-disgust of satire, Sterne proposes a sentimental reconciliation of the mind to its own truancy, the body to its own debilities. Sentiment, romantically interpreted, becomes irony in the next century: not enjoyably painful acquiescence in mental and physical limitations, which is Tristram's philanthropical eighteenth-century meaning as a sentimentalist, but visionary dissolution of those limits, which is his philosophical nineteenth-century meaning as an ironist. Sentiment and irony both, as this chapter will argue, have their origins in Shakespeare's dangerous alliances between tragedian and clown and in his hybrid form. The sentimental Tristram is alternately tragic and comic, sometimes piteous, sometimes absurdly frail; the ironic Tristram is simultaneously tragic and comic, an aspiring spirit weighted by the sad necessities of physical embodiment. Sterne recomposes Shakespeare's collisions between tragedy and comedy, which occur in the congested social space of drama, inside the mind where, instead of remaining in argumentative opposition, tragedy and comedy merge. The drama's social amplitude has contracted into the claustrophobic mental space of the novel[1] and the romantic lyric.

Romantic criticism made a god of Shakespeare, absent and

abstract, and as this deification proceeded his comedy was subdued to his tragedy which in turn was made into spiritual allegory. From theatrical action, from the bustle and verbal agility which are the energy of comedy, the romantics transfer Shakespeare's characters to a dim realm of spirit where Lamb can detach the souls even of Macbeth, Richard III and Iago from their criminal designs and emphasise the purely intellectual adventurousness which "prompts them to overleap these moral fences".[2] Making the tragic heroes spiritual athletes exercising in the air was a prelude to the Victorian interpretation of them (institutionalised by A.C. Bradley) as exemplary victims of the march of mind, exterminated because their idea of themselves is too costly and partial for the lucid universe to entertain. The nineteenth century moves serenely towards Bradley's invention of a genre of Shakespearean tragedy, a ghostly Hegelian paradigm which spiritually unites the heroes and reduces the differences between them to local accidents.

But there is no Shakespearean tragedy. There are only the tragedies; and they are special extensions of comedy. When Yeats called Hamlet and Lear gay,[3] he meant that they possessed a frenzied elation, rejoicing in their own destruction. He should have said that, in one important sense, they are merely laughable. Johnson saw that comedy was Shakespeare's instinct, tragedy his skill, something to be worked at.[4] The tragedies grow from comedy. Hamlet became a romantic cult-figure at the expense of his humorous versatility. Coleridge admitted to having a smack of Hamlet in him,[5] but he had instead a smack of Tristram Shandy, that other self-absorbed and encyclopaedic procrastinator who is a comic Hamlet, truer to the character's irreverence and mental mobility than the pale, drooping misfit of the nineteenth century. Sterne at least saw that Hamlet was funny, and it is precisely this which creates the play's problem. He is a wit and a creature of the theatre, compelled to renounce word games, plots and amateur theatricals for tragic action, and unable to make the sacrifice.

If Hamlet is a comic character miscast in a tragic role, Othello is a man with a tragic idea of himself punished by being made to act out a comedy of cuckolding: an exotic warrior penned in a world of domestic gossip, handkerchiefs, warm gloves and nourishing dishes. Both he and Iago are shamed by comedy. Iago's malevolent response at the quay when Cassio and Desdemona laugh off his railing and discount him as a fool, a cynical zany, exactly anticipates Othello's murderously excessive response to Desdemona's infidelity. Killing her is his way back from this grimy comedy into sombre tragedy, though Emilia is waiting at the end to call him gull and dolt. Killing himself is his way out of this cruel, comic accusation. Lear too begins with the tragic determination to crawl towards death, but the terrible farce through which he is forced reveals in him an extraordinary capacity for life, a boundless resilient vitality. From his initial senescence he grows backwards, as Falstaff claims to do, to the juvenile strength at which he himself marvels when he kills Cordelia's hangman.

Shakespeare's precarious fusion of tragedy and comedy could not be extended or repeated. Satire originates in the seventeenth century, as the novel does in the eighteenth, as the middle form lying between tragedy and comedy. But whereas the origin of the novel is a Shakespearean attempt to amplify, creating the collision of opposites which Schlegel thought central to romantic art, in the seventeenth century the intermediary form emerges not from collision but from collapse. Tragedy and comedy founder into one another: meeting in the middle, they produce satire. The Shakespearean double plot creates space for both tragic characters to undertake their perilous journeys and comic characters to look after themselves: the two meet, but in a mutual incomprehension (the sort of situation Sterne revives) which is moving and complete. The tragic king worries about the fool catching cold, the fool turns tragic madness into a nursery rhyme. They go off their separate ways, you that way, we this, as the direction is given at the end of *Love's Labour's Lost*. In Jacobean plays the same confrontations between tragedy and comedy occur, but instead of opening up an expanse of dramatic territory so ample that people can live in it without understanding one another, like Othello and Desdemona, the oppositions constrict. Tragedy and comedy begin to look alike, and their similitude is satire.

Tragedy teeters into satire: maintaining integrity is now possible only by deceit, rapacity or an aesthetic frigidity. Being true to one's self becomes being true to one's lie about oneself, braving it out like Webster's Vittoria in court. The setting is apt, for these are characters on trial: the plays do every cunning and reductive thing in their power to expose them. The tragic character is an embattled defendant whose only hope lies in the fortification of pretence. Shylock's trial is different, for though it begins like a Jacobean prosecution of a caricature, in destroying him it makes him unexpectedly and dangerously tragic.

Comedy is envenomed into satire, and becomes an exaction of penalties, which Shakespeare so often waives. Freedom is the essence of Shakespearean comedy. The character can contradict himself, and the dramatist even allows him to contradict the play, as Falstaff does the political drama or Hamlet the revenge play or Cleopatra the sternness and dedication of Roman history. But necessity overtakes comedy in the seventeenth century, imprisoning the characters in a satiric conception of themselves from which there is no escape or appeal. The corporeal self-satisfaction of Falstaff becomes a system of humours, medically diagnosed and statically predictable; satire is a corruption or vilification of tragedy because it twists tragic aspiration into self-loathing; it is the revenge of the fastidious, tight-lipped spirit against the body in which it is caged, and in the eighteenth century sentimentalism challenges satire as an uprising of the Falstaffian comic body against the prim disgusted satiric spirit. Sterne's sermon on the Levite and the Concubine demands that the punitive bitterness of satiric wit give way to generosity and benevolence, and Sterne comically heals and indulges the body the satirists had scourged for its foulness.

Satirists are alien and suspect in Shakespeare. Iago's chattering prose diminishes the eloquence of Othello, but Iago's is a small idea – suffer cuckoldry as everyone else does – against which Othello's sacrifice of Desdemona to his wounded honour has a perverse nobility and dignity. Thrusting the situation into tragedy seems better than suffering it to decline into satire. Satirist and clown stalk one another uneasily in Shakespeare's comedies. Feste, the unattached itinerant plaintive clown, is the particular enemy of the puritan satirist Malvolio because the fool has a social freedom Malvolio, as a climber, envies. In *Twelfth Night*, the rivalry is social: Malvolio resents the special privileges Feste enjoys in the household. In *As You Like It*, which is set in no household but in a bitter exposed landscape, the rivalry is accordingly not competitively social but stark and elemental. The fool differentiates himself from the clown Corin: the shepherds are solemn and penurious, unable to see that even their dignity in love and in offering their frugal hospitality is "mortal in nature" and thus "mortal in folly". But both the fool's vision of the "strange capers" of men and the clown's unselfaware exemplification of them are differentiated from the position of the satirist, sour, quarrelsome, an enemy to his own peace of mind. The fool is nimble, opportunistic, forever changing from gravity to flippancy; the satirist has a dogged, diseased single-mindedness. The fool's ingenuity lies in the rapidity of his changes and his ability to tease or disconcert by dodging from one attitude to its opposite; the satirist's ingenuity lies in his ability to turn even pleasure to his savage advantage: Jaques boasts of sucking "melancholy out of a song, as a weasel sucks eggs". Touchstone's is a vision of men absurdly colliding with blunt objects and demeaning obstacles: the batter for beating washing, the cow's dugs milked by chapped hands, the peascods. Jaques's is a vision of men horridly aping beasts: "that they call compliment is like the encounter of two dog-apes".

The satirist envies the fool's licence. The coat of motley frees him from the consequences of his railing; he is sainted and protected. The liberty the fool is granted as his only weapon against the slights of wise men the satirist demands as a special charter. Jaques takes up the medical pretension which, from Volpone and Mosca posing as quacks administering medicine to a plague-ridden populace, yet aware that "to be a fool born is a disease incurable", to Swift's racking of the body as if in an anatomy lesson in the grotesque stretchings and tortured contractions of *Gulliver's Travels*, is the uniform of the satirist. Folly is no longer a Shakespearean or Erasmian universal heritage but a crime or special affliction demanding violent treatment:

> I will through and through
> Cleanse the foul body of the infected world,
> If it will patiently receive my medicine.

Although the satirist hopes for a professional immunity by adopting the role of white-coated consultant, rending his victims for their own good, the Duke's reply is that in chiding others for their sins he is simply indulging his own at second hand, disgorging new poison into the general world rather than curing an infection which already exists there. The satirist tries to make revulsion from his own physical nature clinical and antiseptic, a professional stance of calculated severity; he tries to pass off self-hatred as social criticism.

The Duke unmasks Jaques as a libertine who has himself been brutishly sensual, compounded of embossed sores and headed evils. Satire is diagnosed as the rake's vicious revenge on a body his own dissipations have wasted and on those others who still possess the capacity for pleasure. The Duke has delivered a rebuttal in advance of Restoration and Augustan satire.

Late in the eighteenth century, as Sterne makes Shakespearean folly both a personal virtue and a philanthropic value, the satirist is divested of his armoury of darts and hurtful aspersions.[6] Hannah More disapprovingly enumerates them in *Sensibility: A Poetical Epistle*:

> The hint malevolent, the look oblique,
> The obvious satire, or implied dislike;
> The sneer equivocal, the harsh reply,
> And all the cruel language of the eye;
> The artful injury, whose venom'd dart,
> Scarce wounds the hearing while it stabs the heart;
> The guarded phrase whose meaning kills, yet told,
> The list'ner wonders how you thought it cold;
> Small slights, contempt, neglect unmix'd with hate,
> Make up in number what they want in weight.
> These, and a thousand griefs minute as these,
> Corrode our comfort, and destroy our ease.[7]

Reduced as here to ill-mannered unsociability, satire gives place to the "Sympathy Divine" of sensibility, and as this happens the libertine acquires new meanings. Molière's Don Juan is a knowing satirist, but Mozart's Don Giovanni is a man of sentiment, a hero of voracious sensibility. Wycherley's Jack Horner shares the medical pretensions of Jaques and employs a quack as an inverted pimp, who procures victims for the libertine by reporting him to be a eunuch. Horner, however, becomes what he pretends to be: he is a maimed satirist who congratulates himself on possessing "not only a cure, but an antidote for the future against that damned malady, and that worse distemper, love, and all other women's evils". He is not a comedian but a parody of a tragic hero, not purged and altered by suffering but surgically adjusted and immune to it. In contrast, the damaged Tristram Shandy, a libertine because he cannot help himself and is no more able to control the motions of his physical extremities than the streamy flux of his thoughts, is a reincarnation of the Shakespearean fool, battered, vulnerable, attaining wisdom as he disclaims it.

Satire makes the Shakespearean double plot an engine of public warfare, as the satirist claims prerogatives of tragic insight and revenges himself on the thoughtless comedians. Sentiment, however, introverts the double plot: rather than a device of ideological disagreement, it has become an image of private paradox. Tragedy and comedy are no longer modes of action but aspects of the same heteroclite character, not generic means for classifying character but atmospheres revealing the character's variable sense of itself. Once sentiment has made tragedy and comedy unstable subjective preferences – the man of feeling alternates between them, sometimes morbidly piteous, sometimes frivolously elated, sometimes Hamlet and sometimes Falstaff – irony, the romantic extension of sentiment, could rediscover their equivalence. Like satire, irony is an ambiguous tragicomedy: but whereas satire twists each component parodically into the shape of the other, irony reconciles them by making each the wry, wise image of the other. The tragedians are comic, because they enjoy their deaths, and seize the opportunity for redemptive self-dramatisation, as Hamlet and Othello do; the comedians are tragic, because they helplessly and hopelessly acquiesce in human limitation.

Sentiment finds a likeness, and irony an identity, between

the tragic Hamlet and the comic Falstaff, who together make up Tristram Shandy. Apparently opposed, the tragic mind against the comic body, the chafing ineradicable intellectual being against comfortable, contented absorption in the flesh, Hamlet and Falstaff are secretly alike. Both turn from the activity and self-exertion of the classical hero towards a romantic state of self-forgetfulness, which they approach by different disciplines – Hamlet by absention, Falstaff by over-indulgence; Hamlet by painfully piercing through the flesh to free himself from it and the nauseous unceasing conscious life it imposes, Falstaff by sinking down through the flesh to that profound carelessness and inanition in which Dickens's most impenetrable characters reside, and into which Rossini willed himself when he gave up art to devote himself to eating. The way up and the way down are the same, asceticism has the same end as indulgence. The oriental pampering of the sense, cushioning the nerves in soft yielding fabrics, which Wagner demanded in his domestic arrangements, were, as he explained to Liszt, not gross and carnal but a means of spiritual detach-ment from the body's importunities: "if I am once more to renounce reality, . . . my fancy must at least be helped, my imaginative faculty supported. . . . My excitable, delicate, ardently craving and uncommonly soft and tender sensibility must be coaxed in some ways if my mind is to accomplish the horribly difficult task of creating a non-existent world."[8] This is Falstaff as Hamlet might have defended him; and indeed Wagner's conviction that the state owed him a living which he would repay by the creation of his works of art is close to the political philosophy of Falstaff, who believes that the Lan-castrians owe him a living, even a position of privilege, in return for his creation of the work of art which is himself.

Romantically interpreted, both Hamlet and Falstaff are moving towards that mystic state of extinction of will which Schopenhauer described and into which Wagner projected his Tristan and Isolde. Here tragedy and comedy meet: once a character has been released from the snare of will and aban-doned the desire for life, death has become an object of desire – as it is for Tristan and Isolde – and has lost both its sting and its meaning because one can die by wishing to, "cease upon the midnight with no pain", and descend into the numbness and prostration of the inert, Lethean Hamlet or Falstaff babbling of green fields. Having become voluntary, death is no longer final. Resurrection is always possible: Falstaff gets to his feet at Shrewsbury, Isolde levitates. Romantic characters arrogate to themselves the power of life and death, creating a world of absolute imaginative freedom for themselves to inhabit.

In the crowded space of the Shakespearean play, this area of private fantasy resents the encroachments of the dramatist's notions of form and his requirement of action. The disagreement is resolved by the Sternean novel, which fulfills the dream of the Shakespearean egotist: *Tristram Shandy* is Hamlet's longed-for realm of liberty where, bounded in a nutshell, he can count himself a king of infinite space. *Tristram Shandy* has this very combination of formal compression and associative infinity. The Shakespearan forms are less accommodating. Hamlet and Falstaff both find themselves in the wrong plays, but this only encourages their stubborn self-consistency. Maurice Morgann discerned in Falstaff a detachment and purposelessness which prefigure the romantic interpretation of Hamlet: "He was not involved in the fortune of the Play; he was engaged in no action which, as to him, was to be completed; he had reference to no system, he was attracted to no center."[9] As a self-protective jester he is excluded from the worlds of chivalric honour and political necessity, just as Hamlet – another jester, concerned with preserving the kingdom of his mind as Falstaff is the sovereign realm of his flesh – is from the world of obligatory vendetta. Falstaff "passes thro' the Play", Morgann says, "as a lawless meteor", but the play withstands and eventually expels him. Likewise, Hamlet's challenge to the assumptions of the play is entertained at teasing length but at last dismissed. Shakespeare delights in compromising his forms but never entirely disrupts them, as Sterne and the romantics do to suit the convenience of their lawless characters.

Romantic critics conjured up in Shakespeare the "intuitive and mighty sympathy", as Hazlitt called it,[10] of the man of feeling, who self-effacingly suffers all creatures to live through him. This "innate universality", in Keats's phrase,[11] is the highest moral quality of the sentimentalist. But Keats's notion of the empathetic Shakespeare informing identities other than

his own describes not Shakespeare but Keats's own Sternean
inquisitiveness, burrowing into sensations and secret perceptions. Shakespeare, on the contrary, is not sublimely
impartial, but often seems almost indifferent to his characters.
In cases like Hamlet and Falstaff, he virtually disowns them,
encouraging their defiance of their plays only to desert them
when they most need him. He has the distance of a dramatist,
not the romantic mental intimacy of a novelist. His is the
dramatist's relation to his characters, fickle, discontinuous and
manipulative, because those characters exist to serve a form
which, however subtle and manifold its meanings might be,
knows itself to be a game, a play, something which happens,
not fixed and everlasting. Romantic hymns to Shakespeare's
"capacious soul" have the purpose of converting him into a
poetic novelist, whose insight is everywhere, who understands all and reconciles all – they turn him, as it were, into
Sterne. Sentiment begets irony, the gentle remote knowing
play of perception over the world; and irony, Kierkegaard
said, is the incognito of the moralist. Sterne in the sermon on
the Levite and the Concubine opposes the self-preening intellectual superiority of satiric wit to the absent, ironic moralism
of the sentimentalist, "so pure and abstracted from persons",
and the invisibility of god-like forbearance which the
romantics wished on Shakespeare corresponds to this incognito.

The irresolution of Hamlet and the voracity of Falstaff meet
in Tristram Shandy, whose career is as obstructed and
accident-ridden as theirs. But they are victims of dramatic
incongruity, made to share the crowded space of a play with
people utterly and fatally different from themselves. Tristram,
on the other hand, explores at leisure the vast mental space of a
novel, and his accidents – his entangling himself in systems, his
inability to resist detours – derive from his enjoyment of that
freedom. He inhabits a lawless world (he defies Horace's rules,
and everyone else's), while Hamlet and Falstaff, lawless themselves, are hemmed in by the rigid social law which places
Fortinbras and the steely Hal on the throne.

The romantic theory of comedy begins from this disparity
between character and form. Whereas the comedy of the Jon-
sonian tradition, in Restoration drama and Augustan satire,

counts on reducing its victims to a state of disabled objectivity, depriving them of their freedom simply by the vicious epigrammatic act of naming them, romantic comedy recognises a painful or lyrical subjectivity which will not be cramped inside the numb, unfeeling comic object. In doing so, it vindicates Hamlet and Falstaff. Its generosity is Shakespearean: even the addled Sir Andrew Aguecheek was adored once too. As the romantic critic E.T.A. Hoffman saw, Shakespearean humour is the protest of the sentimental subject against a reality which confines it: "The feeling of disparity between the inner spirit and all the external mundane activity about it, brings forth the morbid excess of irritation which breaks out in bitter, scornful irony. . . . Such characters are the fool in *Lear*, Jaques in *As You Like it*, but the supreme example of them is doubtless the incomparable Hamlet."[12] Hamlet then is a humorist, a metaphysical comedian insisting that he has that within him which passes show, and passes the various roles the play tries to fit him into; most of all he is averse to the humourless role of revenger, which can be made mordantly satiric but which restricts the whimsical liberty of the comedian.

The humorist is a hedonist. His fancies have a charmed pointlessness, they are wit indulged and enjoyed in an epicurean mood. Hoffman's emphasis is misplaced in that he mentions only the bristling irritation of Shakespeare's characters. There is also the excess of playfulness and sheer irrelevance which makes Falstaff so subversive, since his political and military society depends for its survival on the classification of individuals, their submission to their necessary roles. Coleridge implies a relation between this kind of character and the newly elastic Sternean form in notes on wit and and humour prepared for a lecture is 1818.[13] Here he transfers the ludicrous, with its suggestion of Shandyean game-playing, from the reason or moral sense, which are the superintendents of satire, to the fancy; and in doing so he argues that "the laughable is *its own end*". The merely laughable is no more than a matter of disproportion, an action misfiring, an absurb miscalculation. Coleridge distinguishes this from genuine humour which he calls, in tribute to Sterne's German follower Jean Paul Richter, an awareness of "a finite in relation to the infinite". The crude inappropriateness of comedy has been translated into a metaphysical vision. Sterne above all other humorous writers delights "to end in nothing, or a direct contradiction", and this habit of expiring into inconclusiveness passes from comedy to lyricism, becoming a philosophical gesture in romantic poetry. Romantic lyrics, like Shandyean humour, either fade into regretful uncertainty or else salvage a meaning with determined jaunty irrelevance, as Wordsworth does as he strides out of "Resolution and Independence": "'God', said I, 'be my help. . .'". Like the humorist, the romantic poet irresistibly generalises, often from the frailest of evidence. This is the source of the unquiet, demanding movement in Keats's odes, attempting only half-successfully to persuade themselves that they have derived from the nightingale or the urn a consolatory meaning these objects cannot offer. They exemplify the mental motions of Coleridge's humorous man, a person, like Hamlet, of "disproportionate *generality*",[14] who universalises his hobby-horse.

Coleridge's characterisation of Hamlet joins the humorous divagations of Sterne with the lyrical introspection of romantic poetry. His Hamlet is a redeemed Tristram Shandy, in whom the wayward, suspect Sternean morality has been brought under the tutelage of a noble nature. Coleridge's Hamlet is not simply indolent and inept, like Tristram, but "vacillates from sensibility". His mental activity has the superfluity of art, not the resolved direction of thought, and this introspective genius disqualifies him from participating in the action of the play, which despite its urgency is less real than the contemplative calm inside him. Unwilling, like Tristram, to take care of this fate in the world outside him, he too is claimed by accident: he "delays action till action is of no use, and dies the victim of mere circumstance and accident". Sermonising on the drunkenness of the Danes, Hamlet, Coleridge says, "runs off from the particular to the universal, and, in his repugnance to personal and individual concerns, escapes as it were, into generalization". Though this generalising abstracts him into tragedy, it is the same act of imagination which Tristram performs in comedy. The notes on comedy insist, "Each part by right of humoristic universality, a whole. Hence the digressive spirit not wantonness, but the *very form* of his genius". In Tristram digression is wanton, an image of the hunger for experience of the eternally digressing or detouring sensual pilgrim, like the picaresque Don Juans of Mozart and Byron. In the romantic Hamlet, disgression is redeemed as the motion of wool-gathering thought, not distraction-seeking sense. But Tristram and Hamlet both subordinate the form of the works in which they appear to the form of their own associative genius: the connection between the various stations of this diffuse course, Coleridge says, "is given by the continuity of the characters". Hamlet and Tristram constitute worlds which they then explore at their leisure, the "utmost slowness" of the unfolding of action in the play corresponding to the arrested, revolving, regressive procedure of the novel. Dilatory and self-gratifying, with whims of iron they force the works which enclose them to surrender to their rambling convenience. Their moral and aesthetic libertinism will be discussed in the third and fourth chapters of this book.

The progress from Tristram to the romantic version of Hamlet has made Shandyean obsession into a metaphysical freedom of the ego. Humour and lyrical speculation both release the soul into a gratuitous exercise which at once enlarges and diminishes consciousness, giving its random movements the poise and grace of art but, in Sterne, trivialising them by making them predictable, governed by a captious ruling notion. The rider on the hobby-horse becomes the romantic poet, making egotism sublime but recognising as well the imperfections and forlornness of the ego and longing for its effacement, for the selfless certainty of negative capability. Vacillating in this way between prophetic self-assertion and empathetic self-effacement, the romantic poet is necessarily an ironist, flickering like Hamlet between the imperial scope of the mind and its comic condemnation to the prison of the body. "There is *the idea* of the soul in its undefined capacity and dignity that gives the sting to any absorption of it by any one pursuit", Coleridge says of the hobby-horses. But the disproportion has its philosophical purposes: "in humor the little is made great, and the great little, in order to destroy both, because all is equal in contrast with the infinite". This is the half-comic perplexity of romantic poetry, which heroically undertakes to use and exhaust the only instruments a man has for apprehending reality, the mind and the senses, and yet is at every point aware of the flimsiness and unreliability of those organs.

The double plot is now the signature of the ironic romantic intelligence, oscillating between the great and the little, tragic dilation and comic contraction. "Resolution and Independence" is a poem about these difficulties of proportion and perception, in which the poet's sovereign, Hamlet-like power of generalising is impeded and slighted by a reality which declines to be known. The humour of the poem is Sternean. Wordsworth's interrogation of the leech-gatherer resembles Tristram's observation of Toby tapping his pipe on the fender, because in both there is a discrepancy between spoken and unspoken, betwen Hoffmann's "sentimental subject" and an oppressive objectivity. Sterne contrasts the inner bounty of feeling with the minute crevices of particularity through which it squeezes into expression; Wordsworth sets the jealous reten-tiveness and separateness of thought against the humorous inadequacy of conversation, which is prolonged not to help the poet learn something about the leech-gatherer but so that he can transform him into an idea. The great and the little change places, and their confusion is a tribute to Coleridge's "infinite".

"Resolution and Independence" is remarkable because Wordsworth's imperious generalities usually encounter no obstruction. Elsewhere, he commandeers things simply by naming them. In Book XII of *The Prelude* he at first simply notes

> A naked pool that lay beneath the hills,
> The beacon on the summit, and, more near,
> A girl, who bore a pitcher on her head,

and flatly concedes their ordinariness. But then the objects are transfixed by his gaze and remade into elements of his vision, named again and triumphantly taken over. The landscape is no longer merely topographical, with the pool and the beacon above it in the middle distance and the girl closer, but has been imagined and rendered symbolic by Wordsworth's intrusion into it – the pool among the waste,

The beacon crowning the lone eminence,
The female and her garments vexed and tossed
By the stong wind.

The beacon is now the watchtower of the self, the struggling woman now a Wordsworth character, a stoic solitary. The naked pool recurs again, at a later stage in the process of ingestion: now its dreariness and the melancholy of the beacon are irradiated by

A spirit of pleasure and youth's golden dream.

At this third stage the girl has vanished, her place taken by Wordsworth and his loved one: other human beings are aliens in Wordsworth's vacant landscape of mind, and he retreats further and further from them, allowing Margaret to wither into the ruin of her cottage and its garden, Michael and Luke to petrify into the stones of the sheep-fold, and Lucy to be fossilised into the rocks and stones and trees.

At the beginning of "Resolution and Independence" a similar off-hand assertion of ownership occurs. At first the racing hare, the woods and waters are simply noticed, but in the third stanza Wordsworth himself enters the poem to take them over one by one:

I was a Traveller then upon the moor;
I saw the hare that raced about with joy;
I heard the woods and distant waters roar; . . .

Such god-like might is there in this assurance (Wordsworth turns his simple "I was" or "I saw" into the vast exertions of creative will of the god of *Genesis*) that once having imprinted himself on creation Wordsworth can dismiss it or disappear from it:

Or heard them not, as happy as a boy.

But this engulfing ego is blocked and contradicted by another force, an ego so denuded of character or self-consciousness as to be impenetrable, and the poem's ironic double plot represents a Sternean collision of uncomprehending egotists. The poem is a diptych: its two halves regard each other, but stubbornly refuse to be moved from their self-concern. The poet takes the old man for an exemplary figure but, unlike the hare, woods and waters, the old man resists the poet's designs on him, and they converse comically at cross purposes. Preoccupied with his despondent fears and professional self-pity, the poet chooses to interpret the encounter with the old man as fated, guided – the old man seems to exist to be turned into a poem, and Wordsworth promptly begins to abstract him into one of his own characters, reducing him by turns to a stone, a leviathan, an arthritic emblem and an immovable bank of clouds. Yet there is a potentially absurd contrast between the facility with which the poet can absorb the object into a succession of images and the nervous hesitation of his approach through conversation. The condescending banality of "This morning gives us promise of a glorious day", so flat and awkward, is tolerated gently and courteously by the old man, who is determined not to be patronised and reacts with a condescension of his own to the next question, "What occupation do you here pursue?", commanding a loftinesss of utterance ironically denied to himself by the limping and fatuous poet.

Irony such as this is the play of self-reflection. The poet's restless, morbid subjectivity rebounds from the blunt, impervious objectivity of the old man; or, seen another way, the old man's refusal to part with his secret confers on him an astute, remote subjectivity which frustrates the gauche, objective poet, interviewing him in too bland and external a manner. The poem ricochets between the two characters pursuing their separate reveries. Not only does the poet fail to attend to the old man's explanation of himself, he turns him into a dream phantom whose sole purpose is "to give me human strength, by apt admonishment". (That "me", appropriating the old man to its own uses, sounds with the same cannibalistic assurance as the remark that Lucy's death hurts because of "the difference to me".) Eagerly demoting the leech-gatherer to a literary means, the poet misses what he says and has to crudely put the question again, which prompts a tactful, smiling repetition. The coexistence of the two streams of thought and talk is measured in a couplet of extraordinary flatness:

While I these thoughts within myself pursued,
He, having made a pause, the same discourse renewed.

The flatness registers ironically the poet's dismissal of the world outside, his perfunctory glance at the substance of the old man who interests him only as an idea, an image. The final lines mark an odd reversal: the poet laughs at his own failure to credit the old man with a mind, but proceeds regardless to a jaunty final transformation of him into an icon of fortitude:

> "God", said I, "be my help and stay secure;
> I'll think of the leech-gatherer on the lonely moor!"

which stretches the old man into a consolation for experiences he can know nothing about, and casually invokes God to sanctify the act of appropriation.

The poem's inadvertent comedy recalls the double plot – like the poet and the leech-gatherer, Lear and the fool, for all their generous commiseration, merely exchange fantasies rather than venturing towards an understanding of one another. Lear is regally solicitous about the fool's health; the fool makes Lear the victim of hand-dandy epigrams. Shakespeare is instinctively comic, because in his plays the solitary ego which wants to be tragic is always nudged and buffetted into an awareness that it shares the world with others. Even Lear's torments are denied singularity – he is only one of a pair of tragic heroes. But, in contrast with the congestion of the plays, romantic writers turn to forms in which the dreams of the would-be tragic heroes can be made into truth. In the vacancy of the novel or the lyric, subjectivity is unfettered; these private forms are the nutshells in which the characters can declare themselves kings of infinite space, and remake the world in their image.

Richardson and Sterne establish this mental privacy as the form of the novel. The Shakespearean play is an image of society, the novel an image of mind; the one is tragicomic because social extremes collide and are forced into intimacy in its narrow, crowded space, but the other is ironically tragicomic because incompatible thoughts cannot be segregated, and weave themselves together in the incontinent brains of its characters. Richardson and Sterne create the novel as a discipline of detachment, retreating from society towards mental solitude. The novel's purpose, as Diderot interprets it in the *Éloge de Richardson*,[15] is an induction into mystic retire-

ment. Diderot, the first of the European critics to unfold the
romantic significance of eighteenth-century English literature, sees the novel as an opening up of "mental space", to
use the phrase in which Coleridge defined the imaginative
geography of *The Faerie Queene*.[16] Richardson penetrates into
the furthest recesses of the mind, revealing the hideous Moor
in the depths of the cave; Sterne follows him, unmasking the
Moor – when Susannah covets the gown, or the widow is
solicitous about Toby's wound, or Yorick reaches for the fille
de chambre – as a lecherous comic ogre. The same analogy
between literary form and the mind applies in romantic
poetry: Shelley, writing *Prometheus Unbound* in the Baths of
Caracalla and employing imagery "drawn from the operations of the human mind",[17] came to think of the ruins
around him as a Piranesian cranial vault, Hamlet's nutshell
gigantically enlarged.

The confidential, secretive nature of the novel as Diderot
sees it implies a new relation with the reader. Diderot identifies
himself completely with the misfortunes of Richardson's
heroines, and is impetuously willing to sacrifice himself for
Clarissa; Sterne comically exploits the privileges of this new
intimacy in his bantering admonitions to the prurient, officious, sometimes inattentive reader. These works not only
probe the privacy of their characters, but depend on making an
entry into the privacy of the reader, whom Richardson obliges
to become the heroine's confidant. The letters are addressed
from captivity to the reader: hence Diderot's volunteering to
rush into the work to rescue Clarissa. In Sterne, the reader is
obliged to co-operate with Tristram in the composition and
decipherment of the work. Tristram prides himself on his
generous division of the work between himself and the reader,
who is given half of it "to imagine, in his turn". He devotes
himself to keeping the reader's "imagination as busy as my
own", challenging him with blank pages, teasing him with
asterisks, writing the novel backwards so as to make it a puzzle
only the reader can solve.

The movement from the diversions of society to the solitary
concentration of the mind influences the conduct of the narrative. Richardson and Sterne refuse to tell the story econom-
ically and consecutively, because their aim is to educate the

reader out of the desire to be a spectator of events into a mood of patient understanding. They excite impatience in order to triumph over it, because in a special sense the novels are works of ascetic training – preparation, in Richardson's case, for spiritual commiseration, in Sterne's for the mental agility of the ironist. Diderot admits that Richardson's novels seem tediously long-winded to the social person with his countless distractions and inability to concentrate, but they are not so to the tranquil solitary in his shaded retreat, waiting in the silence. The work acts hermetically, translating the reader from society to the meditative peace of solitude; in its effect on him it applies the morality of *Rasselas*, exposing the worthlessness of ambition and achievement, sending the reader back into himself. Its longueurs are a discipline, its longevity an image of the timelessness of the life of thoughtful retirement. It has the emotional virtue of pastoral, making of its reader a peaceful shepherd, who was for Bacon a type of the contemplative Christian soul, "by reason of his leisure, rest in a place, and living in view of heaven",[18] an innocent Abel as against the dangerous dramatic industriousness of Cain the husbandman tilling the soil. Remaking pastoral, the novel removes its solitaries from their bucolic landscape to Coleridge's mental space, and makes suffering passivity (in Richardson) or inanity (in Sterne) the marks of their sanctity.

Modulation from epic to the pastoral of quiet and privacy is an established tendency in poetry. The great English epics all conclude sceptically as pastorals. Spenser abandons the courtly and hierarchical scheme outlined to Raleigh to lose himself in the varieties of love and to remove courtesy from polite society to nature, among salvage men and penurious peasant farmers. Milton expels Adam and Eve from epic into a sad and toilsome pastoral; they set out as the labourer returns wearily home in the evening mist. Christ meekly absents himself from the angelic festivities hymning his victory, and slips out of the poem into his private capacity through the gap created by the enjambment:

> he unobserv'd
> Home to his mother's house private return'd.

Satan is an epic hero, swaggering and militaristic; Christ confronts him with the wise passiveness of pastoral. *The Prelude* too inverts epic so as to make it pastoral, neglecting the French Revolution to retire into the fortitude of the mind and the settled low content of the poet's native landscape.

This reversal of epic and pastoral underlies the morality of the novel. Lovelace has the allure, mobility and treacherous glibness of Comus or Satan; Clarissa, like Milton's Lady or Christ, knows she must simply withstand him, forbearing to move or act, because to do so even in self-defence would be to slip into his world of compromise and dissolution. Her passivity, which frustrates the work's attempt to be a narrative, is a mystic self-concentration, garnering up and meditatively ordering her own powers: she is subjecting herself to precisely the same discipline Diderot requires of the reader. She is the saint, the reader her acolyte. Sterne's religion of sentiment wittily extends this relationship: the serene rectitude of the Miltonic saint abstaining from action relaxes into the tremulous restraint of the man of feeling, paralysed by excess of emotion and expressing his goodness not in action but in effusion, coughs, belches, clumsy stumblings. Tristram's passiveness is a subversive comic wisdom.

Dorval, a character of Diderot's, remarks in conversation with his creator that "theatrical action never rests".[19] The busy and restless inventiveness of the theatre is thus an image of the entropic agitation of social life, the "light fantastic round" of Comus and his crew; the longueurs of the novel, like the Lady's starched reluctance to unlock her lips, are an induction into the calm of solitude. This is one of the difficulties of the romantic Hamlet, who is equal to the swift and versatile course of dramatic action but longs for release into the privacy of soliloquy. His longing makes him novelistic, like Coleridge's Richard II with his "constantly increasing energy of thought, and as constantly decreasing power of acting". As will be noted in a later discussion of romantic criticism, the inverse ratio of thought to action, with one increasing at the other's expense, becomes a formula for defining the novel, and in particular for defending *Tristram Shandy*.

Diderot enjoins the novel to renounce action so as to shift from idle social observation to spiritual understanding. Its purpose is to confound our assumption that we know things, to make us feel them, to reveal their secret intimacy and to make us "*sensible.*" It opens up a microscopic realm of fugitive details and imperceptible nuances, and discerns in human character the same thronging plenitude and subtle inter-involvement Leibniz found in nature, sending us in pursuit of small, minutely-differentiated objects. "In this immortal book", Diderot says of Clarissa, "as in nature during spring, one never finds two leaves of the same shade of green. What an immense variety of nuances!" The household of the Harlowes is as much a tense, vibrant sensorium, a tissue of implication to be apprehended by patient intuition, as the household of the Shandys, who as a family belong less to society then to pastoral. They inhabit the nature of romantic poetry. Their dealings with one another – the pressure applied by Mrs Shandy's hand to Walter's, the gentleness with which Uncle Toby sets down his pipe on the fender, treating it as if it had been spun from a spider's web – are delicate alterations in the balance of an organism, mysterious disturbances of mental atmosphere rather than decisive acts of human will. They anticipate Wordsworth's numinous reverence for

> A motion and a spirit, that impels
> All thinking things, all objects of all thought,
> And rolls through all things

or his sense of guilty trespass while nutting or stealing the boat. The Shandys might be called a group of alternately blithe or dizzy or gravely sensitive Wordsworthians before their time. Their treasuring of associations, their conviction of the sacredness of a fly, their cautious propitiation of the unseen powers and presences (comic poltergeists like the window-sash or the unwound clock) which surround and govern them, are all signs of a Wordsworthian natural piety.

The disorganised comedy of their community derives from their existence as separate and incommunicable centres of feeling. The novel contains a family of different minds, each with its private perceptions and obsessive habits, each generously entertained. Tristram's scatter-brained procrastination is a comic correlative of that god-like impartiality which Keats admired in Shakespeare, but which neither he nor the other romantic poets could attain. Tristram is determined that there shall be room for all in his capacious work (he begins a new volume to give Toby room to expand on his perplexities during the seige of Namur), and he passes in his leisurely way from one impersonation to another, as if acting out the Keatsian notion of the chameleon poet with no identity of his own.

Sterne recreates the amplitude of the Shakespearean double plot by finding space and asylum for all his characters within a claustrophobic household. Humour is for him a guarantee of each character's mental privacy. Yorick's sermons reflect on the literary history treated earlier in this chapter and condemn satiric wit as mere verbal showmanship, "a quickness of apprehension, void of humanity, . . . a talent of the devil", and plead for a return to the festive humour of Shakespearean folly which is tolerant not malignant, and which releases characters into the privacy of their absurdity rather than punitively wearing them down into uniformity. Humour respects, even creates, individuality of character. The Shakespearean double plot becomes a multiplication of separate rooms which, like the radial paths of the garden in Richard Hurd's account of *The Faerie Queene's* multiple plots, do not connect with one another but only with the common centre from which they all diverge, a proliferation of mental spaces.

Likewise, Shakespearean folly is internalised by Sterne. Jest, a dart aimed outwards, is reversed into irony, trained in on itself. The transition from jester to ironist occurs by way of an interpenetration of tragedy and comedy, mental freedom and bodily necessity, the opposed but twin spirits of Hamlet and Falstaff, just as in the seventeenth century the jester had dwindled into the satirist by way of the mutual failure of nerve of tragedy and comedy. Sterne's sermons criticise satirists for dealing in external effects, social victories, misled "by the desire of being thought men of wit and parts, and the vain expectation of coming honestly to the title, by shrewd and sarcastic reflections". Perhaps this explains the strange rules against which Emma transgresses at Box Hill. She is safe while she keeps to herself a sense of distance and superior intellectual agility which are private and ironic; her mistake is to squander this private conviction by making it objective in a lampoon, and to decline into a satirist. Like the sublime, of which romantic theory considered it an inversion, irony is self-referring.

The aesthetics of Jean Paul Richter treat satire as the smaller half of the moral realm because it is constrained by moral responsibilities and dare not risk the arbitrariness of laughter. The realm of laughter is infinite, co-extensive with the vastness of nature. Satire limits, binding us to morality, whereas laughter frees us into poetry, because the ironist's jokes reflect on himself, and have no goal beyond their own existence.

The superiority of irony to satire, which Yorick argues homiletically, Jean Paul justifies metaphysically. Irony miniaturises the sublime. The sublime is telescopic, irony microscopic vision. In the sublime the senses and imagination despair of responding adequately to the grand phenomenon with which they are confronted; in irony they abandon the attempt and instead lovingly contemplate their own weakness.

Irony reconstitutes the double plot inside the paradoxical romantic mind: the tragic half is sentiment, the comic half the sport of that sentiment which Carlyle, in an account of Jean Paul Richter, likened to "the playful teasing fondness of a mother to her child",[21] and found exemplified in Sterne. De Quincey also declared Jean Paul's distinction to be the "the two-headed power which he possesses over the pathetic and the humorous", except that "this power is *not* two-headed, but a one-headed Janus with two faces", because the pathetic and the humorous "assist each other, melt indiscernibly into each other, and often shine each through each like layers of coloured crystals placed one behind another",[22] as in Mrs Quickly's report of Falstaff's death. In this respect De Quincey judges Jean Paul to be the most eminent artist since Shakespeare, and Sterne's superior. Celebrating the ironic fusion of tragedy and comedy, he converts Jean Paul's writings into an aerial pageant, a Shelleyan meteorological fantasy: the ironist is a prince of the air, a disembodied Ariel, an exploding firework or volcano, a compound of images which recur in romantic thinking about poetic creativity. Deriving a cosmic order from the romantic antithesis between the autocratic deity of Milton and the volatile invisible deity of Shakespeare, De Quincey allots to Milton the planets, to Shakespeare and Jean Paul the element of air:

The rapid, but uniform motions of the heavenly bodies serve well enough to typify the grand and continuous motions of the Miltonic mind. But the wild, giddy, fantastic, capricious, incalculable, springing, vaulting, tumbling, dancing, waltzing, caprioling, *pirouetting*, skyrocketing of the chamois, the harlequin, the Vestris, the storm-loving raven – the raven? no, the lark (for often he ascends "singing up to heaven's gates", but like the lark he dwells upon the earth), in short, of the proteus, the Ariel, the Mercury, the monster – John Paul, can be compared to nothing in heaven or earth, or the waters under the earth, except to the motions of the same faculty as existing in Shakespeare.

The double plot is no longer two-headed but two-faced. Jean Paul admires exactly the same quality in the sensibility of Sterne, who "changes Shakespeare's simple succession of the pathetic and the comic into a *simultaneum* of the two". Tragedy and comedy have ceased to be alternative literary genres; they are now contiguous moods of the romantic comedian's heteroclite mind.

Notes

1. I have discussed the romantic conversion of Shakespeare from drama to lyrical novel in *The Victorian Treasure-House*, 1973.
2. Lamb's mental justification of Macbeth, Richard III and Iago occurs in his essay "On the Tragedies of Shakespeare considered with reference to their fitness for stage representation" (1811).
3. Yeats's reference to the gaiety of Hamlet and Lear which transfigures dread is in "Lapis Lazuli", from *Last Poems*, 1936–9.
4. The preface to Johnson's edition of the plays, 1765.
5. In *Table Talk*, 1827.
6. Sterne's contrast between satire and sentiment in the sermon on the Levite and his Concubine is Sermon III in Volume II of *The Sermons of Mr. Yorick*, 1760.
7. Hannah More's *Sensibility: A Poetical Epistle* was published with *Sacred Dramas* in 1782.
8. In a letter to Liszt on 15 January 1854, no. 144 in the two volumes of their correspondence, trans. Francis Hueffer, 1897.
9. Maurice Morgann's "Essay on the Dramatic Character of Sir John Falstaff", 1777, is reprinted in D. Nichol Smith's *Eighteenth Century Essays on Shakespeare*, 1903.
10. "On Shakespeare and Milton" in *Lectures on the English Poets*, 1818.
11. A marginal note referred to in *Recollections of Writers*, 1878, by Charles and Mary Cowden Clarke.
12. *Sämtliche Werke*, ed. Eduard Grisebach, 1900, vol. IV, pp. 51–2.
13. *Coleridge's Miscellaneous Criticism*, ed. T. M. Raysor, 1936, pp. 117–26.
14. The Everyman's Library edition of *Essays and Lectures on Shakespeare*, 1951, pp. 135–56.
15. Diderot's *Éloge de Richardson* appeared in the *Journal Etranger* in January 1762 and is reprinted in Paul Vernière's edition of the *Oeuvres Esthétiques* for Classiques Garnier, 1959.
16. *Lectures of 1818*.
17. Preface to *Prometheus Unbound*, 1820.
18. Sir Francis Bacon, *Works*, ed. Spedding, Ellis and Heath (Boston 1860–4), vol. VI, p. 138.
19. From *Entretiens sur le Fils Naturel*, 1757, reprinted in Paul Vernière (ed.), *Oeuvres Esthétiques*.
20. Described in *Letters on Chivalry and Romance*, 1762.
21. Carlyle's essay on Jean Paul Richter appears in the *Edinburgh Review*, 1827.
22. *London Magazine*, December 1821.

2

Palaces of Thought

Tristram's exploration of mental space is an exploration of domestic space, of a compressed and jumbled interior which is imaginatively extended into worlds elsewhere for the characters to populate with their thoughts. Coleridge felt in Richardson the humid oppressiveness of indoors,[1] in contrast with the breezy exterior expanses Fielding traverses. Richardson's action is closeted in narrow places, and Diderot darkens his cramped household into the psychological cave where lurks the Moor. The Shandy home is compartmented like the Shandy brain, subdivided into retreats for the incompatible existences it contains. The narrative gives a spatial form to that ironic simultaneity of the tragic and the comic which Jean Paul pointed to: it remains constantly aware of other plots proceeding concurrently, of other people living and acting in other rooms. Mrs Shandy is suspended for five minutes "in the dark along the passage which led to the parlour" while the action in the kitchen is advanced, it being one of the mental mechanisms of the house that "whatever motion, debate, harangue, dialogue, project, or dissertation, was going forwards in the parlour, there was generally another at the same time, and upon the same subject, running parallel along with it in the kitchen". Dr Slop and Susannah quarrel about the cataplasm in the parlour, and retire to the kitchen to prepare a fomentation; Walter, in despair about Tristram's nose, walks upstairs and falls onto his bed; on another occasion the narrative winds down the staircase with Walter and Toby, threatening to apportion the number of chapters to the number of their steps. The Shandy house is elastic, at times narrowing into a cell constricting the characters as Toby is squeezed in his sentry-box, elsewhere swelling to enclose the whole of an imagined Europe. It is a nutshell, but an infinite space.

This chapter explores the nature of that space, and its relation to Tristram's character. In the first place, it is an image of his mind, a minute chamber which unfolds into a world. But the random accumulation of the mind's contents suggests, to romantic commentators, another kind of space: Locke called the mind of man at birth an "empty cabinet",[2] gradually filled up, and there is a significant critical tradition which treats *Tristram Shandy* as a cabinet or a museum, each thought a curio, each association an arcane exhibit. Hazlitt applies the same Shandyean metaphor to picture galleries, which he calls "palaces of thought". For Voltaire, Tristram is an antiquarian, storing up pedantic oddities in the lumber-room of his head; for the romantics, he is an imaginary architect, whose chimerical structure has the intricacy but also the insubstantiality of memory and desire. For Voltaire, he is the older kind of virtuoso, collecting objects of vertu; for the romantics, he is the new virtuoso, who does not collect remarkable objects but is himself a remarkable subject, and who plays upon the instrument of his sensibility with the same uncanny dexterity the musical virtuoso employs on the keyboard or his violin strings. Tristram passes from magpie collector to mesmeric performer.

Romantic virtuosity turns *Tristram Shandy* into a fiendish exercise in dexterity of technique; antiquarian virtuosity regards it as a collection or cabinet of specialised and peculiar exhibits. "I write as a man of erudition", Tristram says. The eighteenth-century Sterne pieces together the detritus of a tradition of learned wit, and is a scrupulous adept of hermetic lore and hieroglyphic wisdom; the nineteenth-century Sterne is not the scholarly curator of a miscellany of recondite information but a wizard ironically at the mercy of his own spells, an apprentice sorcerer whose inventions are the impulses of a fevered, teeming brain.

Sterne is treated as the older kind of connoisseur by Voltaire and Scott. Voltaire approaches *Tristram Shandy* as an object in a museum, an inexplicable utensil dug up from the past. It is like an ancient vase decorated with grimacing, misbehaving satyrs, both a fragment of grotesquerie and a cult object.[3] Serving a sacred function inside a profane form, like the indecently decorated Greek vases Sir William Hamilton and his fellow-antiquaries collected with such learned prurience, *Tris-*

tram Shandy enshrines, in Voltaire's description, the ironic, indelicate oppositions of the double plot.

For Scott, the context of style is the Gothic revival, not the classical revival of Voltaire; but the tragicomic improprieties of Gothic, with gargoyles jeering at angels, are another manifestation of the double plot. Scott begins by making the point that is so important to Schopenhauer's romantic version of the work, to be discussed later, arguing that *Tristram Shandy* is "no narrative". But whereas Schopenhauer saw the work opening out into a picture, Scott thinks of it proliferating into "a collection". Narration and collection are opposite impulses, since the former is intelligibly consecutive while the latter follows the fortuitous order of acquisition. *Tristram Shandy* "resembles the irregularities of a Gothic room, built by some fanciful collector, to contain the miscellaneous remnants of antiquity which his pains have accumulated, and bearing as little proportion in its parts, as there is connection between the pieces of rusty armour with which it is decorated",[4] and Scott defends Sterne's plagiarisms as the lucky finds of the antiquarian assembling round him his odd dusty titbits of learning. As a collector of theorems and discredited systems, Sterne is, like Swift's crazed Laputan projectors, an artist of the metaphysical decadence, a late, bemused contributor to the tradition of intellectual antiquarianism which begins with Donne. Donne's conceits are archaeological finds. Picking through the rubble of established truths, the grand Renaissance order of correspondences which has collapsed out of the skies, Donne unearths fragments and tries piecing them together to reconstruct the object they once composed. The conceits are his wittily implausible, hybrid reconstructions of truths fractured by the new philosophy. He has an intense apprehension of details, like the compasses, which he knows to be emblems, but he cannot be sure what they refer to; the poetry tirelessly interrogates its subjects in the hope that they will give up their meaning. Sterne also conducts an intellectual excavation, but the fragments he rescues no longer have any residue of belief: ideas are toys, items in the virtuoso's cabinet, not instruments of knowledge and controversy as they are for Donne.

Tristram Shandy and the *Anniversaries* of Donne build

pyramidal heaps of detail which can never cohere into a whole; they are curiously bifocal, sprawling yet minutely concentrated. Sterne revels in the formal paradox by arguing that the minutest philosophers are those with the most enlarged understandings. The smaller the enquiry, the larger its implications, and the greater the magnitude of soul it requires. As Jean Paul declared irony to be the sublime in miniature, so contraction is the only way to expansion. The view through Milton's telescope is the same as that through Sterne's microscope. To see eternity in an hour or a grain of sand is to promote this literary strategy to a mystic vision. Sterne's perception of the universal in a tiny particular is a continuation of the art of metaphysical poetry. But the difference between Donne's conceits and the pinpricks of sensation and vision in Sterne is that Donne's equivalences are engineered, contrived by feats of preposterous intellect, while Sterne's are impromptu. The one refers with a strained exaggeration which is really nostalgia to an intellectual scheme into which all phenomena fit, the other not to a chain of being but to a more elastic and disorderly pattern of nature, a melting, palpitating sensorium, not a ranked hierarchy. Donne needs to use violence to yoke together ideas which float into connection in Sterne. Donne argues, Sterne effuses. In the Shandy family, Walter with his "close reasoning upon the smallest matter" remains true to the older intellectual habits, longing for a rigid scheme of truths, while Tristram waits on the wayward accidents of romantic revelation.

Conceits are a frail magic, using words as the instruments of their spells, though in Sterne the magic works not through language but through pregnant, hinting silences. The sentimentalist is a sorcerer who is unsure of the power of his arts: because circumstances are set and people incorrigible, his magic tends to peter out into ineffectiveness, which means into irony. He is eternally frustrated, but like Faust he welcomes failure as a guarantee of his integrity. As a romantic, Sterne employs a rough magic which he can neither make perform his will nor agree to abjure. The novel begins with the rude dispersal of the superintending magic presences, and spends the rest of its time attempting to placate them and woo them back. Here, as its antiquarianism turns back into occult-

ism, *Tristram Shandy* recalls another Shakespearean character
who has had an after-life in romantic criticism: the flight of the
animal spirits resembles Prospero's abrupt dismissal of the
phantoms of his masque. Sentimentalism indeed takes up
again the wand Prospero lays down with such weary irony.
He abandons magic because he knows it to be fragile, unable to
deceive let alone change his unregenerate subjects. The romantics return to it – and revive all the disreputable practices
involved in it, forgery, self-deception, narcotic inducement of
visions. But they do not use their poetry to change mankind,
as Prospero or Milton in the masque of *Comus* had hoped to
do. Even Sterne wishes only for harmonious moments of
truce, assuming that individuals will remain in the prison of
their private languages. Romantic magic hopes not to change
men, but to exert power over nature: hence the romantic
intercourse with the spirit-world, comically inaugurated in
Sterne's novel, the invocations of winds, nightingales, rocks
and stones and trees.

Prospero is Hamlet's opposite, an artist who cannot coun-
tenance the shocks and mischances of experience, an aesthetic
tyrant with no talent for negative capability – not Shakespeare's account of himself, but his cruel image of what he is
not. In contrast with Hamlet's Shandyean delight in randomness and exploration of detours, Prospero creates an
exclusively perfect, self-contained, beautifully vacuous work
of art, only to find that it has no point, and that it has expelled
him. Like Flaubert hurt and bewildered by the fact that Emma
Bovary, his creation, will go on enjoying her life after he has
perished, Prospero is left at the end diminished, exposed,
frantic to retain a hold on the art-work which is already
independent of him. His epilogue is not an appeal to the
audience to like and protect the play, but a plea for a transfusion of life from that audience which his self-admiring work
has until now refused to recognise. It is fatally uncharacteristic
and embarrassing in its identification of the audience's right to
dispense approval or disfavour with God's power to grant or
withhold mercy: he literally prays for applause. The arrogant
and invulnerable artificer has become human, and it does not
suit him. He ends in bitter irony, from which he tries to save
himself by sentimental blackmail of the lookers-on:

As you from crimes would pardon'd be,
Let your indulgence set me free.

He resents his lack of control over his art and over the future,
while Tristram accepts his own powerlessness in a comic
correlative of Hamlet's fatalism: if it is not now, it is to come,
and there are special providences everywhere. Prospero's
magic, ideal but unavailing, gives way to Tristram's, inefficient
but healing and reconciling at last.

Prospero's deserted cell turns into Scott's irregular Gothic
room, in which the miscellaneous trinkets, and oddities are
clues to the identity of the collector. The museum becomes a
mental space, because the virtuoso's mind is a museum: he has
a book-lined head, and in conducting one through the defiles
of his learning, as Tristram does, he is taking one on a tour of
his past. Slawkenbergius's Tale is set down as an object of
great scholarly rarity in parallel texts; but its fable *de Nasis* also
has an uncomfortable relevance to the maimings and ex-
crescences of the Shandy family. Uncle Toby's war games or
Walter's arcane science of names are unsteady structures
elaborated by the antiquarian mind, but they are also therapeutic exercises, working off personal dilemmas – Toby on a
treadmill condemned to endless re-enactment of his past,
Walter devising ways of controlling his family's future.

Tristram Shandy reveals the virtuoso's cabinet to be a
memory-theatre, a claustrophobic and subterranean library
stack where recollections are stored and where wisdom col-
lects dust in the form of alphabets, emblems and antique
devices. For all its digressive proliferation, it is a narrow space
tightly packed, a mind indexed and catalogued, a prison of
mnemonic systems – the twenty knots, Toby's maps and
treatises of military architecture, the hobby-horses. Toby's
table is too small for the "infinity of great and small instruments of knowledge which usually lay crowded upon it", and
which represent the orderly and automatic succession of his
ideas: compasses, snuffers, books of fortification, the materials
with which he builds his house of memory which is also a
theatre of war. Walter takes up his residence in the brain itself,
traversing its separate areas – the top of the pineal gland, the
cellulae of the occipital parts of the cerebellum, the medulla

oblongata – in his anxious quest for the seat of the soul. The relations between the members of the family are mental: Tristram is Walter's brain-child. The setback to the process of physical conception with which the novel begins is propitious because Tristram is to be conceived mentally, as an idea springing from Walter's head, not the son of his loins. Walter insists that the act of propagation requires "all the thought in the world" – it is a notion, not an act. As Carlyle was to say, "Manufacture is intelligible, but trivial; Creation is great, and cannot be understood",[5] and Tristram is not to be biologically manufactured but imaginatively created. In his turn he begets his own brain-child, his *Life and Opinions*, which refashions the trivial biological process of living into the significant mental one of remembering and discerning.

Toby's mind is mapped as Namur under siege, a treacherous and obstacle-ridden terrain: "the ground was cut and cross cut with such a multitude of dykes, drains, rivulets, and sluices, on all sides – and he would get so sadly bewildered, and set fast amongst them, that frequently he could get neither backwards nor forwards to save his life". He is trapped inside his own head. Walter's mind also disposes itself in the image of a city, one of the ideally empty urban designs of Renaissance architecture: he learns from the Dutch anatomists that near the medulla oblongata is the place on which all avenues converge (like the centre of Hurd's radial garden, his image for the mental space of *The Faerie Queene*), where "all the minute nerves from all the organs of the seven senses concentrated, like streets and winding alleys, into a square". Tristram's mind is also a town-plan, but it is not a fictional city of obsessive fantasy like Namur or the Angria and Gondal of the Brontës or the Ejuxria of Hartley Coleridge or the Xanadu of his father. Rather it has been extended into a map of Europe, though its topography is mental and two journeys can be superimposed, as Tristram simultaneously walks across the market-place of Auxerre, enters Lyons, and reflects in a pavilion on the banks of the Garonne. His travelling is sentimental, so it may just as well take place in the privacy and convenience of his own consciousness, like that of Des Esseintes in Huysmans' *A Rebours* who, having imagined London, decides that to transfer his body there would be a demeaning anticlimax. He has already made the city a mental possession; the actual journey he can leave to his servants.

The febrile, nervous dandy is the descendant of the man of feeling, except that in him feeling is no longer altruistic or philanthropic but disdainfully aesthetic; and Des Esseintes also inhabits a room which is an image of his mind and a collection of his treasures. But whereas Tristram's room is infinitely expansible, the shape of a rambling and wall-less consciousness, that of Des Esseintes encloses him and protects him from nature. He chooses a decorative scheme based on the morbid acidity and repellence of orange, meant to glare in artificial light. Like Scott's Shandyean collector, he stocks the room with icons of his connoisseurship, but these are not valued for their personal associations, as are the hobby-horses. They compose a forbidding museum of gilded religious artefacts secularised as implements of an aesthetic cult: a church lectern, a singing-desk, silk from a Florentine dalmatic, Byzantine monstrances and some sonnets of Baudelaire copied on vellum in missal lettering.

The action of *Tristram Shandy* passes in the mind, and its discursiveness and episodic muddle are images of the inane eventfulness of consciousness. As Toby lies in bed, "a thought came into his head", and incidents and people start up in the novel with the same inspired inconsequence. It is not narrative because thinking is not. We do not think, in the confusion which reigns inside ourselves, according to the orderly inductive procedure whereby causes have logical effects; rather we guess, diverge, leap to conclusions, circle round aimlessly, apprehend effects without a clue to their causes. The succession of mental events inside Tristram's head is as arbitrary as an arrangement of pictures in a gallery. It has the alogical, causeless, dreamy succession which the lady to whom Pope read *The Faerie Queene* discerned in Spenser's narrative,[6] with each stanza concluded and framed like a picture by its long final line, running down to a halt which compels us to cross the blank gap between this picture and the next. The pictorial incidents do not flow ceaselessly past us; rather we must make the effort to move ourselves from one to the next, and to discover relations between them. The romantic implications of the form of *Tristram Shandy* lead from Scott's antiquarian collection, an index to the contents of its creator's brain, to the picture gallery, which in Hazlitt's criticism becomes both a memory-theatre and a temple.

Visiting the Angerstein collection in 1824, Hazlitt found there the spectral dimness of a sanctuary where "we see the pictures by their own internal light". A gallery is a Keatsian bower where things of beauty are preserved outside time: the museum abolishes time by making all periods of the past contemporary with one another, just as in the jumbled collectivity of the mind all thoughts commingle as equals, and our own history is dissolved since past, present and dreamed-of future have coalesced in our recollections and imagining. In the gallery, Hazlitt says, "we are abstracted into another sphere: we breathe empyrean air; . . . we live in time past, and seem identified with the permanent forms of things". The place is sacred because "the contemplation of truth and beauty is the proper object for which we were created, which calls forth the most intense desires of the soul, and of which it never tires".[7]

The analogy between Sterne's mentally picaresque form and the succession of paintings, and Hazlitt's emphasis on the spiritual atmosphere of the gallery, makes it clear why one of Yorick's successors in sentimental travel, Byron's Harold, should trudge on his pilgrimage from one Italian museum or historical landmark to the next. For this is a romantic reconstitution of earlier journeys to the tombs of saints. The movement from one picture to another in the collection is a traversing of the stations of the Cross. As Hazlitt put it, "A visit to a genuine Collection is like going on a pilgrimage – it is an act of devotion performed at the shrine of Art!" However, although this is the principle of Yorick's leisurely tour and of Harold's pilgrimage, Hazlitt in reviewing the fourth canto of Byron's poem in the *Yellow Dwarf* in 1818 attacked precisely this feature of it. He noted that Byron's "general reflections are connected together merely by the accidental occurrence of different objects – the Venus of Medici, or the status of Pompey, – the Capitol at Rome, or the Bridge of Sighs at Venice, – Shakespeare, and Mrs Radcliffe, – Bonaparte, and his Lordship in person". But this accidental series, indifferent to the logic of narrative, is true to the rhythm of thought, moving ahead through a landscape which is always changing but insistently recurring, to the few images or persons which mark the limits of the poet's mental world. He reviews the contents of the museum of Italy; but in truth he is moodily sorting through the contents of his own mind. Hazlitt feels that this creates "a phatasmagoria, . . . with as little attention to keeping of perspective, as in Hogarth's famous print for reversing the laws of vision". But this point too reacts against Hazlitt and in Byron's favour, for that print will be discussed in the fifth chapter of this book as an intimation of romantic perception. The print refuses to tyrannise objects, to make them obey the specious human law which decrees that they should suicidally diminish as they hasten towards their vanishing points. No longer deferring to the human eye's theoretical plans for them, objects in Hogarth create a chaotic democracy, as thoughts do in Sterne and Byron.

Hazlitt finds in the Angerstein collection "the mind's true home". Similarly he describes the Dulwich gallery as a mental space which turns inside out the crudely tangible appearance of nature: "A fine gallery of pictures is a sort of illustration of Berkeley's Theory of Matter and Spirit. It is like a palace of thought – another universe, built of air, of shadows, of colours. Everything seems 'palpable to feeling as to sight'. Substances turn to shadows by the painter's arch-chemic touch; shadows harden into substances." The Shandys inhabit such a teetering, many-mansioned house, where each room or recess garners up memories or idle associations or solid stories of knowledge. Their chimerical architecture, together with Hazlitt's account of the introversion of the gallery, help to explain the formal logic of certain other Shandyean constructions. The designer of the Dulwich gallery, Sir John Soane, built a palace of thought for himself in Lincoln's Inn Fields, a museum which was also a mausoleum, a Dickensian carapace the embittered architect drew close around himself, a looking-glass world in which spatial relations are determined by the deception of mirrors, a temple miniaturised.[8] Beckford erected another for himself at Fonthill, an abbey in which black masses were celebrated, an attempt to conjure Milton's Pandemonium out of the deep like an exhalation, a top-heavy defiance of natural limits which succumbed promptly to the humbling pull of gravity. Zoffany painted a palace of thought in his "Tribuna of the Uffizi", a study of that room in which as Smollett said, anticipating Hazlitt's notion of the gallery's Berkeleyan dissolution of substance, "a stranger of visionary turn would be apt to find himself in a palace of the fairies, raised and adorned by the power of enchantment".[9]

Zoffany's Tribuna, invaded by covetous virtuosi, is an ironic Shandyean maze in which each man has found his fantasy and stays close by it. The connoisseurs become bemused passengers through a Spenserian emblem-house strewn with an ingenious chaos of warnings, troublingly decorated with both bacchantes and madonnas, popes and satyrs, the Madonna della Sedia and the Venus de' Medici. They are caught in their bewildered effort to make sense of the multitude of temptations and exhortations – some enraptured by the Acrasian nudes, others assessing them as possessions, other vacillating between classical and Christian, still others sketching copies with a blithely literal unawareness that they are surrounded by anything but works of art. The walls are covered with allegories and portents, miracles and horrors of war. Imperial busts and squatting Egyptian figures or an embracing Cupid and Psyche stare back at the virtuosi who are themselves posed and distributed like works of art. The picture hints at the shaming comedy of the wax museum, in which one cannot tell which are the models and which the people looking at them. The difference of course is that people move, but in a painting they are as still, as frozen in attitudes, as the statues, and indeed rather less life-like: the statues embrace or clash cymbals or wrestle, engaged in some activity which is only briefly suspended, whereas the virtuosi are fixed in their inactivity, paralysed by emotions which are purely aesthetic. They have been bewitched, as Smollett predicted the stranger would be. The Keatsian bower in which things of beauty are kept quiet for us is a place of strange sorcery where the works of art look back at those who are looking at them. Hazlitt's reversal takes place here – pictorial shadows have become substances; human substances have wasted into shadows. Virtuosity has ceased to be acquisitive and evaluative, and is now for Zoffany's characters as for the Shandys a devious, hermetic exploration of fantasy.

With Soane and Beckford, a further alteration of the Shandyean mental space occurs. The first chapter has already argued that the delicate, disturbed atmosphere of the Shandy household makes it less a society than a romantic landscape instinct with benign presences and invisible prohibitions; and the palaces of thought of Soane and Beckford are less buildings than landscapes. They are treated in these terms by two contemporary guides, John Britton's treatment of Soane's house as a fusion of the arts, *The Union of Architecture, Sculpture, and Painting* (1827), and John Rutter's *Delineations of Fonthill and its Abbey* (1823). The neoclassical house is set in a landscape which pleasantly confounds it: the Palladian discipline of the architecture is dissipated in the picturesquely rampant garden. But the romantic house itself constitutes a landscape.

The mental space turns into a landscape because landscape is a picture less of nature than of thought. The objects it contains are images of feeling, traces of absent character: Constable's bent trees are icons of pained fortitude, his clouds the gloomy resolutions of the stoic; the lily-pools and rivers of the impressionists are streams of consciousness. Landscape deals in spirit not matter, and thus in air and water rather than earth. Because "air is necessary to the landscape painter",[10] Hazlitt discounts the lakes of Cumberland and Westmorland as subjects for his art (although instead of air they have the sense of watery infinity). In a landscape there are no events, only impressions, and the romantic discovery of landscape implies a change from literary narration, which deals in purposeful time and the active logic of cause and effect, to the forbearance and patience of painting, which simply records objects as they drift across its space. Tristram calls Locke's essay a history-book, but like Tristram's own novel it might more properly have been called a picture-book, of what passes in the mind. A thought comes into Toby's head with the same inexplicable naturalness as a cloud crossing the sky.

Mental impressions can be built as well as painted, and Britton praises Soane's house for its exotic "architectural scenery". He claims that Soane has inaugurated a new epoch in domestic architecture, for in his use of stained glass, mirrors, vestibules, staircases, cortiles and ornaments he has invented an "interior architecture". Like Sterne, he has turned the house inside out, from a confrontation with a public space outside it to a protective casing for the morbid solitary who lurks within. Britton points to its ingenuity in contriving vistas "within the most confined space, and without the least aid of external view". It builds Hamlet's aphorism: bounded in a nut-shell, it creates for itself an illusory kingdom of infinite space.

Soane compresses his picture gallery into Shandyean mental form as well. Peeling away the planes of pictures in the tiny cabinet, a Gothic apartment beneath is suddenly revealed. The superimposition of hinged panels of pictures in the cabinet both expands the space and contracts it, doubling the amount of room for pictures but oddly altering the gallery into a book whose pages we turn in moving the panels. The paintings themselves are subjected to mannerist refractions as they are made to revolve through several degrees of distortion: Soane thought it an advantage that "the pictures can be seen under different angles of vision". Hung in this way, the pictures are perversely animated and, no longer still, move through space, grow and diminish and have other pictures painted over the top of them. Instead of a gallery where objects are carefully separated from one another, this is a mechanical simulation of the palimpsest of memory, which presses down remembered images in layer on layer, the recovery of one image giving immediate access to others long buried and forgotten.

In packing the pictures one on top of the other like this, and having them disclose a cavernous tomb beyond, Soane is impersonating Seti I, whose sarcophagus the house enshrines, collecting his possessions around him to accompany him into his sepulchre. The cramped gallery is a reconstruction of his past and a premonition of the posthumous life he confidently expects. He survives in his collection of paintings, and for this reason they are the centre of the house. In the lectures he delivered at the Royal Academy between 1806 and 1809, Soane virually converted architecture into a pictorial art, which is to turn it into its opposite. The finest building, he argues, is that which needs paintings, because they are representations of spirit whereas architecture is a dull affair of matter and earthly solidity. Adjudicating between the Gothic and the Grecian, Soane declares the former to be inferior because it "leaves only very inconsiderable space, wherein paintings, sculptures and mosaics can be introduced". The only pictures it can accommodate are portraits, the only sculpture busts and individual statues: its self-completeness Soane makes the paradoxical proof of its inadequacy. As an example he chooses Fonthill, "which being partly furnished and the Mansion House in consequence pulled down, the pictures by ancient and modern Masters were sold, being found too large, and unsuitable to the decoration of a modern Gothic Abbey".[14] The superiority of the Grecian manner lies in its plentiful provision of gaps, vacancies which can be transposed into a picture-gallery.

Those empty spaces praised by Soane correspond to the blank pages or suggestive intervals with which Sterne ventilates the text of *Tristram Shandy*. At these moments in Sterne, thought peters out into silence, or breath falters into stillness, or a hand reaches in nervous anticipation to grasp at something which is not named. These are the limits of narrative, the points at which it must turn into something else, into an atmosphere which is too ambivalent and imprecise to be stated or into a reserved inarticulacy which can be either teasing or hushed and awesome. But the blanks are also places left for the insertion of illustrations: what can only be written about clumsily or offensively or tactlessly can be provisionally, conjecturally painted by the reader's imagination. Where the text declines to be specific, the reader is invited to take over the blank space as a screen, a passive *tabula rasa*, onto which he projects the flickering appearance of the scene as he imagines it. That union of the sister arts which Soane thought produced the most "forcible Effects on the intellectual mind" in architectural composition is in Sterne an illicit partnership: he provides the sketchy written evidence, goading us to make the prurient or sentimentally intrusive picture.

Rutter conducts his tour of Fonthill as an exploration of a landscape of fantasy. He leads the reader in through the lowly postern rather than the ceremonial entrance because he wishes to open up the astonishing scale of the place gradually, not to waste its effect in an initial shock which is then dissipated. This husbanding of attractions is said to be "most consonant with those rules of art, which should apply to architecture as to poetry and painting". The various styles which Fonthill brings into proximity are a set of landscapes ranging from the bare and cold to the tropically overgrown and abutting on one another. The landscapes radiate from the Grand Saloon or Great Octagon, with each vista atmospherically differentiated. To the west the eye, detaching itself from the blazonry and the embowered roof, loses itself in the Great Avenue, long and soft and green like a forest glade and naturally lighted; to the north the eye is perturbed the shadowy Sanctuary and the filtered light of the Oratory. The east is decoratively gaudy: "through the *chiaro-oscuro* of the elegant portal . . . flashes the radiance of the splendid *meubles* of the cabinet room to which it leads; and over it rises the superb architectural façades of the Music Gallery and the Organ Loft, pannelled with golden lattice, on grounds of scarlet damask", while "to the south, St Michael's Gallery presents a specimen of the richest combinations, which the genius of architecture has yet invented, beautifully contrasted with the artificial gloom of the opposite gallery, by terminating in an oriel-window of painted glass, exposed to the rays of a meridian sun". The four galleries make up a compass, the contrasted points of which are the varying identities of the building: to the west a dim and empty forest, to the east a golden haze of conspicuous consumption; to the north a religiose gloom, to the south a riot of light and colour.

Scale changes as improbably as style. The monastic austerity of the Gallery Cabinet, a chilly cell where Beckford slept on a narrow couch without hangings, contrasts with the sumptuousness elsewhere. The vestibule of St Michael's Gallery is "the loftiest apartment which domestic architecture can present, probably, in the world!", but other rooms were small, studiously private and secluded: the Chintz Boudoir, for instance, or the octagonal Cedar Boudoir, like Montaigne's tower study with a concealed entrance. Rutter makes a virtue of the contradiction, saying that never before were such sublime feelings evoked with so little space and material, creating the emotional effects of a cathedral within a fraction of the space.

As a palace of thought, Fonthill obeys the arbitrary, associative logic of dream, passing without modulation from a mood of ebullience to one of penitential grimness, simultaneously rejoicing in the multitude of its possessions and sourly rejecting them. Rutter describes the passage from King Edward's Gallery, which Beckford planned to honour his ancestors who had been knights of the garter, to the Vaulted Corridor as a journey through a landscape of mental portents. "We have passed beyond the light, the gold, the marble, and the blazonry; no windows are to be seen", and an involuntary, reverent hush descends in the dimness. From the Sanctuary and the fan-vaulted Oratory "we look back upon the gaiety and brilliancy of the scenes we have left, as a recluse does upon the glittering vanities of a world, whose pleasures he has exhausted and from which he has withdrawn". Flagrantly paradoxical, the building accumulates wealth only to disdain it. For all its extravagance, its architecture is not the expression of lordly hospitality but of misanthropy, like the abandoned cave into which Jaques retires, or Pope's dank grotto. As well, it is architecture fated to collapse. Being the fragile representation of an idea, it scorns the prosaic justifications of utility and soundness of structure. When it fell down, Beckford was positively gratified, and only regretted he had not been there to enjoy the catastrophe. St Michael's Gallery is a heavenly city of art objects, a cathedral transposed into a museum ("Art only has consecrated the spot, and who will afterwards dare to dispute her divine right?"), but again the building contradicts itself, leaving this repository of the civilised past toppling and destitute.

But Rutter finds a perverse, selfless nobility in the absurdities of the scheme. He treats this sybaritic temple of excess as a work of chaste self-sacrifice, and commends Beckford for devoting the whole edifice and not only the entrance "to the splendid purpose of producing a succession of architectural scenes of infinite variety", and for making even domestic comfort subserve this aim. The domestic hazards of the place, rather than evidence of its foolish impracticality, become Faustian challenges, inciting the inhabitants to surpass themselves. Its inadequacies are the ironic glories of its resolution to make a dwelling for the mind and to stint the body. There was only one room in which dinner could be served, but that was impossibly far from the kitchen; of the eighteen bedrooms, thirteen could not be used because they were too high and narrow, poorly lighted and ventilated, and the remainder lacked dressing-rooms; there was no provision for baking, brewing or washing in the basement, so these activities had to be transferred to an outhouse. It is a folly, but an expression as well of an overreaching *folie* like Faust's, a monument to aspiring discontent and dreamy immensity.

The final introversion is to make these mental structures not machines for living in, as Le Corbusier called the modern house, but machines for dying in. Soane's withdrawal from the world into his museum was a premature self-interment, closing himself off in his own funerary urn in company with the grave of the poor monk and the crypt of his wife's cat. Fonthill too was consecrated to Beckford's memory rather than to his existence. It was not until quite late in the development of the scheme, in 1805, that he conceived the idea of living in the place, for its original purpose had been funerary – he planned a tower one hundred and seventy-five feet high, on top of which he was to be buried (a Faustian reversal, however, of the idea of burial, since to be entombed at that height is to turn one's death into a levitation), and a "Revelation Chamber" with recesses in the walls for coffins and an iron grating through which the acolyte might peer.

Hazlitt, interestingly, despised Fonthill, and for a reason very pertinent to the present discussion. He thought it a palace of art but not of thought; and its particular crime was to leave out pictures. His accusation, in the essays of November 1822 and October 1823 in the *London Magazine* on Fonthill and other Wiltshire collections,[12] is the same as Soane's in the Academy lectures already mentioned – Fonthill is unreflective, insufficiently abstract. For Soane it lacks blank spaces for pictures which are the mind's own images, and for Hazlitt too, rather than creating a home for the mind like a picture gallery, it has chosen to display trinkets and gewgaws and metricious oddments in "a desert of magnificence, a glittering waste of laborious idleness, a cathedral turned into a toy-shop, an immense Museum of all that is most curious and costly, and, at the same time, most worthless in the productions of art and nature". Beckford's taste is merely ornamental and, like the older kind of virtuoso, he has assembled a wilderness of dainty and finicky objects which have no more than a material value. His exhibits do not pass from object to thought like pictures or Keats's Grecian urn, for there is no sentiment in a piece of porcelain, no soul in a gilded cabinet or a marble slab. The mind has no room in which to expand as at Dulwich, but is penned in by "frippery, and finery, and tinsel, and glitter, and embossing". A positive enemy of the poetic in painting, Beckford has sold the two Altieri Claudes which redeemed the collection, and revealed a taste in pictures which is "the quintessence and rectified spirit of *still-life*", a taste for surfaces glazed, polished, inlaid, enamelled – "Polemberg's walls of amber, Mieris's groups of steel, Vandermeer's ivory flesh". His delight is in an elaborate littleness, so that the huge pile of Fonthill is divided into a "parcel of little rooms, and those little rooms are stuck full of little pictures, and *bijouterie*". Exerting himself to be infernal, Beckford can manage only to be precious.

Hazlitt's disapproval gives warning of a change in the notion of the virtuoso, whose impulse now is not collection but performance, not scholarly curatorship but self-exhibiting improvisation. Early critics of *Tristram Shandy* often call it, dismissively, a performance, but in meaning to belittle they define one of its romantic qualities. Tristram's associative prodigies and feats of mental dexterity, his acrobatic involutions of literary form, come to suggest the improvisatory monologues of Liszt on the piano or the decorative antics of romantic singers or, in literature, the table-talk of Coleridge, performances in which he erects chimerical, collapsible palaces of thought held aloft briefly by an architecture of mental association.

Seen in these terms, *Tristram Shandy* is an inspired, delirious monologue. Its table-talk is musical: Stendhal's writing on music celebrates the singing voice as an instrument made for improvisation, but Sterne and Coleridge discover a similar power in the speaking voice. Stendhal believes that the voice's ability to shade and vary the spirit of what it sings, exploring nuances of feeling, gives it an emotional effect with which instrumental music cannot compete. Non-vocal music cannot excite pleasure or move us to tears, he argues, because it offers

only the unexhilarating drill of technical accomplishment. A
man need not possess any sensitivity to understand a concerto;
and for this reason Stendhal recommends that Paganini, the
demon of improvisatory virtuosity, should be heard not on
evenings when he is performing a concerto but when, rapt and
yielding to momentary inspiration, he is playing *capriccios*.[13]
Singing is a nervous art, whereas the violinist needs skilful
assurance and patience, and the special genius of Paganini lay
in having treated the violin as a vocal organ, confiding to it, as
if in a dramatic monologue, the secrets of his soul.

In his account of the soprano Giuditta Pasta, Stendhal
praises the reserve and dramatic intensity with which she
employed decorations, and says that she was never guilty of
those interminable ornamental frescoes which are like an
irrepressible talker in a fit of absent-mindedness, wandering
off into vacancy.[14] Though mocking, the analogy is exact. The
art of Sterne or Coleridge turns intellectual exposition into a
virtuoso unfolding of variations of emphasis and inflection, an
argumentative play with ideas like the singer's with notes.
And as the singer can subject the melody to such a labour of
inversion and alteration that it is superseded, so Tristram or
the table-talking Coleridge can divagate or succumb to
associative whim or ramify in networks of complication so as
to forget the point from which they began.

Coleridge, despite a contemptuous remark in one conversation about Paganini's money-grubbing, was conscious
of himself as a performer, a virtuoso extemporiser whose
instrument was his own myriad mind. He knows the vicissitudes of performance, and tells of an occasion when he was
reciting *Remorse* and, though generally proof against the intrusion of "mere external noise and circumstance", found himself
quite put off when a dirty boy burst in and cried, "Please
ma'am, master says, will you ha', or will you not *ha'*, the
pin-round?"[15] Coleridge's tragedies are Sternean comedies of
interrupted performance: the person from Porlock's knock on
the door is the equivalent of Mrs Shandy's question about the
clock. Apologising to a lady for this loquacity, Coleridge said
that he ran on so because his life was passed in the miserable
solitude of everlasting thought so that (like his own Ancient
Mariner condemned to seek out an audience for his recital)

whenever he has a visitor "I can hardly help easing my mind by pouring forth some of the accumulated mass of reflection and feeling". In Coleridge's case as in Hamlet's, the monologue is a therapeutic form, the antithesis of sociable dialogue: hence the inadvertent comedy of "Resolution and Independence", and of the wedding-guest's effort to free himself from the garrulous mariner. Richardson's heroines and Sterne's hero share Coleridge's medical excuse for their continuous discursiveness, since they all find relief in talking aloud to themselves.

Table-talking, Coleridge treats Johnson as a predecessor who was also more a performer than a writer, and who survives not in his literary productions but in the notes others scribbled down during his sessions of improvisation, as musicians owe their immortality to recording devices. Coleridge believed that Johnson owed his present fame to Boswell. His own misfortune was the lack of a Boswell. He is like a musician who antedates the gramophone, and of his talk only jottings remain. On 4 July 1833, Coleridge mentions Burke as another case of "a great and universal talker" without a Boswell. Burke's problem was that, like Coleridge, he talked continuously, which bewilders and exhausts the human reporter (though a bland and interminable tape would not mind), and, at the mercy of his own fluidity, Burke "seldom said the sharp short things that Johnson always did, which produce a more decided effect at the moment, and which are so much more easy to carry off". Coleridge then quotes Burke's opinion that Johnson was "greater in talking than in writing, and greater in Boswell than in real life". He returns to the notion of Johnson as a performer on 1 November of the same year, when he suggests that Johnson's power depended on the presence of an audience, being theatrical rather than literary: "the excitement of company called something like reality and consecutiveness into his reasonings, which in his writings I cannot see". His style had a tedious automatism, a weary reduplication of antithesis, which tended to run on whether it had a meaning or not, while in conversation "he was more excited and in earnest".

On 10 August 1833, Coleridge makes a general rule of the poet's need for praise, for an expectant and admiring audience, and adduces a medical reason for this which recalls Boswell's explanation of Johnson's need for the steadying solace of company: "There is a species of applause scarcely less genial to a poet than the vernal warmth to the feathered songsters during their nest-breeding or incubation; a sympathy, an expressed hope, that is the open air in which the poet breathes, and without which the sense of power sinks back on itself, like a sigh heaved up from the tightened chest of a sick man." Imprisoned in his lime-tree garden-bower, Coleridge regrets the departure of his friends, who have gone off intrepidly to explore the landscape he can only describe to them. Left behind, he can console himself by writing a poem, but that is an occupation of solitude, whereas conversing allows one to create in company.

This chapter has described the development of the Shandyean mental space from an antiquarian cabinet to an abstract, insubstantial gallery of pictures and thus to the illusory architecture of Soane and Beckford. As this happens, the virtuoso changes from a pedantic connoisseur to a visionary architect, suspending delicate, elaborate structures of imaginative association in the air. The process is summed up by Coleridge in "Kubla Khan", which demolishes the exotic architecture of its subject and raises in its place a wishful palace of thought, sustained by the poet's desire. As in his table-talk and conversation poems Coleridge turns the errant discursiveness of Tristram Shandy into an inspired pursuit of association, so in "Kubla Khan" Coleridge promotes Shandyean failure and frustration – the poem is the victim of interruption and expires in enigmatic inconclusiveness – to the prophetic vagaries of the seer.

The poem progressively dissolves and diminishes its landscape of fantasy until what begins as the expression of Kubla Khan's stately decree ends as an image of the poet's excited mind. At first Kubla Khan commissions the pleasure-dome, as the Regent did the Brighton Pavilion or Beckford Fonthill. Then the broadening view of the generation of the place reveals it to be the product not of human will but of fierce natural forces – the chasm hurling up the fountain, the dancing rocks and the sacred river. But the landscape is at last resolved into the creation neither of personal power nor of nature but of art. The dome is finally "a miracle of rare device", an artificial and paradoxical combination of ice and sun sustained by the poet himself. He unseats Kubla Khan as the owner and inventor of the marvel:

> I would build that dome in air,
> That sunny dome! those caves of ice!

The portentous miracle is at last not the dome, the river or the caverns but the poet himself, who has had the vision and emerged from it an object of holy dread. The anodyne prescribed "in consequence of a slight indiposition", to which Coleridge owed his dream, has become in the course of this development honey-dew and milk of Paradise; the picturesque landscape-gardening of Kubla Khan in *Purchas's Pilgrimage*, which the poem begins by paraphrasing, soon loses its solidity. It melts into a mirage on the waves, the synaesthetic product of the music of the fountain and the caves (Schelling's phrase for architecture, "frozen music", might be applied to the dome), and then dissolves into the wishful dream of the poet. Kubla Khan begins by imperiously commanding that the dome be built; the poet ends by faintly asserting that he would build it if he could revive in himself the song of the Abyssinian maid, the magic creative formula which is his secret equivalent to Kubla Khan's exertion of will. The poem is about failure, a vanishing dream, but it succeeds in abstracting the original sensations as they disappear, and holding them as images. Shelley called the creative mind a fading coal: as Coleridge's fire cools it turns into ice. The poet emerges as the awesome hero, a man with flashing eyes like the mariner, from whom people recoil in fear, and in contrast Kubla Khan is no more than a prosaic wedding-guest.

Notes

1. p. 363 of the Everyman edition of 1951, cited chapter 1, note 14.
2. *An Essay concerning Humane Understanding*, 1960, vol. I, p. 15.
3. Voltaire likens *Tristram Shandy* to a vase in the essay on conscience in the *Dictionnaire Philosophique*, 1771.
4. Scott invokes a Gothic room in the 1823 preface to Ballantyne's edition, collected in *Lives of the Novelists*.

5. "Characteristics", *Edinburgh Review*, 1831.

6. Pope's reading of Spenser is recounted in Joseph Spence's *Observations, Anecdotes and characters of books and men*, 1744.

7. Hazlitt's visits to the Angerstein collection and the Dulwich Gallery are in *Sketches of the Principal Picture-Galleries in England*, 1824.

8. *A New Description of Sir John Soane's Museum* was issued by the Trustees in 1955. John Summerson, the curator, also refers to the museum in *The Listener*, 9 November 1972.

9. Johann Zoffany's *The Tribuna of the Uffizi* (1772–8), in the Royal Collection, has been documented by Oliver Millar in *Zoffany and his Tribuna*, 1966. The remark made by Smollet is quoted in this book.

10. In a discussion of Richard Wilson in the *Encyclopaedia Brittanica* article "Fine Arts", 1838.

11. In his first course of Royal Academy lectures, 1806–9.

12. Fonthill is also discussed in Lockhart's review of Beckford's *Italy, with Sketches of Spain and Portugal* in the *Quarterly Review*, 1834.

13. *Vie de Rossini*, 1834, chapter 32.

14. ibid., chapter 35.

15. In *Table Talk*, 1827

3

The Virtuoso and the Libertine

The virtuoso, subduing the forms he employs to the exhibition of mental or physical or musical agility, is naturally a hedonist. He exists by self-indulgently taking liberties with artistic shape and moral precept, and he incites a rebellion of form against content. Garrick, for instance, gave up the self-effacing representation of Shakespeare's characters and made those characters pretexts for a formal exhibition of the fleeting succession of the passions. A character interpreted by Garrick is, like Tristram Shandy, a product of thought and feeling in virtuoso convolutions, a series of minute gestural felicities which work by stretching the text and impeding the dramatic action. But this odd, wayward separation of form from the content it supposedly serves becomes the rule. As romanticism proceeds, form acquires an absolute freedom from content: Turner's later pictures are works in praise of colour and its power to confound and dissolve shape; impressionist paintings make their technical method into a mode of vision, as James does in the New York prefaces to his novels; abstract art at last releases form altogether from the demeaning duty of representation.

Tristram's wayward, frolicsome intelligence has also turned thought into pure form, detached from emotion, inanely contentless. Sterne's fascination with typography, his prurient asterisks or breathless, suspended dashes, reveal him making emotions vanish into the forms which exist merely to record them. The mental antics of Tristram extend forward into the romantic attraction to madness as a pure formalisation of the play of consciousness, and this is another of the musical potentialities of Sterne's novel. For the tragic heroines of romantic opera run mad as effortlessly and as exquisitely as their comic counterparts negotiate scales and trills in their singing lessons, because madness grants them an inspired agility and inconsequence which are Shandyean. This absorption of Tristram into a demented formalism indicates the increasing abstraction of romantic literature, which has as its destiny in England the creation of Nonsense, the local, comic equivalent of symbolism.

From the first, the virtuoso seems dangerous, because irregular and improper. Tristram's early critics attack him as a libertine because he is a virtuoso, flaunting dazzling but scurrilous associations of ideas, and they have a point: artistic licence and moral licentiousness are intimately linked, and this aspect of Sterne's romantic originality will be elucidated in this chapter by comparing Tristram with the various incarnations of the libertine Don Juan, who is, with Don Quixote and Faust, one of the triumvirs of literary mythology. The libertine closest to Sterne, and the most interestingly complicated, is Mozart's Don Giovanni, who proclaims his double freedom, as a virtuoso artist and as an amoralist, in his reiterated cries of "Vivà la libertà!"

Like Tristram, Don Giovanni is alternately tragic and comic. Developing the first chapter's argument about the romantic dissolution of Shakespearean tragicomedy into a heteroclite ironic mood, he may, like Tristram, be seen as a paradoxical fusion of the spirits of Hamlet and Falstaff. From one point of view, he is merely gorging on a banquet of sense, a Falstaff in decline. But from another point of view, he is a tragic creature, harried, deluded, possessed, with some of Hamlet's dubiety in his relation to the supernatural solicitings. He belongs both to the eighteenth-century comedy of voracious appetite and sensual connoisseurship, and to the nineteenth-century tragedy of intellect threatened and tormented, choosing to rule in hell rather than serve in heaven. When Peacock and Shelley saw Mozart's opera together in London (at Covent Garden, 10 February 1818), Shelley asked beforehand if it was tragic or comic. Peacock told him it was a comedy. But when, after the duel with the Commendatore, the dying man's lament, the assassin's wondering commentary and the servant's nervous chatter blend in a trio which questions the same mysteries as Hamlet on the battlement with Horatio, Shelley demanded if this was Peacock's idea of comedy.

Don Giovanni begins in comedy, a man of feeling recklessly pursuing sensations, but ends, at least according to romantic criticism, in tragedy, the victim of the moral law he derides. And yet he is so treacherously ambiguous that his infernal conclusion seems comic as well: he comes upon tragedy inadvertently, by miscalculation, when the spirit-visitor calls his bluff. He is sacrificed to a celestial practical joke. Throughout the opera his most conspicuous dramatic quality is his Shandyean inefficiency. His triumphs are already a matter of historic record, of which Leporello with his catalogue is the custodian, almost the archivist. He fails in all four of the seductions he essays, even with Elivira's maid. His one success occurs when a girl in the street mistakes him for his servant. His virtuosity is by now vocal rather than sexual: he ruefully illustrates that transition from moral to aesthetic libertinism which is a feature of *Tristram Shandy*. For Sterne opens an artful gap between the self-regarding and self-confident virtuosity of the artist and the comic incapacity of his character, Tristram. The distance is the same as that which Byron's *Don Juan* measures between the poet's nimble and licentious command of language and Juan's own inability to make himself master of the situations he finds himself in.

Why does Don Giovanni so consistently fail? Because he doesn't need sexual success; he has a vocal triumph instead. Like Hamlet or Tristram or Byron's Juan, he fails as an agent in order to succeed as an artist. His moral libertinism is turning back into a matter of technical virtuosity. Leporello's catalogue is more a tribute to his master's aesthetic qualities of dexterity and versatility than to his sexual irresistibility, and it is these qualities which Don Giovanni flourishes in his effervescently difficult aria in Act I. The other characters all have arias which are about the emotional state in which the mobile Giovanni has caught and imprisoned them – the piercing icicles of Anna's fury, the long-suffering and long-drawn-out lyricism of Ottavio, the self-betraying affection of Elvira. As a mark of his difference from them, his aesthete's freedom from the emotion in which they are becalmed, Giovanni is given an aria of pure display, "Fin ch' han dal vino". They repeat themselves: each has a pair of arias, one for each act, and the second always shows them to be still the prisoners of the obsessions confided in the first. But Giovanni is constantly fabricating new images of himself, new ways to be himself, and after his first outburst of virtuosity can't be made to remain still long enough to sing an aria.

Existing outside emotion, he turns sex, as the coloratura heroines turn madness, into an opportunity for aesthetic self-exhibition. This transformation of sex into artistry distinguishes him from the pre-romantic Juan of Molière and the late-romantic Juan of Nikolaus Lenau.[1] Molière's libertine is a scientific satirist, exploiting the discrepancy between desire and moral pretence, concerned less to possess his victims than to mockingly anatomise them. His aim, as he tells Sgnarelle, is strategic advantage in the social war, and as a professional hypocrite he depends on deceit, whereas Don Giovanni is boldly, rashly himself always. With none of the stealthy discretion of Molière's Juan, he is a man of feeling, but of feeling stylised – as it is in the virtuoso linguistic games of Sterne and Byron – into the grace of art. Virtuosity of temperament also sets him apart from the dionysiac ardour of Lenau's Juan, whose stormy delight rages and erupts in Richard Strauss's tone-poem. In contrast with the opera, Strauss's version of Lenau is voiceless, because this Juan has undergone the Wagnerian experience of loss of self, immersed in and consumed by those he desires and therefore immersed in and consumed by the orchestra. Don Giovanni's conquests define and embellish that unique self rather than extinguishing it.

Sexual failure ironically vindicates not only Giovanni's aestheticism but his idealism. Don Quixote and Faust also fail, because they aspire to a perfect chivalric heroism or a completeness of knowledge which are humanly unattainable. Their glory and misery is that their reach exceeds their grasp. Don Giovanni's sublimity is sexual and therefore more dubious than their concern for honour and intellect, so that his failure is correspondingly not a tragic concession to mortal limitation, but a comic acquiescence in physical limitation. His sexual frustrations ironically imitate the yearnings and intellectual disappointments of Faust. Eternal literary figures like these revolve through comic and tragic aspects of themselves, as Hamlet does in turning from lecherous or pedantic wit to self-torture and finally resigned calm. Shelley's question to

Peacock cannot be answered about Don Giovanni, or about Don Quixote – a pitiable lunatic from one point of view, a saint from another – or Faust, who in Marlowe's version is as much a mean syllogistic quibbler as a dangerous magus, and who wastes the years until his tragic forfeit is due in comic conjuring tricks. *Don Giovanni* likewise explores all the tragicomic contradictions of its area of experience, searching into the shabby, cynical indignities and the vital splendour of sex.

Tristram Shandy is a comic dependent of these romantic heroes. In him the free range of Faust's speculation unfurls into the comic game of association-seeking, and the ardour of Don Giovanni declines into prurience, while his meanderings make him a comic Hamlet, his resolution sicklied over by the pale cast of thought. Yorick, proceeding with dignity on a meek-spirited jade which is full brother to Rosinante, is Sterne's version of Don Quixote, a character more lovable, in Sterne's view, than the heroes of antiquity. The Quixote of Cervantes is an ironic victim of an illusory and decaying code of manners; Sterne resurrects him as a man of sentiment, the precursor of Childe Harold or Childe Roland, a quester for whom success would be fatal. Harold moping disconsolately through Italy, or Roland realising at the tower that to fail as his predecessors did is the only victory, search for and can never find themselves. They are Sternean figures whose quest is endless because it continues as long as consciousness does. This romantic infinitude of process, comically anticipated in the digressive garrulity of Sterne, recreates the infinitude of medieval chivalric tales like Quixote's, which are endless because there is always more which can be added. Medieval knights can never rest because there is a whole universe of stories for them to work through; romantic knights cannot rest because there is the whole universe of themselves to explore. At whichever arbitrary moment consciousness is arrested, they are still experiencing. There is no terminal, conclusive point, so they are bound to seem hapless inconsequential failures. As the novel ends Mrs Shandy is still asking in bewilderment what the story is about. Sterne's remark about Quixote contrasts, by implication, the finality of achievement which distinguishes the classical hero with the

aspiring incompleteness of the romantic figure, and, accordingly, the heroism of Tennyson's Ulysses undergoes a change
from classical finality to the infinite deferments of romanticism as he sails off wearily with the "will/To strive, to seek,
to find", invited by the somnolent wash of the verse to post-
pone achievement, to join the lotus-eaters.

Eventually the libertine renounces character, which obliges
him to seem completed and consistent in the classical way, and
becomes a process, romantically endless. This is the metamorphosis which occurs in Kierkegaard's account of Don
Giovanni in *Either/Or*.[2] For Kierkegaard the submergence of
character in process is a romantic rescue: the libertine is translated from society to nature, and from tragedy to comedy.
Don Giovanni is no longer a person. Like Hamlet, he is a zero
who turns the others into numbers, while he himself deftly
impersonates a different number depending on whose company he finds himself in. Kierkegaard declares him to be not an
entity fixed and bounded but an ongoing process "of whose
life history one can form no more definite impression than one
can by listening to the tumult of the waves". The fluid and
eternally recurring thought-stream of Tristram Shandy begins
to dissolve character into a mental landscape, and for
Kierkegaard Don Giovanni has the eerie indefiniteness of a
natural phenomenon, not the discrete identity of a social being.
Whereas Faust, being a creature of intellect, can only be conceived individually, Don Giovanni is dashed between individuality and an idea of life, and this storm-tossed uncertainty
Kierkegaard depicts by means of a landscape: "This hovering
is the musical trembling. When the sea tosses tempestuously,
then the swirling billows form images of strange creatures in
this wild upheaval. It is as if these creatures set the waves in
motion, and yet it is the conflict of the opposing billows which
creates them."

Additionally, in becoming a process Don Giovanni is transferred from tragedy to a violent, impulsive, endless comedy,
since his individual nature, the tragic potential in him, has been
merged in the undifferentiated comic energy which throbs
through him. Not even Leporello's list manages to define Don
Giovanni. Kierkegaard imagines it to be hastily improvised –
the "mille e tre" already vanquished in Spain is a suspiciously

irregular number, implying future extension. The list will never reach a sum total, as Giovanni is an untiring and ceaseless power of nature who "as little tires of seducing or is done with seducing as the wind is tired of blowing, the sea of billowing, or a waterfall of tumbling from the heights". He resembles, that is, Shelley's boisterous west wind or Byron's rolling ocean and falls of Terni.

Rescued by romanticism, Giovanni becomes for Kierkegaard a philosophical principle and a creature whose demon can only be expressed by the sensuousness of music – for to his other translations has been added his removal from literature to music. Kierkegaard calls his musical animation an "exuberant joy of life". The phrase recalls Coleridge's account of the levity and harmonised energy of Shakespeare's humour, an elation of animal spirits "like the flourishing of a man's stick when he is walking . . . a sort of exuberance of hilarity which disburdens, . . . a conductor, to distribute a portion of our gladness to the surrounding air".[3] The hedonistic tracing of arabesque patterns in the air with a stick reveals a Sternean delight in form, in freeing language from function and meaning so it can respond to the athletic frolic of emotion. Sterne aims to transform sour and splenetic emotions into playful grace as Mozart transforms the rampant and predatory sexual will of Don Giovanni into exhilarating sport: Sterne's aim, as much as Giovanni's, is physical conquest. He writes in the hope of banishing the spleen by exercising the diaphragm and the intercostal and abdominal muscles in laughter, which forces gall and all liverish bitterness down into the duodenum. He writes in order to have an effect on the bodies of his readers. Like music Sterne's writing seeks to by-pass the intelligence and make itself felt directly in the body, which Burke, as a subsequent chapter will show, had made the measure and the judge of art. Sterne makes the book a score which the reader is to physically perform, a set of exercises in breathing and physical co-ordination which he acts out. The reader plays the novel rather than soberly reading it, both as an actor plays a piece of theatre and as a soloist plays a piece of music. Reading is conceived as a physical rather than a mental activity, almost a performing art. In training or healing his body in the way Sterne recommends, the reader comes to resemble the man

whirling his stick as he walks or the singer hurling forth from
inside himself the notes of Don Giovanni's music. Victorian
novelists expect reading to be work, a labour of verification
and studious evaluation similar to that which produced the
novel. Sterne expects it to be pleasure and performance. The
novel is the conductor, in both musical and electrical senses,
through which his medicinal energy passes into us.

Such an approximation to music accords with Kierkegaard's insistence that the sensuous elation of the libertine
demands not speech but song. Hamlet and Faust are both
unable to escape from language, which condemns them to be
reflective individuals, but Kierkegaard disqualifies Byron's
Don Juan as an account of the libertine because it coarsens him
into a reflective character whose medium is speech. This
afflicts him again with the rational and self-contained identity
the elemental Don Giovanni dissolves: his victims possess
such an identity, but the libertine with his "perpetual vanishing, precisely like music, . . . which . . . is over as soon as it
sounds" ought to evade it. In making language the medium of
an irrational character who has no reliable, single identity,
Sterne, however, endows it with some of the seductive
irresponsibility of song.

Music, despite the efforts of so many composers, has never
been adequate to Hamlet or Faust, because their being lies less
in sense than in intellect. Giovanni seduces thousands, but his
sensuous energy preserves him from ethical judgement. No
such freedom can be granted to Faust: he is judged severely
even though he has seduced only one girl, because in doing so
he has betrayed and trivialised his intellectual self. Faust cannot
enjoy; he values the sensuous only because it offers a diversion,
helping him to forget his loss of another and higher world.
The overworked intellects of Hamlet and Faust lead away
from the tidal impersonality of music towards the dramatic
monologue, where all the small equivoctions and irritated
tremors of thought which make up their pained individuality
can be recorded. Even Marlowe's Faustus is a dramatic mono-
loguist in advance of his time, beginning and ending in
soliloquy and whiling away the years between in horse-play,
which is how Hamlet too occupies the intervals between his
moments of solitude.

The novelty of the libertine's character rearranges literary form. Don Giovanni raises pleasure to the dignity of epic. As Kierkegaard points out, Leporello makes an epic hero of him in unravelling the catalogue of the seduced. The epic quality of that list is its infinitude: it will never be completed. Wordsworth was likewise able to call *The Prelude* an epic of what passes in the poet's mind because, like *Tristram Shandy*, it derives its grandiloquence and proliferation from the infinitude of consciousness, unending and unbounded. As romanticism remakes the picaresque, the mere accidental succession of narrative incidents becomes a formal image of the limitlessly associative nature of experience. Leporello's list is a vindication of the apparently arbitrary succession of romantic narrative which de Quincey criticised in *Vathek*: "as on the one hand, there is no moral *à parte post*, so, on the other hand, there is no determining principle *à parte ante*. Every incident has been separately and capriciously invented, under no impulse from what preceded it."[4] But the career of a libertine could proceed in no other way, since the essence of his character is a random, opportunistic willingness to take pleasure wherever he finds it. The picaresque form allows the artist to follow inspirational whim, as Sterne does, and this freedom to diverge or detour the artists share with their characters. For Byron the picaresque is the promiscuous: Juan's malleable eagerness to slide into any erotic attachment which presents itself answers to Byron's own gleeful irresponsibility with narrative and style. The same is true of Sterne, who allows the *Sentimental Journey* to expire in teasing inconclusiveness as Yorick stretches out his hand towards the fille de chambre's ———. For the picaresque hero, whether he is sentimental like Yorick or erotic like Juan or intellectual like Faust, to reach a conclusion is an admission of defeat.

Freedom of association serves both the character's whim and the artist's formal convenience. Dickens sends Martin Chuzzlewit and Tom Pinch off to America at short notice to extend their range of experience but also to restore flagging sales. Berlioz in the preface to the full score of *La Damnation de Faust* explains why his peripatetic Faust turns up initially in Hungary: "The answer is, because I wanted to get a hearing for an orchestral piece the theme of which is Hungarian, I admit it frankly; and I would have taken Faust to any place on earth had I had the smallest musical reason for doing so."[5] Having to accommodate both the wilful artist and his wandering characters, works of art tend to become miscellanies, held together loosely by the mazy motion of consciousness. The artist's mind is a random collection of thoughts and emotions strangely interlinked, and aesthetic form imitates this genial confusion: *Tristram Shandy*, as the preceding chapter argued, is an image of the mental lumber-room, a mental museum in which curios and accumulations of learning jostle with personal recollections and sentimental treasures, and the store can be added to indefinitely.

This unending process of accession and acquisition marks, for Kierkegaard, one of the differences between romantic and classical art. Sensuousness in the ancient world could be expressed with still, lucid completeness in plastic art, but "in the Christian world the sensuous must burst forth in all its impatient passion", in action which is endless because it is incapable of satisfying the spirit. Romantic heroes act so incessantly and with such dazzling versatility precisely because they are sceptical of action, because introversion afflicts them with an unnatural febrility. Their rightful home, in the Hamlet-like phrase Kierkegaard uses of Don Giovanni, is "in an inward category". Life for them thus becomes a succession of failures to find an outward form corresponding to their inward need. Hamlet's lack of an objective correlative is the badge of his integrity and the play's, not, as T. S. Eliot believed, of an artistic miscalculation, and this lack or absence is virtually institutionalised by romantic narrative, comically in Mrs Shandy's incomprehension, tragically in Faust's objectless aspiration.

Kierkegaard develops his insight about the protracted, inconclusive, chaotically impatient fate of the romantic hero with a perplexed logic which needs to be altered at certain points. For instance, he criticises Byron's poem for failing to realise that, as its Juan is reflective, interest in him can only be psychological. Giovanni seduces a thousand and three because he is energy without a mind or a subtle inside, and we only wish to see or hear him at his furious work. Juan need only seduce one woman, but the artist must show how he does it.

This Byron fails to do, choosing the method, inappropriate in his case, of epic multiplication rather than concentrating on the analysis of a single encounter. But Kierkegaard's mistake is to consider Byron's hero reflective: Juan has the amiable characterlessness of a Fielding hero, pliably picaresque, and the endless epic career is the only possibility for him. The psychological appreciation of motive which Kierkegaard demands belongs not to the imperceptive and *"moyen sensuel"* hero but to Byron in his conduct of the poem. The narrator, not the hero, possesses the hurricane energy of Don Giovanni, which, redirected from sex into art, is expressed in the hectic and irregular sportive velocity of the language.

In Kierkegaard's scheme, Byron's Juan and Molière's decline into comedy because their creators deny them the means to become interesting. Giovanni, living in music, is the master of the medium he employs; the other two are not in formal control in this way, and their failure is not even rendered as a psychological complexity but simply made ludicrous and shaming. Kierkegaard's judgement also needs alteration here, for failure is surely part of the libertine's romantic meaning – his Shandyean component. Even Don Giovanni's mastery of the medium of song is offset by his inability to control the drift of the action – just as Hamlet plays word-games and devises ingenious aesthetic plots while others, less meticulous, ensnare him in hasty but workable intrigues of their own; or as Byron is keen and skilful in his management of the poem, while leaving his hero to flounder through the mishaps of its action. That romantic inwardness which, as Kierkegaard says, prevents Don Giovanni from becoming visible or revealing himself "through the physical form and its movements or in plastic harmony" also obliges him to be ineffective as an actor, in his dealings with the world outside himself and outside art. Success as an artist entails, even demands, failure as an agent.

A complicated exchange takes place between the libertine's sensuousness and his formalism: he is, like Tristram or Yorick, too agitated or impulsive a connoisseur of sensation to bother being a tidy, coherent artist; conversely he is, like Hamlet or Don Giovanni, too refined and immaculate an artist to care any more for victories in action, since his vindication is aes-

thetic. Some of these connections between romantic heroism
and the disruption of aesthetic form are hinted at by Coleridge
who, as the first chapter of this book explained, perceived the
analogy between the literary manner of a character like Tristram and his morals, between artistic licence and moral licentiousness. Technical dexterity and associative virtuosity make
Tristram a libertine, who treats the shape and substance of
narrative and the proprieties of morals with a similar mocking
elasticity. When the libertine next appears in literature, in
Byron's *Don Juan,* artistic licence, whimsical transgression
against the morality of form, has taken over from the moral
daring and self-adventurousness which are the libertine qualities of Tristram (as Coleridge sees him) or Don Giovanni.

In Byron's poem, the artist is the libertine, and the libertine
hero has dwindled into *"l'homme moyen sensuel".* *Don Juan* is
written by Don Giovanni with a hangover; its titular hero is
more like Cherubino, the agitated, inexperienced page from
Le Nozze di Figaro whom Kierkegaard declared to be the
adolescent embryo of Don Giovanni. Byron is as high-handed
and unrepentantly brash with language, as audacious with
rhymes and as unscrupulous in his manipulation of a ductile
stanza form, as his hero is meant to be with women. The
writing of the poem is his rake's progress –

>   (. . .I write this reeling,
> Having got drunk exceedingly today,
>   So that I seem to stand upon the ceiling) –

and the hero is superfluous, chosen at random because brave
and sage men are scarce in the present age, and pressed into service despite his inadequacy:

>   I'll therefore take our ancient friend Don Juan –
> We all have seen him, in the pantomime,
> Sent to the devil somewhat ere his time.

Byron significantly takes his Juan from the pantomime,
rather than from Mozart. Jane Austen's Don Juan has a similar
origin: she describes having seen a play based on Shadwell's
Libertine, and recounts that at the end of the evening she left
Don Juan "in hell at half-past eleven".[6] Her joke and Byron's
about time's foreclosure combine to make an important point

about the libertine. He is one who wastes time, as Tristram idly does, but who is fated to be in his turn wasted by time. Don Giovanni's tragedy is to fall into time. Ageless, ubiquitous, flourishing always in an orgiastic present tense of one "happy minute" (as Rochester, a fellow-libertine, called the instant of sexual pleasure) after another, he suddenly acquires a past when Elvira tracks him down, and as well is forced by the Commendatore's statue to acknowledge a retributive future. Jane Austen's cold jest diminishes Don Juan by turning his time back into her own – she leaves the theatre unmoved at eleven-thirty, like Leporello in the opera's epilogue off to the inn to find a new master. But the libertine recovers from her snub. She makes a purely theatrical figure of him, but theatricality is the secret of his immortality – like Cleopatra's studied "celerity in dying", or Falstaff getting to his feet after being pronounced dead, he emerges unscathed after each performance, perpetually reborn, won back to life by the audience's applause. Jane Austen briskly leaves him in hell, but he does not stay there.

She condemns Juan, while Byron reprieves him. Only in the pantomime, not in the poem, is he carried off to hell before his time. The Byron who writes the poem and intervenes in it to confess his partiality to dark eyes or to upbraid Plato presents himself as the wreck of a libertine, scorched and worn by experience; but the Juan who appears in the poem is not a character made for the abyss. His time will never come: Byron guarantees that by rescuing him for the casually unfurling career of a picaresque hero.

As the poem breaks off, Juan does seem to have reached a terminal point. A door opens before him

> . . .with a most infernal shriek
> Like that of hell. 'Lasciate ogni speranza
> Voi ch'entrate!' The hinge seem'd to speak,
> Dreadful as Dante's rima, or this stanza;

but Juan is not conducted to hell. Rather, when the sable-hooded friar appears, Mozart's conclusion is reversed, so as to make Juan tremble like Leporello, not stand sceptically firm like Don Giovanni. He treats the ghost not as a spirit-messenger but as an intellectual conundrum, pondering the nature of its nonentity. Then, discovering it to be not a harsh and forbidding thing of stone, but a sensuous being like himself, with a sweet breath, pearly teeth and warm breast, he touches the statue into life, instead of being mortally chilled by its grasp as in the opera:

> A dimpled chin, a neck of ivory, stole
> Forth into something much like flesh and blood.

It is no longer his insubstantial enemy but another eager victim, her Grace Fitze-Fulke. The Commendatore, as it were, has been unmasked as yet another metamorphosis of Elvira. Juan parodies Giovanni's end and makes of it an erotic new beginning, like Yorick's extension of his hand. The opera is tragically terminal; the poem's end is comically prurient and provisional, like the ends of Sterne's narratives. Byron has released the libertine from tragedy into the facile freedom of comedy, and transposed his spiritual rebellion into a licensed evasion of the rules of artistic form.

This is why Shaw dismisses Byron's version of the libertine. The Byronic hero is merely a virtuoso, insufficiently immoral, flirtatious rather than defiant, supple and comically flexible, not tragically fanatical. Byron, Shaw implies in the Preface to *Man and Superman*, has backed away in cowardice from the enemy of god to fashion a picaresque worldling, a merely sensuous man whose sexual encounters are glad and guiltless rather than a means of thrusting himself beyond good and evil. Shaw like Byron pardons the libertine. But whereas Byron does so by trivialising him, turning Don Giovanni back into the frivolous anti-formalist Tristram Shandy, Shaw does so by chastening him and converting him from hedonism to politics. He borrows the libertine's posture of moral defiance and declares that the "supernatural retributive morality" which decrees the libertine's fall is the only immoral feature of *Don Giovanni*: "Gentlemen who break through the ordinary categories of good and evil, and come out on the other side singing 'Finch' han dal vino' and 'La ci darem', do not, as a matter of fact, get called on by statues, and taken straight down through the floor to eternal torments; and to pretend that they do is to shirk the social problem they present."

Shaw's Giovanni is a hero of politics not pleasure, a

revolutionary affronting established institutions and deriding the monkish penitence tradition attaches to his legend. He is a worthy antagonist for the Commendatore, existing on the same transcendent plane. They are the mighty abstract opposites of Hegelian history, leaving the other prudes and prigs "on a crockery shelf below to live happily ever after". This political conversion entails the dismissal of Byron's Juan, who for Shaw is merely a picaresque vagabond, "no more an enemy of God than any romantic and adventuresome young sower of wild oats". The last distinctive Juan is Mozart's, because the libertine was rendered obsolete by the more ambitious figure of Faust, whose contest with the gods extends through a sphere altogether wider than the merely erotic one (which Shaw regards with some distaste) of Don Giovanni. Faust has time for only one sexual adventure, and rather than indulging the generalised universal lust of Don Gioivanni devises projects of humanitarian reform: Shaw therefore gives to his own libertine, Jack Tanner, the socialism of Faust rather than the sexuality of Don Giovanni.

Having deprived his Giovanni of a profligacy which, in his view, was never essential to the character, Shaw finds that he has turned him into another of the recurrent creatures of romanticism, Hamlet – but a Hamlet also purged and redeemed, bereft of his self-absorption and giddy theatricality and released from the crude sensationalism of the drama. This new-born character now discards his Ovid and Seneca and reads Schopenhauer, Nietzsche and Westernmarck; he listens to Wagner rather than Mozart. Above all he is concerned, as the preface to *Man and Superman* puts it, "for the future of the race instead of for the freedom of his own instincts." The remark indicates how far the character has been made to outgrow the romantic virtuosity of self-appreciation. Instead of indulging his romantic fascination with himself, as Tristram Shandy, on the model of Hamlet, is permitted to do, he must now attend to the miseries of others. Romanticism now seems, to the man of the late nineteenth century like Shaw, mere moral stupidity, a tissue of fantasies sustained by vanity and selfishness and incapable of producing useful knowledge. Shaw's converted libertine longs to abandon the petty obstructions of personality in which his romantic forbears are so joyfully enmeshed, and to become the disembodied and impersonal conscience of the race.

By a peculiar ingenuity of literary history, Shaw here discounts romanticism by means of a metamorphosis and fusion of the two characters, Hamlet and Don Giovanni, who most forcefully represent the romantic liberation of intelligence and instinct which he deplores. Hamlet, the dilatory intimate of Tristram Shandy, is made into "a true Promethean foe of the gods", whose significance Shakespeare failed to understand: "Hamlet was a developed Don Juan whom Shakespear palmed off as a reputable man just as he palmed poor Macbeth off as a murderer." Juan himself passes from a hero of tenebrous pleasure into one of lucid, ascetic intelligence.

Hamlet is rescued from the role of ineffectual dreamer which Shakespeare allegedly imposes on him, Giovanni from that of compulsive seducer. The qualities of truculence and humorous introversion ascribed to romantic characters in the first chapter, their refusal to change and their digressive delight in themselves, have now become, in Shaw's estimation, crimes against morality and mind. He sees that characters like Hamlet, Falstaff or Tristram Shandy are suspicious of politics and of schemes for rationalising and unifying the world, and he blames their recalcitrance on their creators, romantic anarchists like Shakespeare or Sterne, mere artists (as Shaw disparagingly calls them) as opposed to the strenuous but serene intellectuality of the artist-philosophers, who strive to change the world rather than merely deriving pleasure from it. Shaw detests romantic art for being truant and playful, irregular and subversive: he is finally in agreement with the Commendatore. He reinterprets the Shakespearean double plot so as to suggest that the romantic artist is no more than the artist-philosopher's baser self, possessing a coarse comic wisdom but no organising power of thought. The romantic is the fool to the artist-philosopher's Lear, the Sancho Panza to his Quixote, the Micawber to his Copperfield. These self-preoccupied, irrational romantic creatures constitute, for Shaw, a retarded and fragmented society which must be provoked into consciousness of itself, a society slumbering in dreamy Id (like Giovanni or the childish Tristram) which must be roused into the bracing responsibilities of Ego.

Characters like Falstaff or Tristram Shandy offer repose, the satisfying stillness of basking in one's sense of oneself; Shaw demands motion, purposeful growth, mental effort. The vigour of Don Giovanni is merely physical and pleasure-bound; Shaw's Tanner has none of this sleek, lithe physical attractiveness, but is a prosaic campaigner for enlightenment. Leporello's list – meant, Kierkegaard says, for music, which can turn an inventory into a gently insinuating but torrential force of nature – becomes the handbook for revolutionaries, austerely inaccessible to music. Hedonistically self-absorbed, the great characters of Shakespeare and Dickens are immovable lumps of matter unquickened by mind, requiring external stimulation and contrivance to start them into operation: as Shaw points out, Hamlet, like Micawber, must become a policeman, Macbeth a bush-ranger, and the wonderfully ineffective Tristram is changed into the bustling, parsonical, do-gooding Yorick. The unique informal freedom which derives from the refusal of Shakespeare and Dickens to make plot and character cohere, their creation of spaces in their work where the characters can talk about themselves, unmolested by the nagging punctuality of plot, Shaw can only interpret as mindlessness, an inability to find a motive in things. Shaw's own work has expelled such arbitrary, improvised comic contingencies, which give way to intellectual necessity. Prefaces declare the meaning of plays in advance; stringently specific stage-directions ensure that each servile object is in its place, on duty in accord with the artist-philosopher's intention.

Tolstoy shares Shaw's philosophical contempt for Shakespeare, and he is derisive about the Shandyean carelessness of the plays, their negligence about motive and circumstance.[7] Hamlet is particularly repellent to Tolstoy because Shakespeare gives him no character at all, although this may be said to be precisely the originality of Hamlet, as it is of Tristram Shandy. Like Pope's women, Hamlet and Tristram have no character, no quantifiable set of traits and moral dispositions; instead they have personality, a multitude of variable, alternating selves. Tolstoy deems Falstaff Shakespeare's only satisfactory character, because he is a flagrant embodiment of his creator's vices: in him the quibbling and ghastly punning which were for Tolstoy the staple of Shakespeare's manner are displayed as appropriate to a depraved and shameless person.

Shaw at least concedes that the genius of the art he calls romantic lies in its portrayal of libertines, of "instinctive temperaments", unpolitical and regressive states of mind which are the despair of the artist-philosopher. Among the characters he names as exemplars of this temperament are Falstaff, who is "self-acting: his motives are his own appetites and instincts and humours", Richard III when allowed to indulge in whimsical vaudeville not when sent off to scheme and murder, Faulconbridge, Leontes and Coriolanus. The latter Shaw calls one of Shakespeare's finest comic creations, and he is right. The titanic petulance of Coriolanus is comic and infantile. He is cruelly stung by the taunt of "boy" because it has such unseemly accuracy. His one good and rational act, his submission to his mother's entreaties, is absurdly and fatally inconsistent with his behaviour in the past and, like Falstaff's nomination of himself for high office, it expels him from his comedy of unmisgiving instinct and self-aggrandising fantasy into a severe adult world of responsibility which, inevitably and immediately, destroys him. Don Giovanni's brazen invitation of the Commendatore to dinner is a similar error: like Falstaff's bid for promotion it marks a comic hubris, as instinct attempts to extend its reign into the preserves of reason and moral or political obligation. Giovanni's miscalculation is translated by Kierkegaard into his private theology: he explains that only a ghost can vanquish the libertine because "a spirit, a ghost, is a reincarnation" and Don Giovanni "can withstand everything, except the reincarnation of life, precisely because he is immediate sensuous life, whose negation the spirit is". Or in Shaw's terms he is instinct, extinguished by intellect. His error is to invite the Commendatore to a meal: those calmly rising and falling intervals in which the Commendatore refuses the food Giovanni has been gorging and announces that whoever has eaten the food of heaven will not accept that of mortals are a chilling judgement on the libertine, for they sterilise pleasure and parch appetite to ashes. The charmed life of sense can be ended only by one in whom sense has been petrified.

The character of instinct is his own subject, and resists being used by an artist, even when, as in *Tristram Shandy*, he himself is the artist. But the philosophical character rejoices in the artist's impositions on him, gladly laying down his life, as Mrs Ramsay does in parenthesis or as Leonard Bast does under the bookcase, in the service of an artistic design. Shaw proclaims this slavish sacrifice of oneself to be "the true joy in life, the being used for a purpose recognized by yourself as a mighty one; being thoroughly worn out before you are thrown on the scrap heap" – as their creators wear out and discard Septimus Smith or the sibylline Mrs Moore. The high daring and courageous radicalism which Shaw admires in the characters of artist-philosophers like Bunyan, Wagner and Nietzsche is compromised, though he does not notice it, by their will-less acquiescence in their creators' demands on them. These characters are conscripted, set to forced labour, and eventually declared redundant (as Wotan peremptorily executes Hunding in *Die Walküre*), but are required to rejoice in their enslavement to artistic ideology. The Shavian artist-philosopher is like a philosopher-king, in complete and jealous control of works of art which resemble regularised, enlightened utopias, or Bentham's model prison, every corner of which is visible from a central commanding point of vantage.

Shaw's polemic against romantic inanity misses, of course, the special quality of introversion represented by the characters he disapproves of. It is possible, indeed, to find in the solipsism of Hamlet, Falstaff and Tristram an anticipation of the mental aptitude and alertness which Shaw prizes. His Juan in hell calls Life "the force that ever strives to attain greater power of contemplating itself" – and this is precisely what these romantic idlers are pledged to do. Their instruments are, however, sentiment and irony, tentative early stages in the mind's evolution towards Shavian knowledge. In Shaw's terms, sentiment and irony are retarded because self-referring, inward rather than altruistic. Sentiment is the self's contemplation of its subtle responsiveness as an organism, its elated discovery of new ways to play upon the virtuoso instrument of the feelings. Irony is equally self-reflexive, quizzically marking the limits of sentiment where other people become opaque or the edges of our own personalities are hidden from ourselves. Romantic irony might be called sentiment's admission of defeat. But sentiment and irony join in proclaiming the pleasure of consciousness, whereas, for Shaw's reformed libertine, identity is not feckless and hedonistic but grimly dutiful. The sentimental or ironic vision is always partial and fragile, confessing its own weaknesses, and Shaw's Juan demands in its place the creation of an all-seeing myriad-minded "ideal individual" who will be "omnipotent, omniscient, infallible, and withal completely unilludedly self-conscious: in short, a god". Life is driving, beyond the whimsical self-consciousness of sentiment and the glancing self-knowledge of irony towards what Shaw calls brains, "an organ by which it can attain not only self-consciousness but self-understanding". The romantic characters, however, are so diverted by the self-conscious, self-admiring activity of being themselves that they never admit the obligation to understand themselves.

The race of "higher and higher individuals" Shaw hopes to create, intellects of godly altruism, are a new breed of classical heroes, accepting the ministries of fate and their mission rather than languishing romantically in the pleasures of private life. The force which presides over the careers of romantic heroes is not fate but the comic alternative to it, accident. They grow through impulsive changes of course or leisurely divergences, and the mark of the formal libertinism of the works in which they occur is that these works accommodate the accidents and associative divagations of their progress. Hamlet sends his play off on detours right and left. Falstaff insists on recurring, even posthumously. Sterne's novel follows the untrustworthy, accidental course of rumination: he promises to take up the subject of the midwife within three chapters, if nothing happens on the way, rather as Hamlet by implication promises to avenge his father by the fifth act, if he ever reaches it. The very act of writing is accident-prone and obstacle-ridden, for Tristram as much as for Richardson's heroines, since it breathlessly tries to keep pace with changeful, momentary experience. Art scrambles after a perpetually incomplete life in eager desperation, and from its panic and formal chaos emerge a comic wisdom: living is a readiness to abandon consistency and preconception, to take advantage of each new circumstance into which one floats, as these romantic heroes episodically do. Hamlet does so with witty flexibility, Don Quixote with boundless imaginative hope, Don Giovanni with predatory sensual anticipation, Don Juan in polite deference to those who wish to use him for their pleasure.

This is why these heroes seem failures. They are not creatures of action, sure that there is a tide in the affairs of men, meaningful and determined. They are creatures of performance, who delight because of their ability to cope with the challenge of each new moment, imprinting themselves on it or artfully redesigning themselves in accordance with it. They are at once virtuosi intent on turning life into art, and libertines stretching art into the episodic semblance of life.

Notes

1. Molière's *Don Juan* was written in 1664; the dramatic fragment by Nikolaus Lenau (1802–50), which describes Don Juan's storm of enjoyment expiring not in the fires of hell but in miserable self-disgust, was the source for Richard Strauss's tone-poem, op. 20.
2. Kierkegaard's ethical study of the libertine in *Either/Or: A Fragment of Life* was first published in Copenhagen in 1843, and translated in 1943 by David F. Swenson and Lillian Marvin Swenson.
3. From a report by J. P. Collier after a lecture in 1811–12, reprinted in *Coleridge on Shakespeare*, ed. Terence Hawkes, 1969, p. 121.
4. *Edinburgh Saturday Post*, 8 September 1827.
5. Berlioz's defence of Faust's detours is mentioned by Ernest Newman in *The Sunday Times* for 17 January 1943.
6. Jane Austen had seen the pantomime at the Lyceum in 1813, and dismisses it in a letter to her sister Cassandra on 15 September.
7. Tolstoy's attack on Shakespeare is in *Shakespeare and the Drama*, 1906 collected in *Shakespeare in Europe*, ed. Oswald Le Winter, 1970.

4

The Intellectual Libertine

Shaw's contrast between the two traditions of instinct and intellect, libertinism and determinism, extends the antithesis in Coleridge's criticism between the tradition of humorous digressiveness and that of intellectually rigid form. Although Coleridge is a Shandyean procrastinator, in whom the postponements and collapses of Sterne protect a mystic vision which refuses to be profaned by rationalisation, it is at the same time he who proposes the alternative to the libertine notion of literary form, and who reinterprets the libertine, changing him from a figure of episodic sensuous delight to one of mental acuity and rigorous self-control. In Coleridge the digressive abandon of Tristram ironically coexists with the encyclopaedic exactitude of Walter Shandy. His veneration for systematic literary form is intensified by his own association-seeking or fatigued crimes against it.

On the one hand, as the lecture notes on wit and humour which were discussed in the first chapter imply, Coleridge permits characters like Hamlet or Tristram to indulge their capacity for evasive generalisation, distending or delaying their plots; but on the other hand, Coleridge praises three perfect plots, images of strict moral self-consistency, not improvisatory licence: those of *Oepidus Rex*, *The Alchemist* and *Tom Jones*.[1] For Coleridge, as for Shaw, the choice is moral as well as formal. One tradition is jovially accidental and anarchic, excusing human weakness and idleness; the other is regular and rational, an image of justice, proportion and rectitude. The previous chapter has considered the libertine's affiliations with the former tradition; but Coleridge also interprets the libertine as a figure of indeflectible, sternly logical mental power, which removes him from the digressive pursuit of sensuous distraction and places him in the second tradition of severe formal regularity. This metamorphosis unfolds new romantic meanings for *Tristram Shandy*.

So far as the novel belongs to the first tradition of formal amoralism, it represents character as accidental not purposeful: some men, however earnestly they order their lives, "pass thro' a certain medium, which . . . twists and refracts them from their true directions". Hero and novel reel from one revelatory accident to another. E. M. Forster said that a god sat enthroned somewhere in the chaotic heart of *Tristram Shandy*, and that its name was Muddle.[2] Forster's deity is as potent and as much a presence in romantic art as its associate, the goddess of Pope's dunces, Dullness. Their acquisition of power advances in parallel, and they are the patrons of Coleridge's tradition of indolent humorous digressiveness. Dullness, the state of drowsy numbness and sensuous receptivity, grows from a comic threat in Pope to a visionary delirium in Keats. Muddle likewise grows from comic distraction in Sterne to the disturbed mystery at the heart of things which, as Schlegel said, romantic art approaches. Sterne creates romanticism in comedy: accident is a comic analogue of inspiration, and hilarity of sublimity. Surprise is a revelation, an intimation either of mortality or of the comic chaos in which we live. The news of Bobby's death, like Wordsworth's supposition of Lucy's in "Strange fits of passion", shocks the others into a self-congratulatory thrill of recognition that they, at least, are still alive. Sterne's delays and frustrations – the failure to see Calais or to complete the stubbing of the Ox-moor, the sexual circumlocutions of the widow Wadman, the unresolved question of whether a wound in the knee is more painful than one in the groin – anticipate in comedy those interruptions and postponements to which romantic poets are dangerously subject: the intrusion of the person from Porlock, the nightingale's escape, Coleridge's prevarication in the thirteenth chapter of *Biographia Literaria* about the mystery of the esemplastic imagination which he cannot, ultimately, bring himself to disclose.

But in nominating his trio of perfect literary plots Coleridge is organising the opposition to this tradition of random and malleable libertine form. The actions of *Oedipus Rex, The Alchemist* and *Tom Jones* are regulated by Shaw's god, the autocratic artist-philosopher, not Forster's genial muddler. Plot requires a plotter, whereas accident stumbles and leaps to a conclusion which is dubious or disconcerting but somehow right. The plotter in *Oedipus* is the god, who has pre-determined their histories for the characters. In Jonson the god has turned into the supercilious dramatist whose intellectual (rather than religious) design is strangely in sympathy with the schemes and plots fomented by the rogues. In Fielding the force which ordains the plots is neither oracular nor mechanistically intellectual but sentimentally providential, ensuring that Tom's good nature wins out over his misdemeanours and that he is restored to his rightful social place. Small occasions and stray objects are wound together into a destiny which is benevolent not fatal: accidents and loose ends have no place in *Tom Jones*. The jealous god who is Sophocles's plotter and the ingenious amoral mechanical god who is Jonson's have softened into the charitable, protective god of Fielding, concerned for the social and moral welfare of the subjects. The passage from Sophocles to Fielding is summed up in Napoleon's epigram declaring that the role played by fate in the ancient world had been assumed in the modern world by politics.

From the first, the formal opposition between *Tristram Shandy* and *Tom Jones*, between libertinism and regularity, was an issue of romantic aesthetics. An imaginary dialogue in Reverend Philip Parsons's *Dialogues of the Dead with the Living* (1799)[3] has Courtney Melmoth dispute the subject with Fielding. Melmoth treats as convulsive and glaringly brilliant aspects of Sterne we have been encouraged to think of as winsome and whimsical, and in doing so rescues for us some of Sterne's romantic significance. Sterne, he says, is "the vivid lightning at a distance", whereas Fielding is "the animating light of the sun". The stertorous rhythm of Tristram's narration resembles those lightning-flashes which romantic critics said illuminated Garrick's performances of Shakespeare. Fielding challenges Melmoth in the dialogue by asking if it is not easier to lay down *Tristram Shandy* when reading it than to interrupt the narrative of *Tom Jones*. Melmoth is obliged to admit that Fielding's novel is the more reluctantly renounced – but in this case too romanticism proceeds to create a justification for Sterne. Fielding complacently replies that "the charm which detains you in the one is Method – and it is Irregularity which set you free in the other". Romanticism reverses his judgement. From the point of view of Schopenhauer, whose admiration for *Tristram Shandy* will be discussed in the final chapter, irregularity is indeed liberating, for the profoundest work is one which sets its reader free, encouraging him to lay aside the book newly aware of the claustrophobia of art and his own metaphysically unconfined state. So regarded, the methodical structure of *Tom Jones* is dangerously dishonest, trapping the reader in a neat and comfortable prison, feeding him on the illusion that his existence is organised and necessary, whereas Sterne's chaos reveals that existence to be exhilaratingly contingent; and this heady contingency includes the freedom to close the book at any moment.

At the other end of the romantic movement, the same metaphysical choice between Sterne and Fielding is proposed by George Moore in the conversations with Gosse reported in *Avowals* (1919).[4] Sterne has become for Moore both a wise man, the expression of a permanent mental mood, as essential as the Bible and Shakespeare, and an impeccable aesthete, adduced together with Pater as proof that beautiful prose is possible in English. His genius is preserved by his suspicion of method and his "refraining from story-telling". Unlike the generality of English writers, Moore says, he meditates rather than merely observing; his subject is not particular manners but "the human nature that belongs to all of us – our humanity". Fielding's efficiency, on the other hand, is inhuman, and his regularity mere vacancy: Moore considers *Tom Jones* "an entirely empty book", so astutely impersonal that it seems to be the product of a curious machine, and he declares Fielding to have been "without sensibility of any kind, mental or physical". In contrast with Sterne's scatter-brained generosity and plenitude, *Tom Jones* is grim and denuded, representing "a fieldless, treeless, flowerless planet", a work of anti-romantic monstrosity and unnaturalness.

Coleridge, however, seeks to bring the unruly, impulsive libertine under the tutelage of intelligence and order, and he devotes the twenty-third chapter of *Biographia Literaria* to a redefinition of the libertine as a hero of abstraction, a figure who proclaims the eminence of mind rather than weakly yielding to the caprices of the body. The libertine is to become, as for Shaw, an intellectual. Coleridge had acknowledged, in the manuscript notes for his lecture on wit and humour in 1818, the moral worthiness of *Tristram Shandy* in its delicate rendering of trifles of thought and feeling and its physiognomic tact. He praises there "the moral *good* of Sterne in the characters of Trim, etc., as contrasted with Jacobinism": now it is the vicious Jacobin libertine who is criticised in the twenty-third chapter of *Biographia Literaria*.[5] The chapter contrasts a play by Maturin, *Bertram, or the Castle of St. Aldobrand*, submitted to Drury Lane at Byron's invitation after Maturin had been recommended to him by Scott, with the early monkish play about Don Juan, the *Atheista Fulminato*, and exposes the viciousness of the former, in which the moral rebel reaches his nonsensical decadence, while defending the intellectual abstraction of the latter.

In contrast with the sickliness and moral deformity of Maturin's libertine, Coleridge argues that the reality of the *Atheista Fulminato* is abstinently mental: it is "throughout imaginative", and both its tragic and comic characters are "creatures of the brain". Their abstract quality is attested by comparison with Caliban and Milton's Satan – an odd and significant choice of examples, for both Caliban and Satan are, like the libertine, creatures of physical nature redeemed by being turned into ideas. In the ethereal world of *The Tempest,* Caliban is the coarse remnant of physical nature, abolished when Prospero declares the thing of darkness to be his own. Prospero has revenged himself on Caliban's gross, rebellious physical presence by making a metaphor of him, annexing him to his own tyrannical creative mind, and Caliban at once forfeits his independence, agreeing to sue for grace. Extinguished as a character, he becomes an idea, or what Coleridge calls an "impersonated *abstraction*".

Satan's nomination as the second abstraction is equally paradoxical, for as Caliban is rough and crude substance in a play which is vanishing and impalpable, so Satan is apparently the least abstract and conceptual character in *Paradise Lost*. He has the alertness, urgency and vivid address of dramatic character, whereas Adam and Eve are generic specimens and God is beyond personality and thus beyond embodiment. The impersonated abstraction of *The Tempest* is, before Prospero's revenge, not Caliban but his insubstantial opposite, Ariel; and the impersonated abstraction of Milton's poem is not Satan, it would appear, but God. However, God's revenge on Satan, like Prospero's on Caliban, is to reduce him to an idea, and that is to dismiss him. Beginning as a person, Satan declines into a tawdry and humiliated impersonation, slipping as in a pantomime from one animal disguise to another, until his individuality evaporates and he becomes as much a thin coerced figment of allegory as Sin and Death, with whom he is exiled. The process of impersonating and abstracting is death to both Caliban and Satan. They do not emerge from the works for which they are created to wander off into history, discovering new aspects of themselves, like Don Juan, but are held within those works as prisoners, Caliban inside Prospero, Satan exiled in the furthest distance of the poem. They are anti-types of the archetypal character, who gains his freedom by becoming an idea, since ideas are immortal while characters are desperately mortal.

Like Shaw, Coleridge intellectualises the libertine so as to purge him. Shaw removes from him the merely secondary characteristics of the philanderer and sensual connoisseur, which make him a person, and turns him into an idea of selfless service to the evolutionary world-spirit. Demolished as a character, he is reborn as a principle. Even in Mozart, Don Giovanni tends towards impersonality. He is an unmoved mover who touches his victims into emotional vulnerability but remains himself unattached and unresponsive. His victims sing confessionally in their arias, but Don Giovanni has none of their troubled, private, emotional life, and exists only to bestride ensembles. When he sings alone it is not in confession but in self-exhibition (as in "Fin ch' han dal vino") or, disguised, to play tricks on others, as with Elvira's maid or Masetto. Don Giovanni is sex as self-delighting energy, as its own object, whereas his victims experience sex as desire, as a reciprocal need.

Coleridge similarly argues that Don Juan is endowed with the attributes of personality only so that he can function more effectively as an idea. Characteristics do not make him a character, but serve to keep open all his options as an idea, allowing him to undertake a multitude of practical demonstrations of the principle he represents: "Rank, fortune, wit, talent, acquired knowledge, and liberal accomplishments, with beauty of person, vigorous health, and constitutional hardihood, – all these advantages of noble birth and national character, are supposed to have combined in *Don Juan*, so as to give him the means of carrying into all its *practical* consequences the doctrine of a godless nature, as the sole ground and efficient cause not only of all things, events, and appearances, but likewise of all our thoughts, sensations, impulses and actions." Don Juan is a man without qualities, who impels all those around him to acquire qualities. This is his comic aspect: he is a nothing (which is what Shakespeare's fools, whose Shandyean philosophy was discussed in the first chapter, call themselves) who makes other people into somethings. He shares this power with such other vacant or absent creatures as Wycherley's supposedly impotent Jack Horner, or Molière's Tartuffe, who without appearing in the play can compel the characters to arrange themselves in relation to him, or Gogol's supposed government inspector. Don Juan makes all women declare themselves by provoking them to desire him.

This is why he is an ironist: he is like god in nature, hidden but ubiquitous, withdrawn from his own thronging, distraught creation. The same absence may also make him a satirist: Molière's Juan is superior because he defines everyone while remaining undefined himself. But Coleridge is inclined to a tragic view of the figure, and from this position the abstraction or vacancy of the libertine represents the rigid integrity of a self which will not yield, a principle which refuses to be compromised. So interpreted, Juan draws close again to Milton's Satan, living by the will and the tortured intellectual being. Self-will and the drive towards the gratification of appetite are the sole engines of the figure's conduct, Coleridge says, and in explanation quotes his own translation of Schiller's *Wallenstein*:

> Self-contradiction is the only wrong!
> For, by the laws of spirit, in the right
> Is every individual character
> That acts in strict accordance with itself.

The comedian happily contradicts himself. The tragedian would sooner die than suffer any slight to injure that self, or be caught in shaming inconsistency. Othello, once Iago discloses to him his comic role of cuckold, kills Desdemona rather than acquiesce in it, sacrificing her to his tragic idea of himself. Mozart's Don Giovanni undergoes a late, disconcerting conversion to this tragic rule of self-consistency when he ignores Leporello's pleas to retreat into comic evasion and insists on keeping his promise to the stone guest. But it is not specifically this satanic self-consistency which makes the character an abstraction, Coleridge argues. Morality is increasingly irrelevant to consideration of the libertine, and what raises him to the dignity of a principle is not cosmic wickedness like Satan's "but the rapid succession of the correspondent acts and incidents, his intellectual superiority, and the splendid accumulation of his gifts and desirable qualities, co-existent with entire wickedness in one and the same person".

Don Juan now attains abstractness because he is a hero of intellect, not because he is a sensualist or an apostate. His conduct has a rigorous correctness, mathematically worked out as an exposition of self. He has made love geometrical, as Max Frisch said of his Don Juan, who has become a nuclear scientist, devoted to a Shavian extension of mind into the obtuseness of matter. No longer a hero of Id, Don Juan is now an image of cleansed and rational Ego; and the replacement of Id by Ego was, from Hegel to Freud, seen as the obligation of modern man. Coleridge calls Don Juan an entirely "*intelligible* character: as much so as the *Satan* of Milton", and this places him in the devil's party, for that is the party of mind. Milton's humans have as yet no control over their mental equipment, and his God has a mind already predestinately made up. Satan's mind is at least its own place, whereas the minds of Adam and Eve are empty, impressionable spaces into which angels or devils insert suggestions, and in the mind of God there are only theological rules masquerading as motivations.

The second of Coleridge's reasons for making Juan abstract is "the rapid succession of the correspondent acts and incidents", which intellectualises the picaresque quality of the character. Both Mozart and Byron make their heroes episodic personalities. Mozart's hero is either an eighteenth-century encyclopaedist working his way at leisure through the pleasures of sense, or, as interpreted by the nineteenth century, is fated and driven, condemned to a stale and automatic duplication of sexual conquest in order to live down his weariness and disgust. Byron's character unreflectingly accepts whatever happens to him, letting events and women take the initiative. For Coleridge, however, this episodic expansion derives not from the character but from the principle: it is not that the character chooses to act in this way but that the abstract idea requires it of him. The multiple incidents ray out as a set of differing proofs of the theorem; each new woman Juan adds to his list is another convert to the idea. The character ceases to be a sexual predator and becomes a romantic virtuoso delighting in self-demonstration. An improvising mental and physical gymnast, he joins the line of figures extending from Rameau's nephew and Tristram Shandy to Paganini, in whom the harmless and playful exuberance of his predecessors becomes clouded, for the violinist's contemporaries suspected him of being another of the incarnations of Milton's Satan.

The next argumentative leap Coleridge takes is from the abstract to the ideal. He now compares Don Juan with the "*idealized* figures of the Apollo Belvedere, and the Farnese Hercules", which is to set a hero of sensual strife against the chaste and cold images of perfection and lucidity, to compare romantic inner anxiety with classical abstinence from emotion. Winckelmann pointed out that the sculptor of the Apollo Belvedere had confined the expression of indignation to the dilated nostrils and of contempt to the raised lower lip, leaving the god's glance serene and his brow unruffled: he is a figure of gelid restraint and composure, whereas the romantic heroes are creatures of self-wasting restlessness, fired by contradictions, existing in a state of stress rather than poised and balanced as the classical images are. To compare Juan with Apollo is to turn Caliban into Ariel or Satan into God; it is as if Coleridge has perceived that these are romantic twins, opposites which are secretly doubles, and that Juan is eternal because he can become other people at will – like the romantic Shakespeare who, being nothing in himself, could become all things to all men, or like Byron, to every man mankind's epitome, everything by turns and nothing long. Coleridge links Juan and the Hercules, arguing that "what the Hercules is to the *eye* in *corporeal* strength, *Don Juan* is to the *mind* in strength of *character*": Schlegel describes romanticism as a chaos of formal opposites which collision forces into union, and the difference between the bodily perfection and equilibrium of the classical hero and the violent mental energy of the romantic makes this just such a case of opposites thrust into similitude. Coleridge again fuses opposites in requiring art to balance the general and the specific. Classical art deals in the generic, limiting or excluding emotion (as Winckelmann believed) which derives from the physical frailty of the individual and is inappropriate to the contained idealism of the type. Romantic art, however, fixes on the individual. Coleridge demands both at once: "The former makes the character representative and symbolical, therefore instructive; because, *mutatis mutandis*, it is applicable to whole classes of men. The latter gives it *living* interest; for nothing *lives* or is *real*, but as definite and individual."

Coleridge chooses examples of imbalance between the general and the specific from the painting of his period. He mentions as one crime against the ideal the introduction of a figure which is merely the portrait of an individual into the exemplary convention of history painting, and as its equally damaging alternative the neoclassical technique of obliterating individual truth to leave only the generic outline, "figures which were *mere* abstractions, like those of Cipriani, and what have been called Greek forms and faces, i.e. outlines drawn according to a recipe". Coleridge's own critical art of abstracting and intellectualising is closely similar to a certain romantic artistic practice which kept alive the outline method: this is the cutting out of silhouettes. Turning the outline method inside out, silhouettes change it from a classical diagram of generic form to something both devilish and wistful. The silhouette is uncanny, whereas the classical outline is a severe and reasonable elimination of the inessential. The outline sees through the camouflage of colour and feature to the paradigm of shape beneath. Its dark line is the merest, thinnest stain on the paper. The silhouette, however, obscures rather than clarifies. It is the shadow we cast, not the skeletal idea within us. It is alarming because it traps the spirit rather than the body: or perhaps the spirit after the body's departure. Our shadow has been taken prisoner, which fairy-tales have always represented as an attack on our existence. The silhouette leaves behind a ghost, the imprint of someone who is no longer there – Byron, for instance, in the silhouette cut in paper by Marianne Hunt after his daily ride at Pisa in 1822, with his spurs still on and his riding crop over his shoulder. Byron seems to have stepped out of the hole left by the paper, and the starkness of the contrast between black space and white frame has turned the figure who was there a moment ago into a shade, a spectre. This is the melancholy of the silhouette: it seizes a moment, whereas the classical outline can afford a confident indifference to time.

The outline and the silhouette are pictorial analogues of the literary archetype. Don Juan as Coleridge describes him is a spirit without a body – anyone can slip into that blank space – or a character who has disappeared into an idea. As a person he has been effaced, cut out; but this has opened him up to contain multitudes. As it proceeds, Don Juan's disembodiment separates him not only from any one literary work, which cannot pretend to exhaust him since his apparitions in literature are as promiscuous and inconstant as his dealings with women, but from literature altogether. Coleridge surprisingly declares that the ideal or archetype is so consummately achieved in the figure of Juan that "it is capable of interesting without poetry, nay, even without words, as in our pantomime of that name".

Having deprived Don Juan of words, Coleridge goes on to deprive him of qualities, which pertain to character and so are inessential to him, for he is not a person but an agency, a force, a physical law. The "super-human *entireness*" of the conception, Coleridge argues, keeps it from being morally offensive, as if Don Juan were a tempest or a volcano, which creates havoc but which it is vain to criticise or try to moderate. Although those who share the work of art with the libertine condemn him, his salvation lies with us, since on the one hand we can congratulate ourselves that he is no threat to our own piety, and on the other can indulge a surreptitious envy: "But to possess such a power of captivating and enchanting the affections of the other sex! – to be capable of inspiring in a charming and even a virtuous woman, a love so deep, and so entirely personal to *me*! – that even my worst vices (if I *were* vicious), even my cruelty and perfidy (if I *were* cruel and perfidious), could not eradicate the passion! to be loved for my *own self*, that even with a distinct knowledge of my character, she yet died to save me!"

Coleridge here implicitly withdraws some of his moral disapproval of *Tristram Shandy*. In his lecture on wit, he regrets that Sterne has made "the best dispositions of our nature the pandars and condiments for the basest". Here he makes a similar point, but this time in tribute to the allure of Don Juan, who "takes hold of two sides of our nature, the better and the worse". Discussing Sterne's immodesty, Coleridge recommends a process of denuding and unmasking similar to that by which he justifies Don Juan, although in Sterne's case to process is fiercely critical, not redemptive: Sterne has coupled prurience with drollery, fancy, wit and humour, and has managed to conceal the awkwardness of the fit, but if as a critical experiment we abstract "in our imagination the *characters* of Mr Shandy, my uncle Toby, and Trim, which are all *antagonists* to this wit, and suppose instead of them two or three callous debauchees", the result would be simply disgusting. The innocent whimsy of mental association would then be exposed as vicious, and the sentimentalists revealed to be libertines. Strip the Shandys of their characters and qualities, and they turn into versions of Don Juan.

As Sterne makes the mind the body's officious, inquisitive, genial pandar, so Don Juan forces into intimacy opposite sides of our nature. The emotions the libertine excites can seem improving, as Coleridge admits: "the heroic disinterestedness, to which love can transport a woman, cannot be contemplated without an honourable emotion of reverence towards womanhood". Don Giovanni pretends to such an honourable, ironic reverence in apologising to Zerlina for the raging denunciation of Elvira, who is, he says, pitiably infatuated with him and is pardoned by his bounteous good nature. Although all women are Don Giovanni's dupes, there is a feminine heroism to their folly – Elvira as interpreted by Kierkegaard has abandoned herself to the sensuous life-force, Anna as interpreted by E. T. A. Hoffmann has dared to make a spiritual match with the devil.[6] Increasingly sex becomes a matter of self-consciousness rather than relationship: the libertine is conducting a love-affair with himself, accepting women only as acolytes; the women become sublime not specifically by loving him but by the heady, objectless enthusiasm with which they love. As Coleridge puts it, they love disinterestedly – as if without the self-interested desire for sexual gratification. Shaw made Giovanni an abstinent socialist, and his women turn out to be equally pure, since they are theoretical lovers, pursuing a line of mental enquiry.

In this way the libertine awakens, in spite of himself, the better side of human nature. The other half of Coleridge's proposition, dealing with his baser appeal, is equally intriguing, for he passes from the woman's selfless ardour to the man's petulant, nagging self, that "simply the thing I am" which makes him live, his lowest but most perdurable instinct: "on the other hand, it is among the miseries, and abides in the dark ground-work of our nature, to crave an outward confirmation of that *something* within us, which is our *very self*, that something, not *made up* of our qualities and relations, but itself the supporter and substantial basis of all these. Love *me*, and not my qualities, may be a vicious and insane wish, but it is not a wish wholly without a meaning". That italicised *me* is one of the first times the undying ego, the ill-tempered and demanding successor to the virtuoso, role-playing, adventurous romantic self, stamps its foot in literature. For the man without qualities, the self without a character, is the sick, complaining ego: in Moosbrugger, Robert Musil's man without qualities, Don Giovanni the connoisseur of sense becomes a brutish sex-killer. The grace and delight of Don Giovanni have been turned into the strident hypochondria of the ego which wants to be loved not in order to be released from its malodorous prison but to have that imprisonment confirmed. The hero who finds it a pleasure to discover himself becomes one who exults in his misery and discontent. Leporello's list is now a psychiatric casebook.

Coleridge proceeds to a justification of power as the necessary accompaniment of virtue, and in particular of the power of the mind as "the grand desideratum of human ambition". Here again Giovanni the sensualist merges with Satan and

Faust as a hero of intellect. Knowledge makes a god of him, and his catalogue of conquests is a painstaking experimental investigation of the nature whose secrets Faust hoped to unlock in an instant through magic. Giovanni is the better scientist, more patient and meticulous in conducting his researches. As Milton's Satan insists on thinking for himself, rather than accepting the injunctions of dogma, and as the various Fausts represent the progress of modern man in his long struggle to wrest control of nature from god, so the libertine now becomes, for Coleridge, a hero of "the *first* temptation", which was the desire to know, to break a taboo. At this stage Don Giovanni again draws near to the Shandys, whose sly sexual hints Coleridge treats as a form of primary, childish daring. They dally with the devil, he says, and his analogy of "that tremulous daring with which a child touches a hot tea urn, because it has been forbidden", suggests a crime against forbidden knowledge like that of Faust or Satan, or a crime like Giovanni's against a forbidden sexuality. In the analysis of Don Juan, Coleridge points out that intellectual supremacy in association with guilt has ever been a compelling literary subject, just as, it might be added, the similar association of sex and guilt has always been; and he explains this attraction by declaring that "in this bad and heterogeneous co-ordination we can contemplate the intellect of man more exclusively as a separate self-subsistence, than in its proper state of subordination in his own conscience, or to the will of an infinitely superior being". Intellect or sexual appetite have been purified of moral scruples, and this gives Faust and Juan their hold over art, for the process which has created and made archetypes of them is deeply ambiguous. Artistically, they have been subjected to a refinement and purification, freed from the inessential; but morally the same process is a compounding of vice, the rejection of all restraining and appeasing forces which in ordinary men tame these primary drives.

Tristram Shandy is a comic correlative of these myths, showing libidinous intellect in absurd lordliness, establishing a misrule of whim and random association. Ironically, intellect asserts itself by a wilful incompetence and petulant disorganisation; and this establishes another ground of identity between Sterne and Shakespeare. Coleridge returns to

Shakespeare at this point in his exposition, but to make the opposite point – he attributes to the same guilty tyranny of mental power which thrills through Faust and Juan the "sacred charm" of Richard III, Iago or Edmund, who are "cast in the mould of Shakespeare's own gigantic intellect". But it is precisely their efficiency in plot-making and manipulation which estranges these surrogate, satanic dramatists from Shakespeare's creative intellect. They are dramatists, but not of Shakespeare's kind: his own more indulgent, episodic, improvisatory intellect is perhaps best represented by the inventive but incompetent Shandyean plotter, Hamlet, whose perplexity about his delay mirrors but conceals and justifies Shakespeare's own difficulty in keeping the play going on when it is imperative that his hero, as a reluctant and therefore tragic revenger, must remain inactive. Shakespeare's way out is to provide a series of diversions which Hamlet's mental versatility can both welcome as pastimes and then make into plots of his own, but always subsidiary plots, detours and defiles which hinder rather than advance the prevailing plot of revenge. Unexpectedly converting to the devil's party, Coleridge wrongly implicates Shakespeare in the unfeeling formalism of his villains rather than in the experimental libertinism of Hamlet's treatment of form.

Coleridge goes on to establish Don Juan's mental superiority and to side again with the devil in an illuminating misinterpretation of the myth, commending Juan now for his unremorseful, intellectual disparagement of the imaginative fable he finds himself in. Fearless disregard for the phantoms of the invisible world is, Coleridge says, the most dazzling kind of intellectual power. Most of us, intimidated by its bogeys, submit to being bribed into "a voluntary submission of our better knowledge, into suspension of all judgement derived from constant experience". We "peruse with the liveliest interest the wildest tales of ghosts, wizards, genii, and secret talismans" – Ossian, Chatterton, the odes of Gray and Collins, Gothic novels are presumably intended, for romanticism depends on precisely this gullibility, which Coleridge enlisted to protect his own "Ancient Mariner" in prescribing a trusting suspension of disbelief. This is why romanticism seemed, from Peacock's *Four Ages of Poetry* to Shaw's *Man and*

Superman preface, such a treason of the intellectuals: at a time when knowledge was disproving fable and myth, and instinct surrendering to reason, art encouraged superstition, old wives' tales, mental prostration. Coleridge himself had an uneasy conscience about the matter. He worried that the mental situation in the "Ancient Mariner" might have been obscured by the legendary externals, and is nervously cautious in phrasing his explanation of our state of mind as we watch Juan's encounter with the ghost: "The poet does not require us to be awake and believe; he solicits us only to yield ourselves to a dream; and this too with our eyes open, and with our judgement *perdue* behind the curtain, ready to awaken us at the first motion of our will: and meantime, only, not to *dis-believe*". A series of qualifications wraps the fidgety sentence into a circle. First we are said to be not awake but dreaming, then we are re-awoken since our eyes are to be open and our judgement merely dozing, then it turns out that we are not to believe but rather not to not believe, which is the same thing. Juan is heroic because he cuts through such hesitations and prevarications, which we as readers or spectators are too timid to do. He dares to assert his unbelief in the phantom, while we are left with our cowardly, pious credulity. Additionally, for Coleridge, he is heroic because he has the mental self-sufficiency to dispense with bogey-ridden imagination. He refuses even to make the concession of suspending disbelief. He is artistically as well as religiously atheistic.

Coleridge's admiration for Juan's "cool intrepidity" in mocking the ghost and sneering at its foolish railing recalls Hamlet's attitude to the ghost of his father. Shaw, discussing Don Giovanni, objects that Shakespeare is both coarse and feeble in stooping to exploit religious superstition in the use of the ghost, but had he looked closer he might have seen that Hamlet thinks the same, for like Coleridge's Juan he ridicules the ghost's shabby theatrical counterfeiting, mimics its rhetoric, jokes at the noise it makes in the cellarage while clumsily performing its disappearing act, and pities it as a king of shreds and patches, rigged up as if from the property basket of the travelling players. Like Juan, he defies its morality of retribution and questions its supernatural status; like Juan, he even considers it to be bad, outmoded, makeshift art.

The justification of Shadwell's libertine is, for Coleridge, consistency and intelligibility. Each prodigious event in the story makes a moral point, each of the hero's perverse instincts has a purpose. Against Shadwell he sets the diseased moral inversion of modern drama and the unintelligibility of Maturin, who squanders intellectual significance in a plethora of stunts and tricks. His *Bertram* flourishes supernatural effects without supernatural agencies, groundless miracles, characters (like Eliot's Hamlet) without a cause for the violent emotions or "wry faces, proflated mouths, and lunatic gestures" to which they abandon themselves. Yet, as Coleridge derisively describes it, the play does acquire a certain self-parodying whimsicality. Forfeiting his pretensions to tragedy, Bertram becomes instead a comedian excited by his passions to virtuoso antics of double-jointedness. His contortions, reported by Coleridge, as he vows to assassinate his mistress's husband, link him with Diderot's nephew of Rameau, engaged in a fiendish ballet of attitudes and grimaces: "all this too is for no discoverable purpose on the part of the author, but that of introducing a series of supertragic starts, pauses, screams, struggling, dagger-throwing, falling on the ground, starting up again wildly, swearing, outcries for help, falling again on the ground, rising again, faintly tottering towards the door, and, to end the scene, a most convenient fainting fit of our lady's . . .". Once she faints, Bertram rushes off to seek out her husband before she can warn him. Coleridge points out that she has already had ample time to do so, "but the author rather chose she should amuse herself and the audience by the above-described ravings and startings". The joke is an inadvertent justification: as in *Hamlet* or *Tristram Shandy*, the self-delighting exhibition of temperament impedes the narrative, and is meant to do so. In denouncing *Bertram*, Coleridge has hit on a Shandyean apology for it: the piece is arranged by Maturin as a series of opportunities for his monster to practise its roaring. Bertram is a virtuoso of passion, as Tristram is of mental association or Rameau's nephew of physical dexterity, and all three practise upon their faculties as if they were instruments, their libertinism more of a threat to artistic form than it is to morality.

Valuing consistency, Coleridge finds "a portion of sublimity" in Shadwell's libertine as he "stands out the last fearful trial, like a second Prometheus". Such dogged determination not to learn, such imperviousness to moral warnings, derive, however, from comedy not from tragedy. The mental consistency Coleridge reverses is here a comic truculence: Shadwell's libertine vaunts at the "foolish ghost" and threatens to break his "marble body in pieces and pull down your horse", as Don Giovanni facetiously offers food to his spiritual guest. Our sense of genre and of literary and moral propriety is so far confused by characters like this that their actions ironically superimpose tragedy and comedy. From Coleridge's tragic point of view, the libertine is nobly self-consistent in his refusal to repent; from Leporello's comic point of view, his squandering of himself is an act of foolhardy absurdity.

The first chapter of this book described the dissolution of Shakespearean tragedy and comedy into romantic irony, which makes the formerly opposed genres alternative, coexisting moods; similarly, a character like Juan is an ironic composite, who may be either tragic or comic, just as for Coleridge the Shandys may be either debauchees or frivolous idlers, depending on one's own moral assumptions. The kind of character proposed here, libertine in his evasion of mental, moral and artistic regularity, has a threefold originality. He fluctuates between tragedy and comedy; he is a self denuded of qualities; and he is, as Coleridge now says of Juan, a *"means without an end"*. In him, that is, all the desirable attributes of human personality are combined as the means towards an end which is so inhuman that it is no end at all. This aspect of the libertine again attaches him to Shakespeare, and in particular to Iago, who according to Coleridge's analysis hunts for motives and throws up innumerable irrelevant ones to conceal his essential motivelessness. Iago can no more understand his motive than Hamlet can because the secrets of both are aesthetic not psychological, and cannot be stated without puncturing the deft, evasive structures of their plays. Hamlet delays because Shakespeare needs him to, Iago destroys Othello because Shakespeare needs him to. Their psychological problems are the aesthetic problems of their creator camouflaged. They puzzle over the means, but the end is Shakespeare's.

The three reasons which make the libertine so original a romantic conception may be directly transferred to Tristram Shandy. He too has the freedom of tragedy and comedy, though rather than oscillating between them as Don Juan does, he compounds them: sentimentality or irony is his version of the Shakespearean tragicomedy. He too is a self without qualities: like Pope's ladies he is too infirm and whimsically changeful to have a character, or the qualities which give a character regularity, so he has instead a community of selves and moods, infantile, antiquarian, sensuous, elegiac, humanitarian. He sees other people as characters, encased in qualities like uniforms, Toby with his cannons, Walter with his classical battering-rams; but just as no man is a hero to his valet, so no man is a character to himself. Character is some-thing others – novelists, for instance – endow us with to make us manageable, but Tristram resists the imposition by being his own novelist. Consequently, he remains a chaos of divergent means without an end: not even the completion of his novel is accepted as a worthy end, and, disqualified from action, he is becalmed like Hamlet in meditation on his own motives and preparation for actions which are endlessly deferred.

Notes

1. Coleridge's remark on the three perfect plots is quoted by F. T. Blan-chard, *Fielding the Novelist: A Study in Historical Criticism*, 1926, pp. 320–1.
2. *Aspects of the Novel*, 1927, in chapter 6, "Fantasy".
3. Reprinted in *Sterne: The Critical Heritage*, ed. Alan B. Howes, 1974, pp. 233–4.
4. *Avowals*, 1919, pp. 25–6.
5. Coleridge's demolition of Maturin's libertine, quoted here and on the following pages, was originally a series of letters to *The Courier* on 29 August and 7, 9, 10, 11 September 1816, reprinted in *Biographia Literaria*, ed. J. Shawcross, 1907, vol. II, pp. 180–207.
6. E. T. A. Hoffman's fantastic tale was published in 1814.

5

Arabesque

Comedy conceals its subversiveness by pretending to inconsequence. Kierkegaard called irony the incognito of the moralist, and comedy is likewise the incognito of the imagination
which seeks to extend the bounds of art. Literature's most
dangerous rebels, characters like Falstaff or Don Giovanni or
Tristram Shandy, are careful to adopt comic disguises, so that
while seeming to trifle and waste time in play they are covertly
winning amoral victories never allowed to tragic characters,
who invite and exult in persecution by the frankness with
which they proclaim their ruling ideas. The comic hero's
salvation is inconsequence and inefficiency. He is lost once he
aspires to success in the world of action. Hence Falstaff's error
is hoping to turn his victory of wit into a political triumph, and
to have the laws of England at his command; hence too the
defeat of Don Giovanni. The libertine is safe while he masks
his unsettling rage of the will as mere comic sexual insatia-
bility, but to invite the statue to dinner is to defy openly a god
whose rule he has formerly been content to flout stealthily and
fugitively.

Tristram Shandy at least knows that triviality and ineffectualness will be his salvation, as they are for the capering,
ecstatically frivolous nephew of Rameau in Diderot's dialogue
between sage unity of self and zany comic virtuosity.[1] The
nephew rejoices in his own unregeneracy, hoping to remain
the same for another forty years, whereas Falstaff and Don
Giovanni undertake to grow and change, which is forbidden
to comic characters on pain of death. The antics of Tristram
and Diderot's nephew represent a romantic uprising of comedy against tragedy and, in the nonsensical abandon of Tristram's intellectual and the nephew's physical acrobatics, of
form against content. Their separation of form from content
distinguishes them as virtuosi, and as aesthetic libertines.
Defiantly absurd, refusing to condescend to a meaning, they

force a romantic redefinition of art, opposing pure, wayward, antic, liberated form to the ponderous restraints of content. This chapter will trace the influence of such a Shandyean imbalance on the aesthetic theory of Sterne's period.

The visionary art of romanticism has its origins in comedy. It grows from the low comedy of caricature and graphic lampooning, which in the eighteenth century extend the imaginative range and resource of art, and confer on it a new power to trouble and ensorcell, in Rowlandson's elated scenes of disaster and affray, Cruikshank's bestiary of political monsters, and the ghastly playfulness of Gillray. These artists realise that the test of genius is not to make an ennobled likeness of a subject, as the classical theory of Reynolds proposed, but to transform it, and they do so diabolically. Men become beasts, or bulbous or distended objects; inanimate objects are quickened into threatening life. The graphic satirist's devilish power to humiliate and destroy anticipates in comedy the high romantic's lordliness with reality – inciting it to an orgy of sanguine colour like Delacroix or thinning it into ether like Turner, morbidly darkening it in saturnine tones like Géricault or abolishing substance in a serpentine ballet of line like Blake.

Goya, and his English equivalents Fuseli and Blake, are the artists in whom this transfusion from the low, scabrous imagination of the caricaturists to the high, sublime imagination of the romantic visionary takes place. Goya's squat giant, "Colossus", is an ironic hybrid of satire and sentiment of their transitional kind. The torso of the Apollo Belvedere, which Winckelmann was sure had belonged to some elevated soul "cleansed of the dross of humanity",[2] has had grafted onto it the oafish, brutal head of Caliban. The giant is a creature from the lower depths of caricature, but with a soul transplanted into him. Like Caliban lyrically perturbed by the voices in the air, he turns his head into the moonlight with a grimace of costive anguish. With Goya's skeletal old woman or cannibalistic Saturn or victims of war, he is one of the missing links between the capricious distortions and monstrous imaginings of graphic satire and the entranced nightmares of romantic art.

Caricature derives its comic potency from the magic pow-

ers it employs. As the art-form in which the artist's subject is
his enemy, whom he creates in order to destroy, it keeps alive
art's original dangerous relation to spells and taboos, and it
passes on to romanticism a sense of the violence of the image.
When Shelley ran shrieking from the room at Villa Diodati,
during Byron's recitation of the episode of the witch's
deformed breasts from "Christabel", it was in reaction to a
phantasm poised awkwardly between the ludicrous frights of
Gillray and the psychological terror of Goya: he was haunted
by the idea of a woman with eyes in place of her nipples.
Fuseli's characters are also mutants, hybrids of comedy and
tragedy, of caricature and the manic sublime. His *Macbeth*
witches are doting hags, but they are rendered incongruously
heroic by their mystic, patterned salute, mimicking the con-
certed gesture of David's oath-swearing Horatii. Blake's
spectres belong at once to caricature and to prophecy. His
apparition of a flea, or his Nebuchadnezzer painfully protesting at his transformation into a beast, or his sleek reptilian
Newton, bending a lithe, rippling, boneless body over his
compass, are cartoon figures spiritualised. Caricature no
longer merely defames individuals, like Gillray's porcine
Prince Regent or his blinking Johnson with the body of an
owl and ass's ears. The satiric victims have been generalised, rendered transparent, turned into spiritual emanations.

While the low art confers the imaginative freedom of the
debased, the lurid, the monstrously exaggerated, the higher art
mortifies its practitioners. In Reynolds's Academy discourses[3]
the artist appears unnerved and intimidated, dependent on
sources and prohibited from trusting to his own gift. Originality of vision is, in Reynolds's aesthetics, not the point from
which an artist begins but a final, peripheral luxury, to be
safely indulged only after a long subjection to tradition. The
student emerges from the discourses as one of the buffetted,
demoralised characters of eighteenth-century picaresque, reel-
ing through experiences which one after another warn him to
retract his imaginative expectations, to accept the comfortably
familiar rather than long for impossibilities – a Rasselas sen-
tentiously content, convinced there is no new thing under the
sun. Reynolds prescribes for the fledgeling artist a stern course

of self-mortification similar to that forced on Rasselas. The first stage of apprenticeship involves absolute dependence on a master, from whom the student may learn "to express himself with some degree of correctness". From this he graduates to the task of collecting possible subjects, "a stock of ideas, to be combined and varied as occasion may require", and these are also external to him, a body of situations and images which existed before he did and to which he must adapt himself. He is now under the supervision not of an individual master but of the art itself, but he is forbidden to make decisions about the art of the past or to find himself in it. He must study impartiality, and seek always to attach himself to a precedent, not resigning "himself blindly to any single authority, when he may have the advantage of consulting many". Nor should he exercise his own judgment, which will fatally isolate him: Reynolds turns the intellectual fault into a nightmare by using an image of man unaccommodated, deprived of the rational support of society, like Shaftesbury's rash enthusiast Theocles or Collins's intrepid Home in the highlands – "he must still be afraid . . . of deviating into any track where he cannot find the footsteps of some former master".

A collision between nobility and scurrility, between the two tiers of a double plot, occurs in Blake's annotations to the discourses, which turn Reynolds's programme into a sinister and nonsensical conspiracy.[4] Blake begins with a gesture of sensational exposure, declaring "This Man was Hired to Depress Art", and as in the Gillray cartoons of Boydell sacrificing Shakespeare or Johnson scourged by the muses he slighted, he makes Reynolds an agent of papal guile, intriguing to degrade mankind by destroying art. The grave and judicious caution of the discourses is set against the ferocious slang of the political cartoon: Reynolds and "his Gang of Cunning Hired Slaves" roll in riches while Blake hungers for bread and employment. Artists become slave-labourers, conscripted to make flattering likenesses of the ruling class; Blake casts himself as the brave fanatic challenging interests and institutions: "Where have you hid Fuseli's Milton? Is Satan troubled at his Exposure?"

Blake's graffiti are epigrammatic equivalents of Goya's *caprichos*, stark and acute sketches of the deformities of social life.[5]

Goya's riddling captions to the aquatints, gnomically summing up the inverse wisdom of the images, are products of the same unruly, subversive critical style as Blake's marginal jottings. In Goya's volume, cartoons have become visions of a ludicrous and demented reality; Blake similarly turns graffiti-scribbling and the defacement of a book into the means of proclaiming a critical heresy. The annotations to Reynolds's second discourse translate academic art into the world of Goya's sapient asses and musical monkeys. Reynolds's demand that the student store up subjects becomes in Blake's version a compounding of folly: "After having been a Fool, a Student is to amass a Stock of Ideas, &, knowing himself to be a Fool, he is to assume the Right to put other Men's Ideas into his Foolery." Reynolds's ingenuous artist is now a clown, and his acquiescence in his master's advice to consult no single authority but to learn with wise passiveness from all his edecessors means that "Instead of Following One Great Master he is to follow a Great Many Fools". Reynolds himself in his depreciation of the inventive power is exposed by Blake as an agent of Urizen and the stultifying rule of Baconian philosophy: all his falsehoods are infernal.

In truth, Reynolds is circumspect about imagination, not repressive. He is aware of the danger of unbridling the fantasy, and of the need to concentrate against it the calming influences of rational skill and classical example: "Having well established his judgement, and stored his memory, [the student] may now without fear try the power of his imagination. The mind that has been thus disciplined, may be indulged in the warmest enthusiasm, and venture to play on the borders of the wildest extravagance." Reynolds's prescriptions on style have a similar tranquilising function. Expression, hazardously subjective, Reynolds makes safely impersonal, treating it as a technical proficiency which can be acquired through study and need not be sought within. Once mastered, it is applied to subjects which are also inherited and remembered. Blake had objected to the Greek description of the muses as daughters of memory because it implied that an artistic gift can be trained and managed, but in this case too Reynolds's emphasis is not on stifling and suppressing but on the tense effort to master forces which are refractory and insurgent. The painter applies style so as to subdue his materials: "Style in painting is the same as in writing, a power over materials."

The materials and style of the romantics have, on the contrary, power over them. The mediumistic pretences of romantic artists – Blake taking dictation from spirits, the Gothic novelists discovering yellowing papers in country houses, Coleridge's notion of himself as an Aeolian harp through which creative impulses rustle and vibrate – are stratagems for disclaiming responsibility, disavowals which are both a boast and a subtle self-defence. By thinking of himself as the vehicle for suggestions from a mysteriously external source, the romantic poet does not disown his imagination but divinises it. He makes himself both subject and object, worshipper and god, marrying not only the mind to nature but one part of himself (the intuitive) to another (the artistic), both enacting the rite and watching it in reverent astonishment. In contrast, Reynolds advises self-distrust, not self-celebration: "You must have no dependence on your own genius. If you have great talents, industry will improve them; if you have but moderate abilities, industry will supply their deficiency." The artist may help himself but not believe in himself, and must consider his gift a technical aptitude to be improved upon, without fretting to explain its source or purpose.

Form and style, in Reynolds haughty superintendents of matter, are freed by romanticism for self-exploration. The history of romantic art is that of the fission of the various elements of art, which go their independent, introverted ways. From its beginning in picturesque description, romantic art tends irresistibly towards abstraction; and in abolishing representation it frees the formal qualities of art from that sordid need to simulate and feign which so pained Hamlet. The notable examples are those of line and colour. Line detaches itself in neoclassical art and in the designs of Blake, for whom it is a moral quality, a wiry image of rectitude, and also evidence of spirit: his twining forms are purely linear, volumeless and colourless, because they are diagrams of spirit and must be transparent so the ideal can be visible through them. Colour is a stain on the white radiance of this eternity; and volume too implies material satisfaction, like Falstaff's enjoyment of his own plump three-dimensionality. Even the elements of composition acquire symbolic life for Blake. Symmetry like the tiger's is fearful, because it is a sign of the inexplicable orderly duality of nature as well as a principle of art. In his lectures, Haydon quotes Fuseli's remark that "Colours fade – language becomes obsolete – thought and form remain", and adds that skeletal form is "the vehicle of thought and expression". Anatomical study excites a Blakean wonder for, as Haydon says, "the bones, which give orgin to the muscles, are the foundation of the human form, – the muscles the organs of its actions and thoughts".[6] The linear basis of art is a joyful exposition of the intelligible structure of the world.

The antagonist of line, colour, separated itself in the opposite direction, also making of itself a metaphysical principle. Goethe's colour science dissolved the hard and regular Blakean forms, suggesting that light, shade and colour interweave to create the illusion of an objective world. The value of colour lies, for Haydon, in its gratuitousness, its freedom from linear utility. The great principles of the solar system, the revolution of the planets, the passage of the seasons, gravitation, hydraulics and mechanics, have no need of it, but its very irrelevance makes it creation's most abundant proof of God's kindness, "the property bestowed . . . on all visible substance in earth and heaven to reflect light on the brain, through the eye, under the delusion of various and harmonious colours". If line instructs and patterns the intelligence, colour foments the exclusively aesthetic realm of delighted sense. Whistler called it "a jaunty whore", rioting into "a chaos of drunkenness, trickery, regrets and incompleteness" once free of the surveillance of line. But colour also has a theological propriety. Haydon points out that each of the three primitive colours, red, yellow and blue, is harmonised when set against its complementary, which is itself a blend of the other two primary colours: mixtures of tints declare the mysterious orderliness of nature. The palette is also an emotional spectrum and a network of mental association: red and yellow are warm, blue cold, and Haydon criticises the Chinese habit of wearing white for mourning because "the great law of association" decrees that white is the tone of gladness and black of sorrow and pain.

Romantic art engages in metaphysical speculation about its

own methods and components, just as romantic poets linger over words which possess an atmosphere in excess of their meaning – De Quincey on Wordsworth's "far", which opens a sudden recession into depth in the line, attributing space and its infinities to the human heart, or Keats on the leaden toll of "forlorn". This is a liberation of form from content such as Reynolds warns against. He is critical of the Venetians because they were engrossed by colour "to the neglect of *the ideal beauty of form*", and he argues that "words should be employed as the means, not as the end: language is the instrument, conviction is the work". But the romantics make language literature's object as well as its instrument. Shelley's glancing oblique style, syntactically indeterminate, constantly questions the adequacy of language to represent the immaterial and imageless deep truth of things. Wordsworth, on the contrary, makes words into objects, their blunt solidity and roughness tokens of that state of mute integrity, beneath subjective life, towards which his solitaries sink: "rocks, and stones, and trees". In one sense romantic poetry is styleless, because although the poets make language a reflection of personality, they abandon the notion of Reynolds or Johnson that style is a principle of order, in which a periodic syntax bends words into obedience and etymological learning guarantees correctness of usage: romantic syntax slides and rambles, hoping to discover new meanings in the course of its proliferation, and words are used prodigally, vaguely, conjecturally. But in another sense romantic poetry is about a style which is entirely self-referring: it is a self-inquisition of language.

Reynolds calls pictorial style poetic if it ennobles, omitting small details and improving low ones. Raphael's cartoons give the apostles a more respectable aspect than they actually possessed, but the rusticity of Dutch and Flemish landscapes makes them "unfit for poetical subjects". Fuseli called his own manner poetic, but with a romantically different intention.[7] For him the poetic does not generalise and aggrandise: it signifies in his use a reassertion of the rights of imagination. It is the inventive power he envies in poetry, and hopes to take over for his own art. His pictures often pretend to be illustrating a poetic text, while secretly claiming a poetic freedom of their own. Reynolds imagines the sister arts of poetry and painting amicably dividing the received subject-matter between themselves; for Fuseli this arrangement has broken down into romantic synaesthesia, as one art competes with or trespasses on another or more insidiously adopts its disguise. Fuseli often devised his subjects without reference to poet or historian, only later attaching them to a shadowy, justificatory narrative: the appearance of illustration was his imagination's camouflage or comic incognito. When Byron asked him the source of the Soane Museum picture "Ezzelin Bracciaferro and the Dead Meduna", Fuseli confessed it was his own invention. This morbid vigil over a lithe elegant corpse needs its exotic names and its pretence of narrative to objectify it, to remove it from Fuseli's gloomy fantasy to the shared, reasonable community of literature.

Illustration was a quest for objective correlatives. Iago's motive-hunting is combined with Hamlet's desire to find in the world around him some cause for his anxiety. Fuseli called similacrae like Bracciaferro "philosophical ideas made intuitive, or sentiment personified". The definition admits its own uncertainty by dodging from allegory to metaphor: the one clothes ideas in visible form, but the other more impalpably and hesitantly frames equivalents for feelings. In fact, Bracciaferro is neither an idea nor a feeling. There is no truth outside the picture into which he can be allegorically translated, but neither does he satisfactorily embody a feeling, because the picture's title passes it off as a narrative incident and so obscures whatever metaphorical origin it might have had. Reynolds attacks self-reliance as dangerous and enfeebling: "The greatest natural genius cannot subsist on its own stock: he who resolves never to ransack any mind but his own, will soon be reduced, from mere barrenness, to the poorest of imitations: he will be obliged to imitate himself, and to repeat what he has before often repeated", as Tristram Shandy does. Fuseli dares not frankly resolve to do without the help of other minds, and he therefore fictionalises his relationship with his own creative impulses, as Chatterton did with Rowley or Macpherson with Ossian, attributing his obsessions to some imaginary other and then making an illustration as if the subject did not belong to him.

The artist artificially or even mendaciously separates himself from the subject in the hope of generating unexpected
creative powers, contriving a shock of imaginative surprise.
The imagination is removed to a distance which is safe but also
stimulating, because removal is a prelude to rediscovery. A
ritual pretence like Fuseli's corresponds to the narrative
involution of romantic poems or novels. As the narratives of
"The Ruined Cottage" or *Wuthering Heights* are transmitted
across gaps in time, space and memory, so Chatterton, Macpherson and Fuseli turn their own creative process into a
co-operative drama, in which one part of the mind solicits or
startles another. As Lockwood is drawn into the spectral
centre of Wuthering Heights and finds there a cruel, distorted
image of himself, so Chatterton, Macpherson and Fuseli tread
warily into the dark places of their imaginations and find
waiting for them there Rowley, Ossian, the Ezzelin Bracciaferro. This way the artist convinces himself that his work
has an uncanny, unanticipated power over him, that he is
its medium not its creator. Hence Fuseli's rites of self-
preparation, inducing visions by eating raw pork chops. Like
Chatterton with Rowley he is turning creation into a seance,
making himself the vehicle for spirits he longs to believe have
come from the vasty deep, but which come in fact from inside
him. His prophetic babble is no more than his conversation
with himself. Leigh Hunt mocked Fuseli for being frightened
by his own lay figures, but this too was a ritual attempt to
disown the imagination so as to rediscover it in fear and
trembling.

Reynolds deplores this pretence of involuntariness. He mis-
trusts the artist who claims to be "but a mere machine"
informed by a genius and "unconscious of the operations of
his own mind". But for Blake such deceit is a mystical condition of imagination entranced, a mode of "Spiritual Perception". Landscape commended itself to the romantic artist
by its similar involuntariness. Depriving him of choice, it set
him to scramble in pursuit of its subtly changeful life. Reynolds, however, assumes it to be subject to the artist's dis-
position: meaningless in itself, a mere expanse of incoherent
nature, it patiently awaits the artist who will imprint character
on it. The landscape painter, like the poet, must make "the

elements sympathise with this subject", determining the shape of clouds, the structure of mountains, the inclination of branches, leaving nothing to natural accident. The artist's sovereignty over his subject is most forcefully expressed in his power of light and darkness: he "has complete dominion, to vary and dispose them as he pleases; to diminish, or increase them as will best suit his purpose, and correspond to the general idea of his work". Art's duty is a high falsification, supplying and completing the "natural imperfection of things". But it is this imperfection which romantic art dwells on: the slimy pools and scarred trees of Constable, the clutter and litter of Turner, Keats's swallows gathering in the sky as the scene fades. Romanticism honours the sad temporality of landscape, because that makes it an image of consciousness, fluid and evanescent, not of character, composed and impregnable as Reynolds requires; and *Tristram Shandy* is one of the first literary signs of the same revolt of consciousness against character.

Reynolds extends his argument about artistic embellishment of nature into literature. There are here, he believes, two distinct principles: literature follows nature, or else alters, even abolishes it. In the theatre, farce is merely natural, like upretentious descriptive painting, but the higher kind of drama no more cares for plausible realism than Raphael or Poussin expect their characters to be taken for ordinary beings. Failure to respect this hierarchy creates the critical confusion which Reynolds attacks in those who commend Raphael for a naturalness he never intended, and in Fielding for allowing Partridge, at the play in *Tom Jones*, to imagine Garrick's performance of Hamlet a reality. But again the issue has a romantic complication missed by Reynolds. Partridge's credulity is not culpable ignorance but an inkling of that romantic willingness to be duped, to cast an imaginative spell over oneself by accepting a fiction as truth, which leads Chatterton to identify himself with Rowley, or Catherine Morland to turn a laundry list into a sinister parchment, or Winckelmann to accredit a Mengs forgery as a specimen of antique art. The exploitation of delusion is entirely self-aware: these people will themselves to believe in, even to be haunted by, their lies. Partridge, though he belittles Garrick's acting by saying it is not art at all but nature, is the more intensely disturbed by it for that reason, and for several nights wakes shrieking, convinced that the ghost has appeared again. Naïvely he mimics that artificial but terrifying self-haunting of the romantics, who, in Goya's phrase from the *Caprichos*, send the reason to sleep and urge the mind to breed monsters. Adam effortlessly finds his dream to be truth; the romantics strain to accept their nightmares as truth too. But Reynolds can only see the rite as an admission of ludicrous gullibility.

Like Garrick's Hamlet as Partridge responds to it, Fuseli's Bracciaferro or his nightmare-wracked woman exist in the uncertain region, opened up by romantic art, between tragic terror and superstitious comic delusion. They belong in an ironic no-man's-land between tragedy and comedy. Romantic art creates a new kind of fiction which lies between Reynolds's categories of nature tragically ennobled or comically transcribed. Fiction for Reynolds is either aristocratic licensed falsity or cheap imitation. Either way, it has no hold over the imagination, and it is this dangerous power which romanticism grants it – tragically because the fiction can unsettle the mind, comically because it makes a dupe of whoever believes in it. Partridge's bemused trust is funny; his nocturnal sweating and screaming are not. With a similar ambiguity, the cartoons of Goya or Gillray combine a deformed absurdity which can be laughed off with a morbid conviction which is genuinely haunting. Again *Tristram Shandy* is proleptic, for its hero is a comic but pathetic victim of the fiction from which he struggles to disentangle himself, as Clarissa, recording in infinitely patient detail the process of her destruction which, while writing, she can do nothing to avert, is the tragic victim of her fiction.

The aesthetics of Sterne, irregular, asymmetrical and devious, are treated theoretically in Hogarth's *Analysis of Beauty*,[8] in which art makes its escape from the fixity and grandeur of Reynolds's classicism by means of the wayward, wriggling line of beauty. Introversion is here joined to involution: straight lines, which Hogarth deems not beautiful, lead ahead, and that is the way of character and action, but only a winding, serpentine line can lead inside, for the rhythm of consciousness is discontinuous, digressive, looping and meandering.

Sterne progresses by digressing, because he trusts to the
mind's divagations, not to the body's dull tread; and he illustrates his method of indirection with a number of Hogarthian
lines. Book VI reviews the course of the preceding five volumes, which it sees as a series of initially straight lines vari-
ously perplexed, bumped and fretted, tied in knots, lunging
above and below, shooting ahead or behind in sharp arrows of
anticipation or regressive back-slidings, sprouting bubbles or
opening chasms:

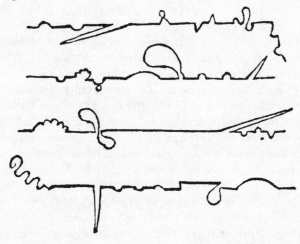

The diagrams seem musical as well as pictorial: the narrative
is imaged as a musical score in which indentation of the line
creates the melody. A simple linear succession of notes is
unmusical; the art depends on leaps, clusters, plunges. The
torments to which Sterne subjects the straight line suggests the
impulsive floridity of early-romantic vocal music, in which
pinnacles or hollows mark the virtuoso performer's decorative interpolations above or below the note. Sterne's fondness
for asterisks may also be musical. They save the situations at
moments when language would be embarrassingly explicit by
turning words into a sly, suggestive humming. The three and
a half lines of dashes which intervene (at Book V Chapter III)
between Uncle Toby's receiving the letter, over which he
hums, and his announcement of Bobby's death, mark musically the interlude, tactfully wordless, in which Toby absorbs

the news. Punctuation becomes for Sterne a form of musical notation.

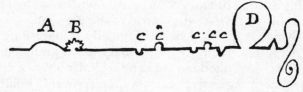

The diagram which represents the fifth book is supplied with explanatory symbols. The bump at A is the trip to Navarre. The prickly-headed curve B is the outing with Lady Baussiere. The fidgety series of small *c*'s marks parentheses, "common ins and outs", distracting variations of tempo. D, the great balloon subsiding via a small pyramid into the beginnings of a treble clef beneath the line, stands for John de la Casse's devils. Sterne hopes to go straight ahead from here, and in earnest of his intention borrows a writing-master's ruler to draw across the page a line of exemplary straightness. This at once wins the admiration of the divines, because it represents the Christian's unwavering path; of Cicero, because it is (as it was for Blake) an image of rectitude; and of Archimedes, because it is the shortest way from one point to another. But despite this trinity of religious, philosophical, and geometrical virtues, it is an unShandyean line, grimly opposed to Tristram's cardiographs of consciousness, in which the quaverings and flickerings of the needle register the shocks and seizures of mental life; the line straightens out only when the patient dies.

In the final volume, a Shandyean line – coiled, looping, trailing, performing acrobatics in the air rather than speeding to its moral destination – is described by Corporal Trim during his discussion of celibacy with Uncle Toby. To illustrate the glory of freedom, he flourishes his stick in the air. Tristram transcribes the curvaceous and exuberant pattern it traces, noting that "a thousand of my father's most subtle syllogisms" could not have been more eloquent. Trim's wand whirls in praise of freedom, as against confinement for life with the widow Wadman or the Jew's widow at Lisbon: like Don Giovanni at his feasts, he is celebrating a hedonistic liberty. At the first of these feasts, during the finale of Mozart's first act, a choral hymn is sung to liberty, and the masked avengers are shamed and disarmed in advance by being made to join it as they enter. They intrude as agents of rectitude and responsibility, and it is as if Don Giovanni suspects their threat and forces them to compromise themselves by toasting the principle of freedom they have come to scourge.

Flourishing his stick, Trim anticipates as well Coleridge's image of Shakespeare's humour as a hilarity which disburdens, a self-delighting ease of motion which has no point, like a man waving his stick in the air. Coleridge calls the stick a conductors: serried ranks of asterisks make embarrassed static sphere, and in this sense Sterne's antic punctuation also creates conductors: serried ranks of asterisks make embarassed static when Toby and Mrs Wadman discuss the location of his wound; a dash gropes into empty space and hangs there suspended as Yorick stretches his hand to catch the fille de chambre's —— ; breathy, faltering dashes musically record rather than plainly describing the last moments of Le Fever.

One of the disputants in Friedrich Schlegel's dialogue on poetry, *Gespräch über die Poesie* (1799–1800) finds the word for Sterne's frisking, knotted, virtuoso line: arabesque.[9] Schlegel considers the arabesque as a definite literary mode, exemplified by Sterne's entwining of decoratively convoluted wit and humid sentiment. He sets against this the unsentimental *Jaques le fataliste* of Diderot, executed with as straight a hand as the line drawn with the writing-master's ruler. Sterne is next compared with Jean Paul Richter, and while he is more arabesque than Diderot he is less so than Jean Paul, because for Sterne the arabesque is only a work of art, whereas for Jean Paul it is the product of nature. Despite Sterne's jocular distortions, his sensibility, Schlegel argues, is placidly English. But Jean Paul's sickly and eccentric temperament spiritualises the arabesque and makes it the frantic, grotesque expression of his abnormal state. John Britton aptly employs the same term in his discussion of the Shandyean introversion of Sir John Soane's house: the Monk's Parlour, its sobriety disrupted by vivid reflections from mirrors cunningly set in dark recesses, mingles irreconcilable styles so as to recall "those playful and graceful sculptural caprices known by the name of *arabesques*, in which animal and vegetable forms are connected with so

much elegance of fancy".[10] Arabesque even acquires a musical
significance, which is also relevant to Sterne: Eduard Hanslick,
in his treatise on the nature of musical beauty, *Von
Musikalisch-Schönen* (1854),[11] employs it as an image of the
formal purity of musical ideas, which have no need of rep-
resentational content. Music sets the linear complication of the
arabesque into motion, constantly making and unmaking its
ornamental shapes: "Behold the broad and delicate lines, how
they pursue one another; how from a gentle curve they rise up
into lofty heights, presently to descend again; how they widen
and contract, surprising the eye with a marvellous alternation
of quiescence and mobility". Like Sterne's blizzards of
punctuation-marks or his vacant or marbled pages, the mobile
patterns of Hanslick's musical arabesque declare form's
romantic liberation from content.

Hogarth's *Analysis of Beauty* finds the same quirky, twisted,
arabesque oddity in nature. He admits, for instance, a Sternean
predilection for odd rather than even numbers, because nature
intimates her own fondness for them: "in all her works of
fancy . . . where it seems immaterial whether even or odd
numbers of divisions were preferred, [nature] most frequently
employs the odd; as for example, in the indenting of leaves,
flowers, blossoms, etc." The progress of romanticism from
the comedy of irregular patterning and tortuous intricacy to
scientific rationality can be marked in the change from
Hogarth's or Sterne's discovery of the plurality of worlds,
minute and misshapen, to Ruskin's resolution of this comic
complication into reposeful order. The boughs of trees, Ruskin notes in *Modern Painters*, "always . . . bear among themselves such a ratio of length as to describe with their
extremities a symmetrical curve, constant for each species; and
within this curve all the irregularities, segments, and divisions
of the trees are included". The most wayward lines are obe-
dient, in Ruskin's scheme, to the moral consonance of nature.

Hogarth's theory of serpentine beauty, working in alliance
with Burke's theory of the sublime, confounds proportion in
nature and art. The scale of aesthetic perception is changed as
Hogarth and Burke insist on contrary extremes of tiny pecul-
iarity and turgid immensity, an irregularity which is either
minute (Sterne's divagations or Hogarth's indentations) or

threateningly awesome (Burke's Alps). But whether constricting or distending nature, both resolve objects into emotions, and make the external world a precarious construction
of the observer's fantasy. Works of art can no longer be
classically barricaded off from the desires and appetites of
readers and spectators. Art caters to those appetites, confessing
its solitary incompleteness and pleading to be quickened into
life by an outsider's response. Whereas in the doctrine of
Reynolds nature is mean and unsatisfactory until made
respectable by art, for Hogarth and Burke art waits anxiously
for the natural man to rescue it by adopting it into his own
physical and mental life. A mountain is not sublime until a
romantic viewer reacts sublimely to it; art exists only in the
eye or on the pulses of its beholder. Hogarth proposes physiological causes for aesthetic effects: the love of pursuit is a
human characteristic, and eye and mind delight equally in
being led "a wanton kind of chase", and this alerts us to the
challenge of unravelling riddles, allegories and involved plots.
Tristram Shandy is an indolent or incompetent artist who
trusts to such susceptibilities to do his work for him: his
disconnections and postponements transfer the burden of
organising the narrative to the reader.

Schlegel remarks that the wits of England introduce into
reality an absolute freedom. Sterne's formal chaos is such a
state of freedom, bewilderingly random, exhilaratingly contingent. The English wits "live wittily", Schlegel says,
"hence their talent for madness. They die for their principles."
Sterne, writing wittily, discomposes and destroys his novel
for his principles. He and Hogarth both question the formal
elements of their art, irritated by the artifice of representation
which mimics emotions and objects rather than embodying
them. But, by an inspired abuse of these elements of form,
imprisoning artifice becomes a heady natural freedom. Slavish
formalism, in Sterne's typographical games and Hogarth's
study of perspective, is the ironic alibi for a romantic form-
lessness. In setting art to quarrel with and disrupt its own
formal constituents, Sterne and Hogarth are anticipating in
structural terms the self-contradictions of the romantic ironist,
who is possessed, as Schlegel says, by a disorderly spiritual
rage to overcome himself, to violate restrictions of formal or

moral consistency. The ironist treats his life as Sterne or Hogarth treat their work; his rule, in Schlegel's words, is that "we must be able to rise above our own love; in our own thoughts we must be able to destroy what we worship; other- wise, no matter what other capacities we have, we lack a sense of the infinite and of the world". The ironist has made Sterne's witty chaos a spiritual imperative.

Sterne's transgressions and incongruities deform the letter of his text, but with the ironic purpose of making it express the unconfined, contrary spirit. His marbled, blank, or mourn- fully blacked-out pages are complaints about the inadequacy of literature, which must give way at moments of rage or delicate intimacy or bereavement to silence. Yet while making their protest, these caprices extend the range of literature by incorporating silence into it. They open up pregnant gaps, respectful pauses to be filled in by the reader, as an unwritten cadenza leaves a space for the performer's improvisation.

Similarly, Hogarth's satiric print of false perspective (the frontispiece to a simplification of perspective method by Joshua Kirby)[12] defends a convention, but with the ironic purpose of setting form to bemuse and disrupt content. With the excuse of criticising the disarray of art unregulated by perspective, the print creates a dizzying fantasy in which objects refuse to recede acquiescently towards their vanishing point, like recalcitrant words in Sterne rising up to torment those who use them. The design is slippery and disorienting, impossible to read consistently: there is no solid ground on which to found one's view of it, since surfaces drop steeply and illogically away. Near objects and far slide into proximity as if by a Sternean magic of association – a crone in the foreground leaning out of a window with a candle lights the pipe of a traveller on a distant hill; fishing lines are launched across vast distances and cross in mid-air; tumbling barrels in a pile are seen at once from beneath and above. Each object makes sense in isolation, but its relations to all other objects are incon- gruous. Things trip over or contradict one another in an arbitrary space like that of *Tristram Shandy*, another work in which perspective fails: characters, words, documents, inserted narratives revolve in bewilderment there, with no design to make connections between them or to explain them to one another. A bird in the distance of Hogarth's print looms as large as a dog in the foreground, a swan as a horse. But the clumsiness is ironic rather than satiric: it recreates the episodic joy of the naïve eye, contemplating each object for itself, not grading and differentiating as Reynolds insists; and this is the enchanted chaos of Tristram's mental state. This existence is out of proportion: the smallest detail for him swells into enormity, while the towering issues of life dwindle into minutiae.

Perspective and proportion conspire to keep objects sedately in place; for Hogarth, however, nature is not a static hierarchy but a democracy of motion. He points to movement and gesture as evidence that nature repudiates categories, and desires each of its creatures to grow into uniqueness: "To the amazing variety of forms made still more infinitely various in appearance by light, shade and colour, nature hath added another way of increasing that variety, still more to enhance the value of her compositions. This is accomplished by means of action." The modes of action he mentions are playing, dancing and fencing: self-delighting exhibitions of the capacity, not action enslaved to a purpose, the expression of a fortified and directed character, but action as the pointless, playful, self-exploring image of consciousness; not the action of Fortinbras marching across the country but that of Hamlet, volatile, unattached, conjuring with experience, writing a script for his life and performing it as if it were a play. Hogarth adduces the dancing Perdita as an example of bodily grace, and his choice is apt: Florizell's desire that

> When you do dance, I wish you
> A wave o' the sea, that you might ever do
> Nothing but that; more still, still so,
> And own no other function

transforms action into ballet, beautifully gratuitious (Valéry was to call walking a mode of prose, and dancing of poetry), as a moment before he transforms action into opera, when telling her to buy and sell in song. Action is turning into decorative arabesque. Richard Hurd, a contemporary of Hogarth and Sterne, dismissed the classical notion that epic unity consisted in "the representation of one entire action" in his defence of

The Faerie Queene, and argued that Spenser's poem derived its unity not from one single thrust of decision and ambition but from the exfoliation of small actions all contributing, however tangentially, to a common purpose. Its unity was a matter of design, a Gothic principle resembling the radial plan of William Kent's gardens, in which the branching walks appear to have their own destinations but are joined "not to each other, but to their common and concurrent centre".[13] Hurd turns from action to design; Hogarth turns action into design.

In *Tristram Shandy* a graceful mobility is granted to the mind, agilely swooping from one point to the next. The body is more enslaved to system, cumbrously regular: Walter's body thrown on the bed composes itself into an attitude, a static point of a map. Trim, however, in preparing to read the sermon, relaxes into the Hogarthian line of flexibility and sinuousness: Sterne is particularly anxious to save him from seeming merely perpendicular and upright, with the sermon clenched in his left hand, and he allows Trim to persuasively incline his body, bending and swaying "just so far as to make an angle of 85 degrees and a half upon the plain of the horizon". Trim does not determine this angle by calculation, as Walter would, but by happy instinct. The clauses in which Sterne captures his exact stance suggest his trembling motion, a movement in one direction countered at once by a steadying modification towards the other, every assertion of foot or knee immediately reconciled to the fluid rhythm of the whole, restrained before it can become disruptive. The sentence itself teeters to and fro, uneasily balancing its sets of semi-colons and dashes. Punctuation becomes choreography.

> He stood, – for I repeat it, to take the picture of him in at one view, with his body swayed, and somewhat bent forwards, – his right leg from under him, sustaining seven-eighths of his whole weight, – the foot of his left leg, the defect of which was no disadvantage to his attitude, advanced a little, – not laterally, nor forwards, but in a line betwixt them; – his knee bent, but that not violently, – but so as to fall within the limits of the line of beauty; – and I add, of science too; – for consider, it had one-eighth part of his body to bear up; – so that in this

case the position of the leg is determined, – because the foot could be no further advanced, or the knee more bent, than what would allow him mechanically to receive an eighth part of his whole weight under it, and to carry it too.

The sentence sways with a willowy, wavering motion, shifting its weight across those dashes from one foot to another, exactly balancing its equations.

Sterne's lines of beauty either teeter in mild intoxication, as Trim does in reading the sermon, or swell into corpulence like the squat Dr Slop, who is "of about four feet and a half perpendicular height, with a breadth of back, and a sesquipedality of belly". Dr Slop's embonpoint is referred to Hogarth's *Analysis*, and those who have not read it are advised to do so. The same globular form recurs in the adipose, complacent people of Rowlandson, who develops Hogarth's principle by giving to his characters a satisfied, drowsy rotundity which suggests Falstaff's philosophy of immersion in the warm, mindless protection of the body. Hamlet and Falstaff have been mentioned in preceding chapters as romantic opposites secretly in agreement. The one struggles out of the body in which (like Shelley's Ariel) he is imprisoned as in a grave, the other declines through it into his quietus, becoming a thing endued with sense. Both are deeply antisocial, the one because he retreats into the privacy of the mind, the other because he takes up residence in the fortress of the body. Both withstand a painful siege, Hamlet the persecution of those who wish to draw him out of the seclusion of intelligence into dutiful action, Falstaff the persecution of those who enviously assault his bodily self-sufficiency. Fuseli represents the torment of Falstaff as a battle of Hogarthian lines: the plump globe is beset by twisting serpentine enemies, lines of beauty which have curled into malevolence. Fuseli's Falstaff in the buckbasket (1792) or unmasked in the forest by the merry wives (from the Rivington Shakespeare edition of 1805) is a rotund form at the mercy of angular, predatory women. The wives in the first scene circle him with looped trains of linen, their slippers equipped with stabbing points, their hats plumed and crested like helmets; in the later illustration they lay hands on him as if to tear him apart. The Falstaff of 1789 with Doll Tearsheet on his knee is a mountain of rounded flesh with a head so small it seems lost in that immense waste of fat. Twined round him, Doll is menacingly serpentine. She has taken hold of his tiny head as if imagining it served to her on a platter, and huge feathers flaunt themselves from her hat like victorious banners. The expression in her eyes is of steely rapture; Falstaff's are beadily wary. The great globe of his body now has an elephatine immobility which makes him a ready victim for her sharper angles and lither lines.

Curves are for Hogarth generously appetitive: "who but a bigot, even to the antiques, will say that he has not seen faces and necks, hands and arms in living women, that even the Grecian Venus doth but coarsely imitate?" In Fuseli they become the contours of sexual war. His women turn the line of beauty into a weapon. Diderot's nephew of Rameau is also, but less threateningly, composed of Hogarthian lines, exuberant s-curves of body and mind. Perpetually in motion, he is driven to act out whatever he describes: if the subject is gavottes he sings them, if a house he stretches his arms to measure it, if a bed he reclines on it, if a coach he lifts a leg to enter it, if a pretty woman he fondles bosoms in the air. Feeling is no longer a matter of life arrested in a drooping, sentimental tableau; the nephew has transformed feeling into a performance. He plays on his thoughts, feelings and physical responses as on instruments. Like the musical virtuoso, the man of feeling must be a physical prodigy, more keenly sensitive and nervously alert than others are, just as the musician needs a freakishly wide hand-span to grasp at outlying keys or strings. The nephew has punishingly trained his body to perform: his wrist, fingers and tendons used to be dry and stiff, but he has "pulled them about, strained and broken them in", and he demonstrates their nimbleness with a fearful cracking of joints. When Diderot objects that he will maim himself, the nephew replies that his extremities must be bludgeoned into obedience, must learn to finger keys or pluck strings accurately, and he has tormented them to this end: in the same way, the physical accidents to which Tristram Shandy is subject are ordained to render his body and mind incapable of action but exquisitely and tortuously capable of feeling.

The sublime and the beautiful also, in Burke's philosophical enquiry into the origin of our ideas of them,[14] are seen as means of playing on and extending the body's powers. The shortened title, usually employed when Burke's essay is mentioned, carries with it a misconception about the work's purpose. It is not a treatise on the sublime and the beautiful as aesthetic categories, but, more hesitantly and at several removes of impression and reaction, an enquiry into the origins of our ideas of what they might be. Burke aims not to define them but to follow them back to their physical sources within us. His argument emphasises the feelings which create a work of art and those which it inspires in an individual exposed to it. Art is kinetic, and can never rest in completeness: itself a reaction to some original emotion, it seeks to induce a corresponding reaction in another. Hence the abject, helpless attitude of the narrators in novels of this period: they beg the reader to bring them alive, by listening in Clarissa's case, by deciphering in Tristram's.

Burke makes the experiencing individual the measure of a work of art: his senses are the instrument on which the bare score of the work's text is played. Thus the nephew of Rameau is an Aeolian harp reversed: with the wind-harp, there is an instrument but no visible performer; in the nephew's case, there is a performer but no visible instrument. He plays on non-existent violins and keyboards, because the instruments have been retracted into his own body. Having been made the seat of moral judgement by Sterne, the body now becomes, for Burke, the arbiter of poetic excellence. A specialisation of sense occurs as the body allots different aesthetic responsibilities to its various faculties: the sublime, Burke argues, communicates itself specifically through the eyes and ears, not through the other organs; taste, the subject of his introduction, is promoted from a gustatory to a critical term.

Returning art to the body means embroiling it in emotion, allowing it to be contaminated by its audience. Burke points out that "the most powerful effects of poetry and music have been displayed . . . where these arts are but in a very low and imperfect state. The rude hearer is affected by the principles which operate in these arts even in their rudest condition; and he is not skilful enough to perceive the defects." This is Caliban's response to the voices in the air, and Caliban is increasingly vindicated by criticism, as ignorance and the mental prostration of terror are declared the ideal state of mind for reception of the sublime. Wilde defined the nineteenth-century dislike of realism and romanticism as the rage of Caliban at seeing or not seeing his own face in a glass. The ecstasies of the late eighteenth century in that case must be, like the grimace of Goya's Colossus, the whimpering delight of Caliban at hearing the twangling instruments and sweet noises in the air.

Such a recommendation of trusting ignorance in an audience is dangerous, because the artist is tempted to practise on this gullibility. This is a period in which art indulges in forgery and fraud, in which the imagination comes near to seeming no more than pretence and high mendacity; and art's manipulation of our vain and wayward natures is more prominent in Burke's theory than its address to knowledge and fine feeling. Since Burke regards the passions as shabby stock responses beyond the control of reason, he refuses to assign "the cause of feelings which merely arise from the mechanical structure of our bodies, or from the natural frame and constitution of our minds, to certain conclusions of the reasoning faculty on the objects presented to us". Emotion is both cheaply conditioned and promiscuously careless of its object. Art makes every man a cynically faithless libertine. And as in Coleridge's analysis of the libertine as a hero of mental power and ruthless self-will, Burke's exposure of the "glorying and sense of inward greatness" which well up in an individual experiencing the sublime entangles art with power, will and their corruptions. "Power is undoubtedly a capital source of the sublime", and art plumes up our sense of ourselves, enticing us into Falstaffian satisfaction with the sheer effortlessness of our being, absolving us from the need to do anything. Art's disreputable compact with its audience, playing on our shabbier characteristics as a way of excusing its own imperfections, is written into the structure of *Tristram Shandy*: Tristram makes the reader both a prurient eavesdropper and a dull factotum, charged with repairing and reorganising a narrative for which the artist disclaims responsibility.

With a knowing intimacy like Tristram's, Burke defends his

theory by confiding such well-kept psychological secrets as
the delight we take in the pains and misfortunes of others.
Since both beauty and sublimity pander to our egotistic self-
congratulation, the one exciting our sense of possession, the
other rallying our ambition, the agonies of others can only
enhance our self-assurance as, like the servants when Bobby's
death is announced, we smugly remind ourselves of our own
safety. Such mean thrills are comic counterparts to the exal-
tation of the sublime. Art itself is a shadowy substitute for the
blatant sensations of life: no matter how sublime and affecting
the performance of a tragedy may be, Burke says, the theatre
would instantly empty if a public execution were announced
in an adjoining square. Together the sublime and the beautiful
draw on our psychological history so as to stimulate a phantasmagoric play of sensation and desire in us. "There is a wide
difference between admiration and love. The sublime, which
is the cause of the former, always dwells in great objects, and
terrible; the latter in small ones, and pleasing; we submit to
what we admire, but we love what submits to us; in one case
we are forced, in the other we are flattered into compliance."
Like the libertine, art either threatens or cajoles its victims. The
connection between the two experiences Burke calls admiration and love is the unholy one of power, self-obliteration by
a power superior to our own, or else the jealous, acquisitive
demand, to which Coleridge attributes the dubious charm of
the libertine, that something give itself up to us. Blustering or
wheedling, crushing or caressing, literature has an intimate
hold on us which is regressively explained through its analogy
to our earliest relations with our parents: the sublime mimics
the forbidding authority of the father, the beautiful recalls the
indulgent affection of the mother, and they conspire to keep us
all in the bullied, otiose and infantile state of Tristram.

Sterne converts Burke's theory to comedy, revealing that
there is a sublimity in minuteness as well as in vastness (which
Burke concedes when he notes that in tracing diminishing
scales of existence we are confounded by the wonders of
minuteness), and that the attributes of the sublime – dis-
arrangement, disproportion, chaos – may be comic as well as
awesome. Burke allows words an emotional aura quite independent of the sensible images they may propose to the brain,

and this is a justification of muddle as well as of mystery, of nonsense as well as inspiration. He calls Virgil's description of Vulcan's cave sublime, but warns that "if we attend coolly to the kind of sensible image which a combination of ideas of this sort must form, the chimeras of madmen cannot appear more wild and absurd than such a picture"; and Burke's dazing obscurity has its comic correlative in the dullness and inanity which befuddle Tristram.

Notes

1. Diderot's *Le Neveu de Rameau*, circumstantially dating in its first form from mid-1761, has been translated for the Penguin Classics by L. W. Tantock, 1966.
2. J. J. Winckelmann, *Beschreibung des Apollo in Belvedere*; Fuseli translated this in the *Universal Magazine*, February 1768.
3. The Royal Academy Discourses by Reynolds, given between 1769 and 1791, were first collected in 1820.
4. Blake's annotations are printed in his *Complete Writings*, ed. Geoffrey Keynes, 1966.
5. Goya's *Los Caprichos* are reproduced in a Dover edition, 1969.
6. B. R. Haydon, *Lectures on Painting and Design*, 1844; Lecture VI: "On Colour."
7. Fuseli's criticism has been collected by Eudo C. Mason in *The Mind of Fuseli*, 1951.
8. The most recent edition is by J. Burke, 1955.
9. The *Dialogue on Poetry*, with the *Literary Aphorisms*, has been translated by Ernest Behler and Roman Struc, 1968: this is the source for the passages from Schlegel treated in chapter 8.
10. See chapter 2, note 8.
11. *The Nature of Musical Beauty*, trans. Gustav Cohen, 1891.
12. Hogarth's "Satire on False Perspective", February 1754, was the frontispiece to Joshua Kirby's edition of *Dr. Brook Taylor's Method of Perspective Made Easy, Both in Theory and Practice*, dedicated to Hogarth.
13. *Letters on Chivalry and Romance*, 1762.
14. The most recent edition of Burke's *A philosophical enquiry into the origin of our ideas of the sublime and beautiful*, 1757, is by J. T. Boulton, 1958.

6

Libertine of Painting

Hogarth's line of beauty describes a pattern not of action but of capriciously involuted thought; Burke's beauty and sublimity are likewise mental and emotional chimerae, not categories of aesthetic evaluation. As the region of art contracts to Coleridge's mental space, even painting, apparently dependent on observation of the external world, is made to undergo a Shandyean introversion. Fuseli, as the preceding chapter explained, set himself to paint thought, the obsessional internal world of fear and desire, and he reduces the external paraphernalia of literary sources and characters illustrated in grandiose action to alibis, defensive incognitos. But having turned the art inside out, he is obliged to deal with a series of critical complications, all of them bearing on literature as well as painting, and these problems and paradoxes are to be unravelled now.

Determined to personify sentiments and paint the world within, Fuseli is obstructed by theoretical qualms. Is the pictorial imagination trespassing on the field of literature, which can make the interior drama of sentiment intelligible in a narrative, while painting is restricted to a single image which it has no time to decipher? How shadowy can painting, supposed to be a record of the solid surfaces of objects, safely become? What are the rights of the imagination? Fuseli's critical essays and aesthetic speculations attempt to manouevre a way out of these difficulties.

Early essays on Cowper's Homer and Roscoe's study of Lorenzo de' Medici protest against the overlapping of poetry and painting, but Fuseli was never able to rid his own art of its timid dependence on literature.[1] The convenience of literary sources is that they supply his paintings with a cautionary motive; they excuse his violent images of personal fantasy – his malevolent Pucks, horned amorinos and muscular women – as excerpts from some independent narrative. His art is nervously literary. It crosses Lessing's border between the arts because it dare not stand on its own, because the appearance of literary content allows it to pass off confession as characterisation, as Chatterton passed off his dreams as antiquarian scholarship. Fuseli battens on his subjects but flouts them, flaunting the distance in spirit between his version and the text it illustrates but unable, for all the liberties he takes, to risk separating one from the other.

Fuseli deforms the texts he illustrates by making them images of his own nightmares; the blatancy of the imposition is, paradoxically, his protection, because he disowns his neuroses by attributing them to someone else. Shakespearean drama contracts, in his illustrations, into a psychological prison, a mental space of threatening narrowness. The death of Falstaff is purged of lyrical babbling in Fuseli's version and becomes sinister and predatory. The unconscious knight clutches at the bed-clothes with hands like paws while his chamber is invaded by obscurely dangerous visitors: a man in a cap peers round the curtain of the bed, his nose casting a grotesque, belligerent shadow; a woman with keys and a rosary at her belt and a stiff flat hat on her head reels startled as she is discovered searching in the bed. The merry wives become brutal tormentors. Titania, surrounded by insect-headed fairies and cold gloating duennas, nestles against the asinine bulk of Bottom, trapped in a dream of bestiality. The picture of Garrick as Macbeth emerging with the bloody daggers to be hushed by the Lady Macbeth of Mrs Pritchard translates the play's savage gloom into the chaste transparency of neoclassical line, and makes the characters electric apparitions, blue-green ghosts shivering like lightning in the air, pestilentially hued. In other sketches for Fuseli's Shakespeare Gallery, the lunettes of the compositional scheme are the cramped chambers of the victims in *Macbeth*, one of whom is being run through while the knife is poised over the other. Fuseli here invades that private sanctum, concealed in the depth of Shakespeare's play, where the murders are committed. This is no longer illustration, but a rewriting of the play: Shakespeare's Macbeth is a contemplative metaphysician, pondering at a reflective distance the consequences of deeds which seem not to belong to him; Fuseli's is a ravaged inhabitant of nightmare, and his sleep-walking Lady Macbeth is a maenad.

But the paradox of such art is that, despite its interpretative daring, it is a product of shifty, timorous compromise. Charles Lamb remarked on the besetting cowardice of modern art,[2] and Fuseli seems feeble despite his violence, secretive despite his sensationalism. In Coleridge's phrase, he is vigorously impotent.[3] He resembles Hamlet and Tristram Shandy in his combination of frantic energy and depressed purposelessness. Like them, he is self-disabled: his own aesthetic theories conspire to impede him.

In his discussion of Cowper's Homer, Fuseli declares that poetic imitation must move in time, dealing with objects in action and not with still surfaces, which are the prerogative of painting. He particularly attacks the "descriptive tribe" in literature, "who imagine that they paint what they only perplex, and fondly dream of enriching the realms of fancy by silly excursions into the province of the florist, chemist, or painter of still life". The essay on Roscoe protests that the boundaries between the sister arts are no longer respected, and argues that it is the duty of the painter to take the external form of an object, frozen in an attitude, while the poet "surrounds his object, pierces it, and discloses its most hidden qualities". But this specifically literary penetration into a psychological drama, which Fuseli forbids to the painter, is all the same the purpose of his own pictures. For instance, his version of Pope's "Cave of Spleen" from *The Rape of the Lock*: with its bilious colour and sickening swirling lines, its comatose enchanted population of insects, elaborately coiffed squatting dwarfs and huddling figures headless under their shawls, and its darkened recess of inanition, it is a picture of a state of mind, not of a place. This makes it, in Fuseli's analytic, internal use of the term, more "poetic" than Pope's original. Pope is, on the contrary, pictorial: his living teapots and chattering goosepies and maids turned bottles suggest the animistic mutants of graphic satire.

The theory works against the creations. The images of the painter are required to be "inert and motionless", which Fuseli's own never are, except when spell-bound like his dreamers. His Satan plunging through the air, his Tell leaping from Gessler's boat through the foam, his twisting, bounding Roland sounding the horn at Roncesvalles, or his balletic Undine in flight from the fisherman's hut, are all figures of motion, suspended in mid-air. They refuse to remain still, which would mean imprisonment. Their desire is to struggle free of all constraints, to evade not only their persecutors but also their lowly containment in a human body. Fuseli's Roland seems about to leap out of his skin.

These characters are aware of the shame of being "enchained hopelessly in the grovelling fetters of externality". The phrase, aptly, is that Lamb used against those "deeply corporealised" persons who could tolerate illustrations of Shakespeare's plays. His objection is that illustration robs Shakespeare's characters of their freedom of mental space, and shackles them in "exterior accidents". Falstaff pictorially is no more than an image of corpulence, Othello of blackness. In stirring up such hectic, unsatisfied motion, Fuseli's characters seem to be expressing his own and Lamb's reservations about the form, protesting against their enclosure in a picture. Disrupting the composition, they prepare themselves to leap out of their cramped space in a storm of frustration. Their rage of dissatisfaction resembles Tristram Shandy's protests against the bother of having to write the novel, and his objection, like theirs, is that the form condemns him to an existence in exterior accident. Lamb derisively called such an existence pictorial. The poetic, on the other hand, is the realm of "unseen qualities": Lamb's phrase is close to Fuseli's, for both, like Hamlet, define poetry as that which passes mere pictorial show.

As earlier chapters have described, the libertine has an equally unsettling effect on artistic form. He finds his home in opera because, as Kierkegaard points out, music moves ceaselessly in time and yet overcomes it by organising it. Thus it is able to satisfy the romantic libertine's longing to be released from time's tedious succession. Fuseli's characters stage a similar rebellion against the constraints of space, which are the formal limitations of painting; and they are released into ballet, for dance organises space as music does time. Fuseli was fascinated by ballet, and the possessed, whirling motion of his characters derives from the dance. The sinister enchantment of romantic ballet lay in its victory over gravity, and Fuseli's dancers – the nymphs surrounding Bottom and Titania, the merry wives with their pointed slippers, the spirits entwining above the head of the dreaming shepherd – have a fiendish weightlessness.

Fuseli's theory, however, attributes the qualities of his own pictorial art to poetry, and he thinks of painting in terms of the "painted statues" of neoclassicism, static and frigid. Poetry is volatile, mobile, mutable: "it lives and moves; it is expanded or compressed; it glares upon the imagination, or vanishes into air, and is as various as Nature herself". He agrees with Roscoe that poetic diction is a representation of objects in motion, in time. But this confinement of poetry to time and painting to space is a restriction which Fuseli's own art and that of the romantics contravene. Romantic painting is anxious about time and eager to keep pace with it: the serial form of Constable's dated and numbered cloud studies or of Monet's haystacks and water-lilies represents an attempt to make images continuous, to overcome the frustrated imprisonment in a moment of the figures on Keats's urn. Romantic literature creates effects of space, of distant recession and remembered depth, within poems: avenues open suddenly in *The Prelude*, steep perspectives whose vanishing point is a moment of recognition far in the past. Although classical theory keeps each art within the bounds of its speciality, romanticism moves towards a transformation of each art into its opposite. Epic becomes lyric, and so does drama. Painting becomes poetic and poetry pictorial. Prose is quickened into blank verse and verse slackened into ruminative prose. Fuseli is one of the first artists to think of painting in terms of music. He said that the pinks, greys and light greens of Titian "soothe, charm and melt like a sweet melody", and described the Veroneses in the Louvre as "a scale of music"; the austerity of unbroken colour in Poussin's "Transfiguration" he called euphonious.

Fuseli's sources are equally hybrid. Oppressed by inherited material, documentation, inset narrative, scholarly footnoting and exegesis, Tristram turns out to be hardly the hero of the novel devoted to his life and opinions; and Fuseli similarly blocks himself inside the proliferation of his narrative sources, classical, Nordic, Shakespearean or Miltonic. He does not deal in significant, revelatory actions designed by himself, but takes over at random the actions prescribed by his sources and hopes to find himself there.

One of Fuseli's aphorisms illuminates this attitude: "Things came to Raffaelle and Shakespeare; *Michael Angelo* and Milton came to things."[4] Fuseli has extended a pervasive romantic critical antithesis to the visual arts. In the romantic critical theology, Shakespeare and Milton represent two opposed, complementary kinds of godliness. As Coleridge put it, Shakespeare is the "Spinozistic deity – an omnipresent creativeness", while Milton is "the deity of prescience; he stands *ab extra*".[5] Shakespeare creates by effacing himself, rendering himself invisible as he passes into each object of his universe. Criticism of Shakespeare becomes an exercise in animism. Milton is not absorbed, but retires to a distance as supercilious supervisor of the world he has created. Fuseli ironically compounds the two attitudes – things come to him in that he is content to illustrate whatever material is proposed; but he comes to things by distorting and deforming his sources, in a parody of the Miltonic imperiousness. He finds in Shakespeare a cold comedy of sexual aggression and suspicion, and disturbs the equilibrium of Milton's poem by moving Satan to the centre. His version of Satan is afflicted by some of Fuseli's own contradictions: although Satan is conceived as a hero of motion, he seems vigorously impotent, expending his energy in frantic running on the spot. Swooping, diving, gesticulating, agitating himself but achieving nothing, he is an image of Fuseli's own explosive ineffectualness – an infernal Tristram Shandy. By his own definition, Fuseli's is the Miltonic or Michelangelesque kind of creativity, since he takes things and bends them to his purpose; but though arrogant he is ineffective, and his Miltonic will seems mere impatience. He comes to things, but in the end finds himself unable to move them. As Haydon said, he deserts nature with a massive petulance "because she disdained to bend herself to the frenzied irregularities of his own spasmodic conceits".[6] He frets and struggles, but vainly. Leigh Hunt indeed considered him "an ingenious caricaturist of . . . Michelangelo", absurdly domesticating the muscle-bound apostles and prophets of the Sistine ceiling: "the quiet tea-table scene in Cowper he has turned into

John Henry Fuseli, *Satan, Sin and Death*, 1776.
Ashmolean Museum, Oxford.

John Henry Fuseli, *Satan, Sin and Death, c.* 1790.
Los Angeles County Museum of Art.

a preposterous conspiracy of huge men and women, all bent on showing their thews and postures, with tresses as fantastical as their minds".[7]

As Fuseli chooses subjects which resist him, but on which he struggles to imprint himself, so Sterne's are characters who do not define themselves in action but betray themselves in incidentals and asides. Walter maintains that "there a thousand unnoticed openings . . . which let a penetrating eye at once into a man's soul; and . . . a man of sense does not lay down his hat in coming into a room, – or take it up in going out of it, but something escapes, which discovers him". Fuseli's self-revelations have a Shandyean fugitiveness and furtiveness. He is given away by hints, nuances of difference added to his received subject-matter, not so much by the laying down of a hat as by those monstrous coiffures which are clues to his sexual temperament: the hat of one of Falstaff's tormentors, bristling with feathers like an alighting bird; the hard pyramidal head-dress of the naked woman in the "Allegory of Vanity"; the cannon-balls of bunched hair of Chriemhild embraced by the kneeling Siegfried. Feet are also a signature in Fuseli's pictures: the spiked ballet slippers of the merry wives, the laced sandals of Titania against the outsize bare feet of Bottom. Obliged to serve the imaginations of others, Fuseli fastens on sly details such as hair and feet and uses these fetishes, like Shandyean hobby-horses, to absorb the source into his own curious and devious private drama.

Although much of Fuseli's criticism is an attempt to define phenomena which are abstract, sentiments personified, but which can still be painted, he admits the near-impossibility of achieving this. His theory is prepared for failure. When Roscoe argues that the ancients were less skilful than the moderns in embodying abstract existences, Fuseli disagrees. Despite the airy nothings which haunt his own pictures, he calls ancient prosopopoeia more natural and credible. Milton is his example of modern confusion in the matter: "will it be denied, that by personifying the *act* by which his heroes were to fall, and the *punishment* attendant on that act, Milton has, as far as in him lay, destroyed the *credibility* of his poem?"[8] Whereas Homer employed abstractions which are already personified, and which could therefore associate naturally with human characters, Milton needs to invent mobile abstractions of his own, and they remain shadowily intellectualised, like Sin and Death, lacking the epic substantiality of Adam or Satan. Milton's personifications are condemned to wander in the impalpable worlds of spirit and sentiment, bodiless revenants, unreconciled to the human world of action and endeavour.

Fuseli has discerned in Milton a contradiction between imaginative truths on the one hand and facts, narratives and physical substances on the other. The fission is relevant to his own art, and to Blake's. Both are concerned with making painting, which deals in surfaces and substances, represent the invisible. The traditional answer to the problem is allegory, but this Fuseli discounts because an allegory is a fiction belonging only to its inventor, unable to compel general belief. Fuseli commends Homer for admitting no "*new-personified beings*" to his poem as actors. His own art, however, depends on such inventive liberties. Had Homer "introduced *Wisdom* seizing Achilles by the hair, and *Beauty* ravishing *Paris* from the combat, the Iliad . . . would be little more than the rival of the Pilgrim's Progress". But despite the embargo of theory, Fuseli himself regularly combines two planes of being. His slumped dreamer, whose body has the elegant elongation of a Parmigianino heroine, is assaulted by a grinning imp and a fiery-eyed horse from the world of Gillray. His dreaming shepherd lies innocently unaware of the malicious gnomes and insect sprites around him, and of the sly Pandora unwreathing a circle of temptresses from her box. His two naked women, in the sketch of a nightmare, lie on their crumpled bed, one recoiling in shame, the other relaxing in pensive gratification, as a dark horse and rider escape through the window: the nightmare here is literalised in the way Fuseli mocks in Bunyan.

The difficulty of reconciling spirit and substance explains Fuseli's reliance, in pictures like these, on sleep and dream. The dream of reason breeds monsters, and in conjuring up the figures of the dream around the hapless sleeper Fuseli has found a legitimate way to introduce demons into nature, to relate sentiments personified and the embodied persons they persecute. While it would be ludicrous for a representative of one world simply to appear in the other, for Wisdom to seize

Achilles, the process can be disquietingly revealed as an invasion. In sleep, reason's guard is down, and Goya's "impossible monsters" materialise. Fuseli disliked allegory because it was the reason's tactic for regimenting these monsters and attaching moral captions to them. By turning allegorical diagram back into dream vision, he is releasing the disturbing fictions from the control of the dreamer who is – in Goya's case as in his own – the artist.

The artists of Fuseli's period are fascinated by Milton's Sin and Death because, slithering between inner conceptions and embodied characters, this problematic pair express the frustration of an artistic attempt to make the ideal, the visionary, the hallucinatory and the sentimental into subjects for painting: to give form to the airy nothing of a mental state.

Satan's encounter with Sin and Death was painted by Hogarth as a grisly contest between three cartoon fiends. Death is a flaming skeleton, Satan a wolf with red eye and glinting claws, and Sin between them is a melting-eyed baroque figure whose ample body swells into a girdle of snarling hell-hounds. Hell is a Hogarthian brothel or madhouse. Gillray adapted Hogarth's composition to graphic satire, casting Queen Charlotte as Sin with wrinkled dugs.

James Barry's version exchanges the rabid ugliness of the cartoon for neoclassical solemnity. His Satan is a classical torso, Death is enveloped in a winding-sheet, and Sin, with a woeful open mouth, thrusts them apart. Her hair and the cloak twisted around Satan fly in the wind which rushes through the scene, but the figures themselves are poised and monumental, painted statues.

Blake is exuberantly linear. The serpentine lower reaches of Sin lie along the bottom of the design like a coiled spring storing energy, and tongues of flame wave in the air: the transparent Satan seems to taper into a flame. Whereas Barry gives the characters bulk and presence, with Death's spear striking at Satan's shield, Blake isolates the contestants from one another. Death is a wraith, an idea, whom the dazed Satan seems to be dreaming; Sin is the intermediary between the natural world and that of demented vision. Blake's characters are paralysed in eternal opposition. This Satan is not mobile: his arms are pinned in the air in the mocking posture of a crucifixion, and on his face is a look of apathetic dismay.[9]

Fuseli's 1776 sketch of the subject, now in the Ashmolean, turns this incestuous tangle into an erotic dream. A quivering swarthy Death and a blonde elegant Satan, whose body swings with a lazy Praxitelean curve while Death lunges forward to launch his spear, are rivals for the affections of a blowsy Sin. Her scaly nether parts and ring of barking hounds are disguised in a swirling line which has the serpentine contours of beauty. Thrusting Death back, she strokes Satan's cheek. His wings envelop her, and her hair is tousled: they appear to have been caught *in flagrante delicto* by her jealous husband.

A later painting of the subject by Fuseli, in the Los Angeles County Museum, still portrays Sin as a demon mistress. But Death is now a goblin, a close-up of one of the repellent insects Fuseli delighted in rearing, and Satan is a perversely sinuous creature with flowing hair and a sullen baleful pout. His body meanders in the same decorative curves as that of the woman in the "Nightmare", and like her he holds at bay the monsters of the sleep of reason: he confronts them in calm despair, acknowledging them to be his own.

Hogarth makes a cartoon of the scene, Barry a history painting, Blake a vision, Fuseli a bad dream. Such a scale of stylistic alternatives is possible because the subject vacillates between Milton's usual epic massiveness and the flimsy internal reality of psychological portent.

This episode in *Paradise Lost* is a dim psychomachia, externalising a state of mind. Sin springs from Satan's head, and in reminding him that

> Thy self in me thy perfect image viewing
> Becam'st enamour'd

she is analysing his moral illness, the rejection of the good in favour of a false image. The partnership of Sin and Death is a conjunction of ghosts. Together they constitute an idea, and this is why they are inseparable:

> Thou my Shade
> Inseparable must with mee along:
> For Death and Sin no power can separate.

Sin is a "meager Shaddow", and needs Death to lead her towards earth. Johnson noticed how awkwardly this miniature allegory is attached to the epic when the causeway is built. Milton hopes his phantasms will acquire solidity in working on the architecture of his universe, but there is an inconsistency of literary mode; and this inconsistency is the imaginative opening through which the illustrators make their various entries. Satan's passage across Chaos was physical and sensible, but the bridge ought to be figurative. Instead, as Johnson says, Sin and Death "worked up a mole of aggregated soil, cemented with asphaltos, a work too bulky for ideal architects".[10] A further inconsistency attends their intrusion into Paradise. Here there is a clash between their divided existence as characters and as conceptions. Sin as a state of being became part of the consciousness of Adam and Eve as soon as they tasted the apple, and Death was the automatic consequence; but as persons they arrive later, and in this form are already redundant. Milton quibbles apologetically, arguing that Sin had been there before in act but has only now appeared in body; but the disreputable couple interrupt the moving account of the mind's absorption of these alien states of being, as Adam struggles to understand the significance of death.

Milton is caught between epic and allegory, between character in action and the personification of theological reasons as motivations. His uncertainty is developed by the late eighteenth century as a division between narrative and self-exploration, between solid objects and the ideal, imagined world beyond them. Fuseli criticises Milton for giving currency to personifications which have no agreed objective status and are only abstractions posing as entities. He might perhaps have excused his own art from the same charge by pointing out that his phantoms are not ideas masquerading as persons but sentiments, the apparitions of the inner life, a dreamy tribe of mind not theological qualities. And he can even, on another occasion, vindicate Milton. Discussing Cumberland's "Calvary" in the *Analytical Review* of 1792,[11] he defends Milton against Johnson: "The Sin and Death of Milton are real actors, and have nothing allegorical but their names. The poet unskilfully gave to positive beings names adopted to theology and common language to convey notions of mental qualities, ideas of privation. The portress and guardian of the infernal gates are not more allegoric than Force and Labour, when they chain Prometheus, or the grim creature which Euripides introduced in his Alcestis; not more than the twin brothers that convey Sarpedon's corpse from the field of battle in Homer, or the dream that visits Agamemnon." This defence moves dubiously, however, between the two poles of Fuseli's own art. He begins by saying that Sin and Death are not allegorical figments but characters; yet he goes on to compare them with a succession of dreams and portents. He cannot be sure whether they are persons or chimerae imagined by Satan, just as in his own "Nightmare" it is impossible to tell whether the gnome and the leering horse are Gothic persecutors or images of the girl's troubled sleep, whether they are without or within, her tormentors or her lovers.

Poetic language connects the invisible realm of influences and emotions with the visible one of objects and actions by means of metaphor. A literary correlative of Milton's causeway, metaphor either actualises the immaterial or decomposes a material thing into an abstraction. It is this intermediary territory of metaphor which Fuseli's poetic paintings explore. His figures are imperfectly realised because they are dissolving into spirits; his narratives are puzzlingly inexplicit because they are an enigmatic shadow-play of sentiment and sorcery. When Canova remarked that Fuseli had *la fiamma* whereas Raphael had *il fuoco*, Wordsworth added that there was a third element, *il fumo*, of which Fuseli had plenty: he meant to be disparaging, but in fact he had defined the obscurity, the immaterial pall, which envelops Fuseli's smudged and obfuscated figures. This sets him apart from Blake, who traces his imagined world with naïve linear clarity. Blake presents his visions as facts: spirits slide down from the air to converse with him in his suburban garden. Fuseli's visitants are more undefined in status and hazier in outline: they are metaphors.

It is therefore apt and revealing that Fuseli's Milton Gallery includes so many illustrations of metaphors. The centre of *Paradise Lost* is uncluttered, spare, intimate: it has the rigorous exclusiveness of epic and the concentration of tragedy. But it contrives to mime the haphazard meanderings and wool-gathering accumulations of romance in the similes and metaphors which arch out from its simple, grand actions. The manifold allusiveness of these inset comparisons permits Milton the literary freedom of expanses of myth, fable and pastoral which his theology and his nobler purpose intellectually deny him. Milton the epic philosopher can admit to his poem only what is true, and cannot allow notions and traditions to float about in it unverified and uninspected, as Spenser does. But the similes work sceptically or wistfully through the censored material and include it under the pretence of correcting it, as in the legend of Mulciber's fall onto Lemnos. Fuseli possibly senses that Milton's problem, like his own, is one of conviction, of literary truancy from intellectual certainty: he scuttles crabwise back, as Peacock accused the romantic poets of doing, into a fairy-land of "mysticisms and chimaeras", longing to have his gods and reject them too.[12] Hence Fuseli's provocative emphasis not on action but on dream (Eve's dream in which she fancies she has tasted the fruit; Adam's narrative of her creation, the dream which became truth), vision (the lazar house, the deluge and the vision of Noah) and metaphor.

The metaphors Fuseli chooses to illustrate are concerned with Satan, whose perplexed questioning and reconnoitring and insatiable restlessness of mind make him the centre of metaphoric expansion in the poem. Because he is so mobile and treacherously manifold, he resists containment in any single image. Similes frighteningly dissolve into other similes as he sheds his influence around him, each new comparison extending his range and reach. As he moves towards the shore of the fiery lake, his shield turns into the moon observed through Galileo's telescope, and his spear shoots up with dreamy abruptness into a Norwegian pine. He encompasses Europe, his spear stretching north, his shield touching Fiesole or Valdarno but from there still seeking "to descry new Lands". However, this metaphoric exfoliation is not only a means of territorial aggrandisement, but an emblem of instability. Satan's legions suffer metamorphoses into autumnal leaves, then into scattered sedge, then into the blood-boltered waves on which floated the carcases and broken chariot-wheels of the Memphian chivalry. Satan himself, constantly

changing shape, slips by degrees down the ladder of being into
the likeness of a beast. Exiled with Sin and Death, he is at last
reduced to a metaphor, diminished (in the terms of Coleridge's argument from the fourth chapter) to an abstraction.

Fuseli's sympathy for Satan is stylistic, rather than the moral
or political affinity to which romantic critics admit. Satan has
the indeterminacy which is characteristic of Fuseli's own art.
Haunting the twilight intermediary zone between one state of
being and another, Satan is an influence made into a character,
or rather a composite of innumerable characters: a sentiment
personified. Fuseli dissolves him into his circumambient haze
of metaphor. Among the metaphors he illustrates are that
referring to the contracted forms of the spirits in Pan-
daemonium, like fairy elves whose midnight revels a
countryman spies on; the birth of Sin, and the building of the
causeway; the Lapland orgies of witches, a simile for Sin's skirt
of hell-hounds; a Gryphon pursuing an Arimaspian, a simile
for Satan's exertions in forcing his way through Chaos; and
Ulysses between Scylla and Charybdis, representing Satan
straitened in his passage to Light. There is also a tempera study
of "The Night Hag", who rides through the air in anticipation
of infant blood to join in the Lapland orgies: not a grotesque
but an elongated bisexual figure with a Blakean expression of
helpless despair, clutching its flying pigtails, an incubus of
irrationality.

Metaphor slights the action of Milton's poem by illustrating
only its dim penumbra. Narrowed and beclouded, the epic
becomes a morbid dream. Metaphor also snubs nature, pre-
ferring insubstantiality and hypothesis to actuality. Fuseli
commended the visionary art of Blake because he saw in it an
impatience, like his own, with nature. Praising Blake's edition
of Blair's *The Grave*, he complained that art has been so long
burdened by its servile mimetic and exemplary functions that
"reason and fancy have exhausted their stores of argument and
imagery", and art has grown stale because natural phenomena
have been pillaged for correspondences to human concerns.[13]
Nature is enslaved to man, and myth declines into a game:
"The serpent with its tail in its mouth, from a type of Eternity,
is become an infant's bauble; even the nobler idea of Hercules
pausing between virtue and vice, and the varied imagery of

Death leading his patients to the Grave, owe their effect upon us more to technic excellence than allegoric utility." The art of the late eighteenth century turns myth into charade, and hopes to make an ironic virtue out of its sense of inadequacy: Reynolds's Garrick as Hercules wavering between the tragic and comic muses, his Mrs Sheridan as St Cecilia, or Romney's attitudinising Lady Hamilton, are conscious of the tactlessness of their impersonations, but accept it with a knowing shrug.

Blake, in Fuseli's view, rescues art by inventing fables of his own. He "has endeavoured to wake sensibility by touching our sympathies with nearer, less ambiguous, and less ludicrous imagery, than what mythology, Gothic superstition, or symbols as far-fetched as inadequate could supply". His metaphors domesticate the spiritual: he spreads "a familiar and domestic atmosphere round the most important of all subjects, to connect the visible and invisible World, without provoking probability, and to lead the eye from the milder light of time to the radiations of Eternity". Blake's art is innocent. Its prosaic literalness is the source of its spirituality. The excited incoherence of Macbeth's image of Pity as a naked new-born babe still powerful enough to stride on the blasts is, for instance, naïvely turned into fact. In Blake's version, the manikin with glad spread arms is lifted into the air from its dead mother by the cherubim on their sightless couriers. The Shakespearean entanglement of images is tidied into literal truth. The metaphors are taken on trust, as statements of fact, not intimations of fancy. Fuseli's Miltonic lazar house is an agitated drama of pitch dark, blinding light and ferocious movement; Blake's is a diagram of a spiritual state, a lucid mystical cartoon: a blind god, whose twisting beard rays out like a sun into a zodiac, extends his arms over the orderly rows of the diseased stretched on their mats. Fuseli's art is a product not of innocence but of sour, corrupted experience, as suspicious as Blake's is trusting, blurred and spoiled and uncomfortable where Blake's unfurls its marvels with linear grace and decorative joy. Blake converses with spirits, Fuseli with bogies. Blake sees the world unfolding into loveliness, Fuseli sees it contracting into ugliness and filth. The prophecies of the one are the obverse of the pornography of the other.

Blake with extra-sensory eye sees through reality: Fuseli

finds it opaque and punishes it for being so by defaming it. "I see Every thing I paint In This World", Blake wrote to Trusler.[14] Fuseli however said "Nature puts me out". His art is in Blake's terms an impious libel on reality. Imagination envenoms Fuseli, equipping him to settle with the nature which refused to accommodate him. His 1788 caricature of the artist leaving Italy turns the creative process into an organic one, not in the beneficent romantic sense but messily and vindictively. Art dirties reality, and this artist's winged genitals detach themselves and make their way back to Italy in ejaculatory haste while he, an overgrown classical statue, defecates on Switzerland. Mice scurry across England, scratching at his rivals, Ozias Humphrey, Romney and Benjamin West.

Fuseli's scatological rage against nature, and the hectic, combative impatience of his pictorial style, are qualities he shares with the libertines of this book's earlier chapters, and he was indeed accused of libertinism in a philosophical criticism of painting published by the Rev. R. A. Bromley in 1793.[15] Bromley attacked Fuseli's subjects, especially the "Nightmare", while praising the improving art of West and Barry, who redeem a reality Fuseli distorts and besmirches:

> What good has the world, or what honour the art, at any time derived from such light and fantastical speculations? If it be right to follow Nature, there is nothing of her here, – all that is presented to us is a reverie of the brain. If it be allowable to cultivate fancy, that which has little or nothing of nature in its composition becomes ridiculous. A man may carry the flights of imagination even within the walks of the chastest art or science, till they become mere waking dreams, as wild as the conceits of a madman. The author of Observations on *Fresnoy de Arte* very properly calls these persons, 'Libertines of painting': as there are libertines of religion, who have no other law but the vehemence of their own inclinations, so these have no other model, he says, but a rodomontado genius, which shows a wild or savage nature that is not of our acquaintance, but of a new creation.

As if not sure whether Fuseli is to be mocked or dreaded, Bromley's attack vacillates between the sublime bragging of the rodomontado and a nature dangerously wild and savage, between ludicrous fancifulness and the madman's deranged excess of fantasy, between frivolity and vehemence. The indecision is perceptive, because Fuseli, like the libertine, moves bewilderingly between tragedy and comedy. His art strives to be haunting, but recoils into a confessional libertine comedy like that of Tristram Shandy, who also treads the perilous line between the scatter-brained virtuoso indulging waking dreams and the morbid, disturbed genius at the mercy of those dreams, and whose novel is what Bromley calls "a reverie of the brain".

Romantic criticism is equally unable to decide whether Fuseli is tragically irrational or merely comically conceited. Haydon disowned him for having too much imagination.[16] In his autobiography he praises Fuseli's "inventive imagination" but criticises the superfluity of it which led him into mannerism. Romanticism has renounced Fuseli's metaphoric liberation of painting, and makes the artist nature's humble, observant acolyte. Haydon considers Fuseli a creature of the air without foundations on the earth: "in conveying his conception he had all the ethereal part of a genius, but not enough of the earthly to express his ideas in a natural way". The integration of faculties is for Haydon a moral balance: "we are made up of body and mind, and one of the greatest proofs of a complete genius is the evidence it gives of this union".[17] But not, perhaps, of a romantic genius: the essence of romanticism is imbalance, dissension between mind and body. This is the origin of that Shandyean romantic irony which flickers between tragedy and comedy, between the free range of intellect and vision and the lowering necessities of action and bodily existence. This is the problem of Hamlet, who might have been the author of an aphorism of Fuseli's, which declares that "reality teems with disappointment for him whose sources of enjoyment spring in the elysium of fancy". Hamlet like Fuseli has an excess of inventiveness; is a spirit of the air not the earth; and ends as a mannerist, rearranging his world in imagination but not in action, transforming a cloud into a camel, a weasel and a whale as it suits his convenience.

It is this high-handed transformation of reality – whether with witty perversity as in the case of Hamlet's cloud, or in imaginative earnest as in his desire to be free of the flesh and its ills and of a troublesome identity which binds him to the world – which Haydon attacks in Fuseli. The artist has "no business to make nature as she never was: all we have to do is to restore her to what she is according to the definite principles of her first creation; further we have no right to go". Haydon assumes that Fuseli's aim was arrogant improvement of nature. But it may be that his desire was alluring or alarming comic deformation of nature, an activity of scurrilous fancy, not reverent imagination.

"The basis of my character was earnestness of feeling", Haydon states. The characters of Fuseli and Sterne are, like Hamlet's, based on very different qualities: idleness, the indolence of speculation, experiment with one's own capacities. Haydon is as stolidly single-minded as Fortinbras, identifying art with leadership and national prestige, not with playful, provisional exploration. Haydon's is the complaint of society against Hamlet: he is repelled by Fuseli's self-absorption, his querulous refusal to be instructed, the unpredictable sports and frenzies of his imagination. In 1825, after Fuseli's death, Haydon called him "an egotist, as all mannerists must be". But mannerism is not the product of egotistic confidence. It is the baffled attempt of art to find its way out of an impasse, over-emphasising quirks of style in the hope that these will transform an intractable reality. The mannerist's strategy is devious, insecure, desperately laying hold of each passing chance: it is the method of the cornered Hamlet. Fuseli's mannerism like the antic dispositions of Hamlet or Tristram Shandy is a retreat into irresponsibility. Because the courtiers think Hamlet is simply behaving oddly, as Johnson thought of *Tristram Shandy*, they don't notice the subversive inspection of their society he is carrying out. From a similar pretence Fuseli gains the freedom to dramatise his fantasies: he adopts in public the guise of exaggeration and unreliability in order to conduct in private an exploration of personality which would otherwise be prohibited.

Like Bromley, Haydon considers Fuseli a libertine in art, a philanderer whose "great delight was in conception, not in embodying his conceptions; and as soon as he rendered a conception intelligible to himself and others by any means, he flew off to a fresh one, too impatient to endure the meditation required fully to develop it". This is also the career of the libertine: as soon as a conquest is cursorily made, he sickens of it and is driven to repeat the experience elsewhere. The infinitude of the conceiving spirit demands that the libertine should never rest satisfied with any one relationship, and that the artist should never see a work through to the end of stultifying completeness. Morally, this makes Fuseli a Don Giovanni; intellectually, it makes him a Hamlet or a Tristram, for they too are conceivers who feel that their freedom resides in never embodying their conceptions.

Fuseli's "Nightmare" is regularly scorned for being laughable rather than terrifying. But, given the libertine qualities of Fuseli's art – its impropriety, its promiscuous fancifulness, its use of narrative as an alibi for the indulgence of personal fantasy – the comedy of the painting may be seen as a mark of its peculiar success. Its most sinister and suggestive quality is a prurient joviality, and its methods are comic distortion and incongruity. The version in the Detroit Institute of Arts turns mental terror into a sly conspiratorial comedy of sexual invitation. The dreamer is not in agony: her arms and legs impossibly extended in languorous abandon, she stretches herself under the glaring monster as if convinced that, as a nightmare is inevitable, she may as well lie back and enjoy it. In Goya's caprice of the sleep of reason, the dreamer is the victim of his own imaginative creations, which turn on him with aggressive beaks and beating wings: his is the romantic tragedy of imagination, which singles out whoever possesses it for delights and agonies beyond the normal. But Fuseli's dreamer has relaxed into a comedy of imaginative acquiescence. Goya's figure casts aside his pen in trepidation and self-distrust: he is not asleep but summoning energy for the war of consciousness against its enemies. Fuseli's woman, however, has found in sleep both her opportunity and her excuse. The horse's gloating laugh and the gnome's goggle-eyed pout imply that their victim may be shamming sleep in order to discreetly welcome their embraces.

Comedy reverses relationships. The affable demons are humanised. The horse's gleeful eyes, cosy rounded snout and ruffled lock of hair make it a panting, dishevelled rustic lover,

while the gnome with his hand philosophically under his chin
is a sullen Caliban who has at last won Miranda. The woman is
dehumanised. Her huge, sinuous, tapering body makes her
more of a monster than her domesticated tormentors. Stylistic
inconsistency also detaches one level of the picture from the
other. The woman's posture and the looping drapery beneath
her are fluently Italian, but the upper tier is a bestial cartoon: a
Gillray gnome has alighted on a Parmigianino nymph.
Although Fuseli intended the painting to rank with Mor-
timer's apocalyptic death on a pale horse, it is not a grand
machine but an alarmingly humorous cartoon, and Cruikshank assimilated it to graphic satire in parodying it.[18] His
"Louis the Fat Troubled with the Night Mare and Dreams of
Terror" poises the ape on the summit of Louis's belly. Dream
armies charge through the room and the king's listless bed-
fellow, gazing at the chamber-pot, manuals of sexual technique and phials of eau de Cologne, complains of his snoring
and reflects that if he makes war no better than he makes love
the Spaniards have no reason to fear.

The wraith of Napoleon in Cruikshank's cartoon justifies
the parody of Fuseli by pointing out that "there is but one step
from the sublime to the ridiculous". Gillray also considered
Fuseli's art as one of collapsed sublimity: he referred to Fuseli's
"Mock Sublime 'Mad Taste'".[19] But Fuseli's sublimity is not so
much collapsed as inverted, and the inverse sublime is not
absurdity but irony. Burke's diminution of the sublime into a
mental category has already been discussed; the final chapter
of this book will show how Sterne's romantic critics further
miniaturise and introvert the sublime and derive from it the
new kind of perception which they call irony. Fuseli does not
mock sublimity or ineffectually ape it, but turns it upside
down into a bathos which prefigures romantic irony. His is the
art not of soaring but of diving. His nightmare subsides into a
leering erotic comedy, but that descent is the source of its
disquieting confessional intimacy. The downward lunge of
bathos turns into an excavation of the vast profound which is
the den of Diderot's Moor. Just as Pope's slumbrous and inane
state of dullness was to be transvalued into a visionary experience which romantic poets took drugs to induce, so the bathos
which his hack Martinus Scriblerus calls "the bottom, the end,

the central point, the *non plus ultra* of true Modern Poetry"[20], is transvalued and becomes in romantic art a plumbing of dark secret depths. "Is there not an Architecture of Vaults and Cellars, as well as of lofty Domes and Pyramids?" Scriblerus asks, and this is the architecture of romantic fantasy: Diderot's cave; the caverns beneath Kubla Khan's pleasure-dome; the dank sepulchral Monk's Yard of Soane's house; the subterraneous regions of Walpole's Otranto, hollowed into cloisters, a "labyrinth of darkness".

Verbally romantic poetry transfigures bathos. Keats's "feed deep, deep upon her peerless eyes", Wordsworth's "Oh,/The difference to me!" or Shelley's "Bird thou never wert" are all bathetic; but the sudden relapse into self-centredness which makes the first two examples bathetic is the source of their intimacy and truth, and in the third case language risks bathos by working at the edge of possibility to transform a creature into a spirit. The way down is the way up for Fuseli too. His winking comedy and the smutty ugliness of the image enable him to probe further into the equivocations of sexual fear and desire than high-mindedness would. The "Nightmare" is the more disconcerting for being laughable, since laughter attaches us to it and sends us to investigate the reason for its hold of derisive fascination. Empyrean sublimity and the bathetic profound are, like the airy Hamlet and the earthy Falstaff or the lyrical Ariel and the growling inarticulate Caliban, opposites which complement one another, whose antagonism turns into similitude: soaring and plunging, the exhilaration of the heights and the mystery of the depths.

The introversion of pictorial form which results from Fuseli's attempt to paint metaphors has the same paradoxical conclusion as the introversion of literary form discussed in the first chapter. There, tragedy and comedy are involuted, scaled down from alternative genres to overlapping moods, and then fused in the double vision of irony. In Fuseli's case, the same happens with sublimity and bathos. They are first introverted: as Haydon's criticism of Fuseli implies, sublimity is the magniloquence of the conceiving spirit, bathos the impatience and technical ineptitude of the executing body. Then, intricately interdependent as they are, they become indistinguishable: sublimity turns into bathos in Fuseli's "Nightmare", and the union, like that of tragedy and comedy, creates irony – the irony by which Fuseli suggests that the mental frights of Gothic terror are fomented by the incontinent body, and unmasks the tragic phantoms of sublimity as comic ogres from the bathetic cave of unconsciousness.

Notes

1. Fuseli, review of Cowper's *Homer*, *Analytical Review,* January 1793; review of William Roscoe's *Lorenzo de' Medici*, *Analytical Review,* April 1796.
2. Lamb's complaint about the "Barrenness of the Imaginative Faculty in the Productions of Modern Art" is one of *The Last Essays of Elia*, taken from *The Athenaeum*, January and February 1833.
3. Recorded by Henry Crabb Robinson in his diary for 6 June 1811, p. 34 of E. J. Morley's 1938 edition.
4. John Knowles, *The Life and Writings of Henry Fuseli*, 3 vols., 1831, Aphorism no.125, vol. III.
5. *Table Talk*, 1830.
6. *The Autobiography and Memoirs of Benjamin Robert Haydon*, ed. Tom Taylor, 1853, vol. II.
7. Leigh Hunt, *Lord Byron and Some of his Contemporaries*, 1828.
8. From review of William Roscoe's *Lorenzo de' Medici*.
9. Both Blake and Barry reproduced in Marcia R. Pointon, *Milton and English Art*, 1970.
10. 'John Milton' in *Lives of the English Poets*, 1779–81.
11. Review of Richard Cumberland's "Calvary or the Death of Christ", *Analytical Review*, June 1792.
12. Peacock's *The Four Ages of Poetry* appeared in *Olliers' Literary Miscellany*, 1820.
13. Fuseli's preface to Blair's *Grave,* illustrated by Blake, 1805.
14. Blake to Trusler, letter 23 August 1799.
15. Rev. R. A. Bromley, *Philosophical and Critical History of the Fine Arts*, reviewed by Fuseli in *Analytical Review*, July 1793.
16. Benjamin Robert Haydon, *Diary*, ed. W. B. Pope, 5 vols., 1960–3; his *Correspondence and Table Talk* appeared in 2 volumes in 1876.
17. This and the following quotations are taken from *The Autobiography and Memoirs of Benjamin Robert Haydon*, op. cit., vol. I, p. 32, p. 105 and vol. II, p. 101.
18. George Cruikshank, "Louis the Fat, Troubled with the Night Mare", 1823, reproduced in Nicholas Powell, *Fuseli: The Nightmare*, 1973.
19. James Gillray, letter to Rev. John Sneyd, October 1800.
20. Pope's inversion of the sublime, *Peri Bathous: or the Art of Sinking in Poetry*, appeared in 1727, and was edited in facsimile by E. L. Steeves in 1952.

7

Pictorial Forms

Fuseli justifies his own poetic, metaphoric art by constructing, in his lectures, a genealogy of pictorial forms which continues the process of formal introversion discussed in the first chapter of this book·by successively converting epic, drama and history into mental categories and implicitly redefining the purpose of art. Now, instead of imitation of nature, art aspires to imitation of the mind. But the theory has a self-disabling irony: Fuseli enslaves himself to literature by insisting that painting needs an illustrative pretext, but at the same time liberates himself by his inversions of literary genre and by his impudent infidelity to the spirit of the texts he uses. He begins by arguing that art dare not create, and can only obsequiously invent or copy; but this deference is his excuse for a reckless pictorial invasion of the unpaintable mental space of literature.

Painting is made subservient to literature because, in this early, ironic phase of the movement, the romantics disavow creativity. Although revering Shakespeare and Milton as primary creators, who make whole worlds by enigmatic disappearance or by thunderous force, the romantics see themselves as secondary creators, deprived of the imperative will of their god-like predecessors. Romantic Shakespeare criticism is a body of religious lore, pondering in Shakespeare the mystery of the first mover who is himself unmoved. In worshipping him, the romantics admit their own unworthiness. Shakespeare has created them, along with his characters: the romantics can enjoy an empathy with one or another of Shakespeare's people, since these are their fellow men, but they never dare to feel they have a smack of Shakespeare in them. They can create nothing: they can only invent. In a lecture of 1801, Fuseli makes a self-mortifying distinction between the two states: creation, the secret from which even Coleridge draws back in foreboding, is "incompatible with our notions of limited being"; invention is the humbler and more appropriate notion, being merely the discovery of something which exists already. For the painter, it exists already in literature.[1]

However, Fuseli's theory tries to mark out some small area of liberty for the artist, asking if it is possible for him "to find or to combine a subject from himself, without having recourse to tradition or the stories of history and poetry?" It galls him that the "immediate avenues of the mind, open to all its observers, from the poet to the novelist" should "be shut only to the artist". Imitation of nature must be secondary mimicry, but imitation of the mind permits a certain inventive independence. The mental space Fuseli appropriates for the painter is that of fantasies or visions, "unpremeditated conceptions". These he identifies as the source of Shakespeare's power, which consisted in a spontaneous and intuitive fashioning-forth of characters who belong to him alone. Fuseli calls this power an "intuition into the pure emanations of nature", but his definition slithers evasively between abstraction (intuition, emanation) and embodiment (nature); purity cunningly begs another question, because it can mean either refinement and disembodiment or the essentialising Fielding intended when he said his characters were species not individuals. It appears to suggest that Shakespeare's characters are spirits thrust into human form, as Carlyle imagined Shakespeare himself to have been, rather than intriguing and many-faceted individuals; it etherealises whereas Shakespeare, who was intuitive without needing to be visionary, embodies and makes concrete; it translates character back into dream.

Fuseli's criticism of classic art subtly romanticises it, and these transforming misconceptions about Shakespeare correspond to the modification of history-painting which justifies his own shadowy and uncertain genre of poetic painting. In an aphorism about dreams, Fuseli dissolves the lucid art of Raphael and the Miltonic solidity of Michelangelo into dim personifications of sentiment: "the Prophets, Sibyls and Patriarchs of Michael Angelo are so many branches of one great sentiment. The dream of Raffaello is a characteristic representation of a dream; the dream of Michael Angelo is moral inspiration, a sublime sentiment." But the sober reflective prophets and burly sibyls of the Sistine ceiling are not like the witches in *Macbeth* or the smirking goblin of Fuseli's nightmare. They are not portents of fantasy but participants in an intellectual design which unfolds the history of faith across the ceiling. They have a place and a function, the prophets preaching to the Jews, the sibyls acting as auguries among the Gentiles, whereas Fuseli's monsters are the phantoms of the mind, not truths of theology. Despite his attraction to Shakespeare's witches, Fuseli seems to have resented their being forced to do the play's work of dynastic prediction, as Hamlet resents having to do his play's work of revenge: he thought them not truly terrifying in the play, presumably because they have a function and are not unattached spirits, and hoped in his illustrations to return them to their rightful significance as figments of the visionary imagination. He was particularly proud of the mystic triangular form of his version of the cauldron scene.

His psychological interpretation of classic art leads Fuseli to argue that Raphael in the "Incedio del Borgo" subsumes history in a study of "the effusion of the various passions aroused by the sudden terrors of nocturnal conflagration". This reading of Raphael acts as justification for Fuseli's own cavalier impatience with his subjects: he exploits them so far as they coincide with his own psychological interests, but has no interest in doing justice to their historical content. Once they have been made over into the idiom of his own obsessions he discards them.

The genealogy of pictorial forms constructed in Fuseli's lectures suggests a lineage for his own poetic art. He distinguishes three orders of artistic invention, the epic, the dramatic and the historic. These are at once converted into psychological categories, differentiated by their varying emotional effects: epic art is sublime and therefore astonishes; the dramatic is impassioned and therefore moves us; and the historic, circumscribed by truth, proffers information. Through these three forms classic art proceeds in the direction of rationality and education, moving from the violent primary response of wonder at the sublime to the tepidity of instruction. Fuseli's own practice implies that he saw truth-telling historical painting as the wrong conclusion for the evolutionary process, because it enthralled art to prosaic imitation; he intended his poetic painting as an alternative third state. History chastens dramatic emotion and turns intuition back into reportage: poetic painting is the proper successor to the dramatic because, while drama can only deal with its characters as actors, achievers in the external world (the Julius II of Raphael authenticating the miracle at the mass of Bolsena, and his Leo facing Attila are two of Fuseli's examples), poetry can penetrate their lyrical internal lives. This way, art's destination is not journalism but an ever more refined division and insubstantiality. From the rude massiveness of the sublime it moves towards the sketchy haze of mental life, from epic, which exists prior to human individualisation, concerned with racial generalities, not personal discoveries, through drama, which studies the individual objectively in his relations with others, to poetry, which releases him at last into subjective individuality.

The evolution of the forms is the evolution of the individual. The epic painter, Fuseli argues, impresses a general idea – as, for instance, war in Homer – with elemental simplicity and without condescending to record detailed subdivisions of character: "as in a conflagration we see turrets, spires, and temples illuminated only to propagate the horrors of destruction, so through the stormy pages of Homer, we see his heroines and heroes but by the light that blasts them". The theocracy of the Sistine frescoes is rigorously generic, an affair between god and man which never stoops to the local or personal. The romantic interpretation of epic – questioned by Haydon, who points to the gradations of character in the treatment of the oracles – makes a dubious historical point in order to make a covert emotional one: the attraction of epic, as of the sublime, lay in the forceful extinction of individuality, the relief of self-obliteration.

Jean Paul Richter in the *Vorschule der Aesthetik* (School of Aesthetics, 1813)[2] gives to epic a character of sleepy dullness which is the obverse of the agile ironic wakefulness of romantic intelligence. "Long and slow, broad and creeping", epic suggests the lumbering weight of a Falstaff, as against the volatile Hamlet-like motion of drama. In place of dramatic differentiation of character, epic delights in the proliferation of objects. Whereas the primal epic poem involved two races, the primal tragedy involved two men. The *Odyssey* turns epic into novel, but manages to escape concentration on the subjective existence of its single hero by replacing numbers of actors with numbers of countries visited. The picaresque hero of eighteenth-century novels – which are, in Hegel's terms, a recurrence of epic – remains in the epic state of non-individuality because he has encounters and episodes rather than experiences, and at the end is no more than the sum of what has happened to him. Even when left alone on his island, Robinson Crusoe contrives not to become a person by turning his attention scrupulously outwards, busying himself in building, planting and taking inventory. Picaresque wandering need not mean self-exploration: Tom Jones is returned at the end of the novel to the position he occupied at the beginning. So much happens to him almost, it seems, in order to refuse him the leisure to absorb events and incorporate them into himself. Tristram Shandy transfers picaresque rambling into mental day-dreaming. His inconclusiveness as a thinker and indeterminacy as an actor, his multitudinous projects interrupted or deferred, his journeys without arrivals, are the equivalents in his world of thought to the endless extensions of epic: for epic, as Jean Paul argues in quoting from Schlegel, can stop at any point or continue in any direction (like Leporello's list). *Don Quixote* was twice continued, by Alonso de Avellaneda as well as by Cervantes; *Tristram Shandy* was continued in random directions at random intervals. Characters like Don Quixote and Don Giovanni are epic in that they can be built onto in this way, like Gothic cathedrals, being no single artist's possession.

Possibly because its impersonality makes epic the most anti-romantic of forms, it is the one which the romantics most persistently attempt to re-define. Romanticism transvalues artistic forms. The ironic necessity of rising above oneself into Schlegel's "sense of the infinite and of the world" leads these artists to turn each form into its opposite (as mythic characters like Don Giovanni are turned into their opposites: Mozart's sensualist becomes Shaw's socialist) in the hope of liberating literature altogether from the prison of form. Hence Fielding's hybrid of epic and comic prose, or Byron's of chivalric quest and grand tour, or Keats's of Grecian statuary and the evolutionary morality of Gothic.

The romantic assimilation of epic begins in the novel, which takes over its slow expansion. *Hamlet* is relevant here: Coleridge called it the most retarded and protracted of Shakespeare's tragedies in the unfolding, in contrast with *Macbeth*, which reaches its climax with importunate speed, like vaulting ambition overleaping itself, and ends virtually before it has begun. Macbeth himself acknowledges that the beginning of his career is its end, that he will live hereafter marking time in sterile anti-climax, when he wishes

> Had I but died an hour before this chance,
> I had lived a blessèd time.

Pace is the prerogative of drama, and Macbeth wishes to succeed dramatically in a life of precipitate action and decision, the velocity of which consumes him. Slowness, the self-immersed Lethean drowsiness of which Hamlet accuses himself, is the rhythm of epic and of the novel. Jean Paul maintains that the best story is the most complicated, which means the slowest, but that in turn must mean the most accelerated. The work must be, like life, at once both short and long. This is the metaphysical aspect of Shakespeare's double time: the work seems to unfold with infinite, teasing slowness, but the period of time in which it does so is extremely brief. Jean Paul takes as his examples the fifth book of *Don Quixote*, which deals with one evening at an inn, and Yorick's journey through France, which has a real duration of only three days. From this point of view, *Hamlet* has the characteristics of epic and the modern form adjacent to epic, the psychological novel, rather than of drama: the hero's instinctive feeling that he is out of place in a play is justified by criticism.

The first chapter of this book mentioned Diderot's vindication of the longueurs of Richardson. For Diderot, the tedium of the narration was an exercise in virtue, a model of the patient fortitude Clarissa herself is obliged to learn, and an induction into pastoral quiet and content. For Jean Paul, the same longueurs resemble not pastoral but epic, recalling the multiplication of episodic decoration on the shield of Achilles. His imagery is domestic not rural, evoking sentimental warmth and comfort not, like Diderot, meditative calm and conventual solitude: we are heated, he says, by the long circuit of the stove pipes, rather than by the fire's blaze. In *Candide*, incidents hurtle past without troubling our sympathy; but in *Clarissa*, the very slowness with which the sun rises warms us completely by degrees.

This is how epic is taken over by the novel. It is also assimilated by romantic poetry. Wordsworth's lyrical epic about the formation of his poetic intelligence is the successor to Sterne's history of what passes in the mind. In Wordsworth adventure is internalised, and action, in the temptations of the French Revolution and London, is eschewed for retirement. The endlessness of epic becomes, in romantic narrative poetry, the inexhaustibility of thought. The picaresque seekers of these poems, the sullen Harold, the ardent Endymion or the misty Alastor, represent the vagaries and eternal disquiet of consciousness; they, like the indefinitely extensible poems in which they grow, are continuous with the poet's own mental life, and can have a stop only when that does.

The romantics individualise epic. From the most communal it becomes, paradoxically, the most private of forms. The second of Fuseli's categories, the dramatic, is also turned inside out by romanticism. Fuseli sets the dramatic Raphael against the epic, undifferentiated Michelangelo, and argues that if Raphael had painted the Sistine Last Judgement (which Haydon thought "infamously deficient"), he would have introduced a more varied pathos in the manner of Dante, with individualised figures of "connubial, fraternal, kindred connexion". As a dramatist, Raphael also introduces the portrait into allegorical compositions, so that, stamped with and ennobled by character, the portrait is raised to the dignity of drama. In the Stanze, Raphael's Julius II or his Leo with Attila "tell us by their presence that they are the heroes of the drama, and that the action has been contrived, is subordinate to them, and has been composed to illustrate their character. For as in epic, act and agent are subordinate to the maxim, and in pure history are mere organs of the fact; so the drama subordinates both fact and maxim to the agent, his character and passion: what in them was end is but medium here."

Fuseli's definition forces a contraction of drama, assuming that it exists for single individuals, since the actions are contrived to explore and illustrate the peculiarities of a character.

Jean Paul also argues that there cannot be too many characters in epic or too few in drama, and comes close to disqualifying Shakespeare as a dramatist because of the superabundance of his people: the history plays are turned back into dramatic epics. This is the problem of the romantic Hamlet, who is driven to compose a monodrama for himself inside the tense, crowded, demanding society of the revenge play. Hamlet obliges the drama to abandon its concern for character in action and relationship and to isolate character in self-contemplation, and the stasis of the dramatic monologue is, in Fuseli's sense of the term, pictorial. The still moments painted by Raphael are not images of action but of interior will and revelation, of soliloquy. In dramatic painting the agent has triumphantly separated himself from the indignities of the maxim (the prosing morality of Hamlet's father) and from the obtuse tyranny of historical fact (the solid world); he is in Tristram Shandy's happy state, in which self-analysis is both play and art.

The third of Fuseli's styles is the historic, which also under-goes a romantic introversion. *Tristram Shandy* is a history of what passes in the mind. Sterne makes clear the shift from action to thought, from events to mental associations, by his sly introduction of Locke when, early in Book II, he is filling in crevices through which critics might invade the work. He calls Locke's *Essay Concerning Humane Understanding* "a history", which excites a volley of expectations in the hypothetical critic, who wants to know "of who? of what? where? when?" A history, the critic assumes, must pass in the world of action and circumstance, but Sterne makes him pause by revealing that it happens in the mind. Likewise, in Fuseli's practice, history-painting, originally a commemoration of moments of significant action, evaporates into shadowy personification. One of Fuseli's patrons requested a picture of "some mentally heroic action", and was supplied with Marcus Curius at his frugal repast.

Epic gives way first to drama, which is in turn superseded by the novel, for this is the form which, in Jean Paul's analysis, emerges from the transformation of either epic or drama. The epic novel is a realm of pure imaginative caprice: a fairy-tale is the liberation of epic, while a dream (Fuseli's "most unexplored region" of art) is the liberation of the fairy-tale; and in this sense *Tristram Shandy* is an epic novel, made of whim and imaginative conjecture. In contrast with this dreamy dilation, the novel deriving from drama is tauter and more concentrated on the problems of its characters. One of Jean Paul's examples of the dramatic novelist is Richardson. But *Tristram Shandy* might be related to this form as well, or seen as an inspired destruction of it, as *Hamlet* is of the terse and precise drama of revenge. Sterne begins with a domestic situation as replete with antagonisms and affections within its cramped space as that of Richardson, but his manner of narrating frustrates dramatic expectation at every point, as Hamlet elegantly prevents his play from developing in accordance with the logic of revenge. Drama disintegrates into fantasy and into soliloquy. Jean Paul remarks that the stray incidents which occupy an epic novel like *Don Quixote* can hardly be called episodic, since the novel conceives of life itself as episodic. Episodes, on the contrary, are anathema to drama. This is why Hamlet's episodic welcoming of each chance which arises – to gull Polonius, to hear the players recite a favourite speech, to travel to England, to quiz the grave-digger – is so subversive; and Tristram too has a mind which is incorrigibly episodic.

Fuseli admits that the three styles he has distinguished are seldom pure and, anticipating the romantic fusion of formal opposites, mentions numerous hybrids. In Homer, the conception of Hector and Andromeda is dramatically particular and affecting, rather than epically astounding. Shakespeare crossbreeds epic and drama in making the ghost stalk the ramparts like the shade of Ajax. For all the severity of Tacitus, his Octavia encircled by the centurions is as moving as Ophelia. Raphael allows himself personifications of the genius of the river when Joshua passes through the Jordan, and at the inauguration of Solomon, and Poussin conjures up before Coriolanus a grim vision of Rome in arms attended by Fortune: personification is the critical point of Fuseli's aesthetics, since it is in embodying conceptions that the painter approaches the status of creator.

The triad both reduces classic art to its emotional sources and conducts it into a dead-end. As Burke returned the sublime and the beautiful to their origins in the senses, so Fuseli converts artistic styles into physical responses: epic thrills the senses, drama arouses the emotions, history instructs the mind. The triad is elegiac as well as reductive, for it records the taming and eventual obsolescence of imagination, as epic's grand power of generalisation is narrowed into drama's isolation of single cases, until in the third phase invention is overtaken by accuracy in reporting. Fuseli's own effort to establish a style of poetic painting has the effect of revising the succession. Poetry now replaces history, and the evolution of the forms is truly a recapitulation of the evolution of the individual. Epic enclosure in a general idea and in a community leads to the dramatic discovery of a personal self, which drama still conceives publicly: in the works of Raphael which Fuseli praises as dramas, a specifically political fortitude is being exercised; and he thinks the tapestry cartoons of Raphael supreme because there "the drama, divested of epic or allegoric fiction, meets pure history, and elevates, invigorates, impresses the pregnant moment of a *real* fact, with character and pathos". But this need not be the terminus: the process now concludes in poetic art, which unlocks the private self inside the historical actor and embodies its secret life of dream and sentiment.

Poetic painting emerges from a dissolution and introversion of classic art. Its particular forbear is allegory, which Fuseli thinks of as a dangerously questioning force, sceptically unsettling the reality surrounding it wherever it is introduced, as Sin and Death create an abstract alternative to Milton's otherwise substantial epic universe. Allegory is an outlaw, because once admitted it tends to convert all else into its own system: if Sin and Death are merely ideas clothed misleadingly in human form, the anthropomorphism of Milton's God the Father and Christ is also suspect. The critics and artists of Fuseli's period are fascinated by Sin and Death, as the romantics were by Satan, because they sense here an entry into the poem's forbidding structure and a means of reversing it. In his lecture on invention, Fuseli argues that "Allegory, or the personification of invisible physic and metaphysic ideas, though not banished from the regions of Invention, is equally inadmissible in pure epic, dramatic, and historic plans, because, wherever it enters, it must rule the whole". Allegory is introverted by Fuseli: deprived of its ideological function and its hieratic structure, it turns into a means of mental characterisation. Fuseli declares that "the principles of allegory and votive composition are the same; . . . both surround a real being, or allude to a real act, with symbols by long general consent adopted, as expressive of the qualities, motives or circumstances that distinguished or gave evidence to the person or the transaction". In this sense, the "Nightmare" is a version of allegory. Votive celebration of historical actions has become exploration of fantasy: the icons are now ogres, and instead of being supported by orthodox "long general consent", the meanings of the symbols are disturbingly new and ambiguous.

This psychological inversion is a possibility which Haydon, in a corresponding lecture on invention, cannot admit.[3] For him allegory remains a decorative accessory, justifiable in a long series of paintings, like the Luxembourg Gallery of Rubens, because it prettifies the composition. The agents of allegory are always, Haydon assumes, beautiful girls, cosmetic creatures who can hardly be expected to bear the burden of a meaning: "who on earth, when they see a beautiful girl with a castle on her head, ever thinks of a city? Thus has Rubens represented Lyons, congratulating Mary de Medicis on her safe accouchement". Haydon believes that Rubens would have done better to present "a deputation from Lyons, with fine senatorial heads".

Introversion is complicated by internal dissension: as well as controverting each form he employs, Fuseli incites the elements of his art to disagreement. Matter and form, the literary source and its pictorial treatment, are goaded into enmity by Fuseli's wilful inconsistencies. His illustrations to *Macbeth*, for instance, fragment the play into three dissimilar pictorial styles. For the witches he adopts the solemnly laughable deformity of the cartoon, for Lady Macbeth the hard outline of neoclassicism, for Macbeth the vertiginous sublimity of romantic landscape. Each choice has its logic, but the result is to foment stylistic disruption within the literary source and to imply that painting can only subdue literature by dividing and ruling, by stylistic perversity.

Fuseli's witches are gross bawds, reassimilated to caricature, where they belong, by Gillray's parody.[4] This cast Pitt and two of his ministers as the weird sisters fingering their beards as they watch the moon, which shows on one side the grinning sickle-shaped face of the queen and on the other the dormant, bloated shadow of the mad king. Fuseli's sleepwalking Lady Macbeth is a neoclassical maenad, a stark ballerina immobilised in her memories. His Macbeth is, however, removed from the play's encroaching interior into a landscape. Hecate and the witches are dismissed, because "it is not by the accumulation of infernal or magic machinery . . ., by surrounding him with successive apparitions at once, . . . that Macbeth can be made an object of terror, – to render him that you must place him on a ridge, his down-dashed eye absorbed by the murky abyss; surround the horrid vision with darkness, exclude its limits, and shear its light to glimpses". But this choice is as contradictory as the reduction of the witches from oracles to bawds or the linear purification accorded to Lady Macbeth, for character is loosened into and unmade by the landscape and, in the treatment Fuseli describes, Macbeth's tragedy is appropriated by the elements. Relieved of tragic accountability, he dissolves into a spirit. In a discussion of the backgrounds to Reynolds's portraits, Fuseli discriminates between "whatever connects the individual with the elements", which is sublime and therefore astonishing, and "whatever connects [the individual] in the same manner with, or tears it from the species", which is pathetic. It is appropriate that Haydon's examples of epic sublimity in scenery[5] should mainly concern Milton's Satan – rearing his mighty stature off the pool, moving towards the shore, sailing through surging smoke, buffetted and plunging ten thousand fathoms into the "vast vacuity" of an air-pocket, only to be thrown again into the heights by a nitrous cloud – because, as Fuseli reveals in his prescription about Macbeth, sublimity consists in the individual's disappearance into a landscape, and Satan, airborne, indistinct, treacherously chameleon, defensively becomes whatever landscape he finds himself in. Macbeth too is made to renounce his tragic singleness and, disembodied, haunts an obscure and vacant landscape.

Fuseli's decomposition of *Macbeth* betrays his assumption that the subject will be intractable, forcing the pictorial style to conquer it by misrepresenting it; that the subject will be a mere external record of events which the style must deform and deface in order to reach the secret mental life inside. The enmity between matter and form underlies Fuseli's construction of a triad of possible subjects, which he grades as positive, negative, and repulsive.[6] The first group he significantly calls "the voluntary servants of invention", docile and ductile, although the examples he gives are mostly of emotional distress or agony. The Laocoön, Niobe and her daughters, the death of Ananius, and Elymas struck blind qualify because they "speak their meaning with equal evidence to the scholar and the unlettered man, and excite the sympathy due to the calls of terror and pity with equal energy in every breast". The second group consists of subjects which style may redeem, although nothing of general human truth may be found in them. Here, with extraordinary dismissive coolness, Fuseli mentions the sorts of subjects which make the greatest classical pictures. St Jerome presenting the translation of his Bible to the infant Jesus, or St Peter kneeling before the Madonna to receive the thanks of victorious Venice, like all other votive altar-pieces, only make an impression, he claims, because of "the dexterous arrangement, the amorous or sublime enthusiasm of the artist". He has turned the classic tradition he inherits and illustrates inside out, making it a representation not of historical action or moral precept but of his own "amorous or sublime enthusiasm". Style appropriates subjects for its own self-dramatising purposes. Hence the encyclopaedic range of Fuseli's sources: he ransacks literature and mythology in a frantic search for new worlds to conquer, new material to be colonised by his idiom, as Don Giovanni tours Europe in pursuit of additions to his list.

Yet the freedom Fuseli's stylistic licence claims for him is enfeebling rather than invigorating. The other side of his vigorous impotence is a powerless omnipotence. Like Tristram Shandy he vacillates ironically between irresponsible, whimsical absolutism and inanition, paralysis, timid enslavement to the sources he is free to flout. For when you can fill the pages with writing on any subject, you first lose yourself, as Tristram discovers, in the anarchy of thoughts competing to be expressed, then gradually succumb to silence, leaving more and more blank spaces or sketchy unfinished pictures, since if everything is possible nothing is worthwhile. The libertine's omnivorous appetite withers into sated disgust.

Negative subjects, Fuseli's third category, offer a particular challenge, defying pictorial style to subdue them since they depict "an action or event that receives its real interest from a motive which cannot be rendered intuitive", for instance Alceste expiring or the cause of Demetrius's disorder. Fuseli's subjects are predominantly negative, and his aim is to penetrate the intuitive truth of situations which literature can treat from inside but which painting generally obscures by embodying, to hint at motive rather than transcribing acts and effects. Hence the suggestive impropriety with which his style alters its sources, making Eve, with her coiled and castellated hair, temptingly invite the love-sick serpent, or transforming Ugolino from the staring, haunted madman of Reynolds into a huge and saturnine totem figure whose overgrown hand jealously clutches at the sacrifice lying across his knee.

Depending on distortion, on an infidelity to the spirit of the literary source which compensates for enslavement to the letter, and on a mannerism which galvanises characters into extreme states of violence or abandon, Fuseli's is an art of the fancy rather than the imagination. Fancy disrupts and improvises with the idle, skittish, reckless irresponsibility of the nephew of Rameau; imagination is a solemn ordering force, a principle of quiet natural growth and shaping. Coleridge in framing his theory of imagination needs to demote fancy, which for him has an inferior levity. It is the trickster's art:

> the fancy . . .
> the fancy cannot cheat so well
> As she is fam'd to do, deceiving elf

and it divides what the poet's synthesising imagination aims to bring together. It is odd, as Johnson thought *Tristram Shandy*, whereas romantic imagination aspires to a naturalness which will render it unobtrusive, a silently and invisibly working power which germinates poems like trees. In this sense Shakespeare's plays were natural objects, as de Quincey described them, so fully imagined as to leave no trace of their creator, although the creator is always anxiously present in Sterne's novel or Fuseli's pictures, officiously supporting his fragile invention or damaging it in order to gain the freedom for a new start. The divisiveness of fancy is close to the state of mind of the ironist, who cannot rid himself of the fear that his work is weighing him down or penning him in, who obtrudes and gesticulates so that no-one will be tempted to take his work for himself.

Fancy is the style of Falstaff, who gives to his every caprice the force of law and makes himself king by fancying himself to be so, although unlike Keats's Adam he awakes at the end of the play and finds that the dream was a fiction. Irony is the style of Hamlet, an untiring inventor who still cannot convince himself to believe in his fabrications, but waits for them to destroy him. Burke, irritated by the habit of digression in *Tristram Shandy*, complained that "the book is a perpetual series of disappointments",[7] which is no criticism but a perfect definition of the novel and, incidentally, of *Hamlet*, for they are both ironic compounds of misconception and misadventure. Tristram's fancifulness is as absolute but as unavailing as Fuseli's. The elation of imaginative freedom is countered by the dull oppression of bodily necessity, the fertility of mental conjecture betrayed by the failures of physical performance and the suspicion of impotence. The rampaging libertine declines into a nervous, hapless ironist. *Tristram Shandy* is harried and disorganised within, besieged from without. It needs a reader to rearrange it into sense, and yet is at the mercy of inattentive readers like the lady who fails to understand that Mrs Shandy is not a papist and admits first to having skipped a page, then to having been asleep. She is sent back to re-read the chapter as a penance, but still does not find what the author claims is there: Tristram then reveals that the fact was not baldly stated but merely implied, and laments the misfortunes his wretched book must suffer from those low-minded or over-hasty readers whose only concern is for "the gross and carnal parts of a composition" and are insensitive to "subtle hints and sly communications" – those, that is, who read it as a novel and not as a lyrical poem, who crave business and intrigue and are unresponsive to the motions of thought.

Fuseli as well seeks to release the spiritual from the literal, the sly communications of literary psychology from the gross and carnal externality of painting; and it is this ambitious romantic introversion of form which leads him, paradoxically, to acquiesce in the servile role of illustrator. The image is a bland surface which can only acquire an interior by attachment to a literary context. Later romantic painters continue to seek the protection of literature. Turner added to his paintings fragments from his interminable poem on *The Fallacies of Hope*, turning the images into dramatic gestures, speeches of stoic defiance or sententious contempt.[8] The image acquires a voice, the painting becomes a soliloquy. For instance, the note to "Slaves Throwing Overboard the Dead and Dying – Typhon Coming on",

> Before it sweeps your decks, throw overboard
> The dead and dying – ne'er heed their chains.
> Hope, Hope, fallacious Hope!
> Where is thy market now?

with its nautical swagger and its swift change from the slave-trader's brutality to the professional fatalism of the old tar, makes the picture strike an attitude, turns it into a rudimentary dramatic monologue. Quotation supplies the absence of human characters, and makes the landscapes a continuing commentary on tragic nature.

As romanticism begins, all the arts aspire to the condition of literature, the treasury of moving or ennobling subject-matter, so that painting is assigned the task of illustration; as it ends, all the arts aspire to the condition of music, which has no subject. In between, the subject has been progressively reduced. Haydon did not feel at home in his painting-room unless accompanied by Dante, Petrarch, Homer, Shakespeare, Milton, Spenser, Tasso and Vasari, who smiled on him "like phantasmagoric visions" while his brain teemed "with associations of their sublimity or charm", and when he pawned his lay-figures and studies of the Elgin marbles he could not bring himself to part with his darling authors. His error was to assume that the choice of a noble subject from literature guaranteed an epic achievement in painting. But increasingly the romantics feel no need to wait on a significant subject, and positively boast of their ability to find a subject anywhere, to discover eternity in a grain of sand or sublimity in slimy planks and stagnant mill-ponds. This is the easy resourcefulness which Collins, in the "Ode on the Popular Superstitions of the Highlands of Scotland",[9] envies in his friend Home:

> To thee thy copious subjects ne'er shall fail;
> Thou need'st but take the pencil to thy hand,
> And paint what all believe who own thy genial land.

Romantic art is diffused, sketchy, serial, not trusting to a single all-consuming achievement but recording a continuing life of perception and sensation through intermittent glimpses, shots at certainty not Haydon's epic finality.

Painting discovers this suggestive subjectivity in literature. Fuseli has a shadowy complicity with his sources: he apologises for his bad dreams by attributing them to the authors he illustrates, although the encounter between his fantasy and the narrative of the source generally produces shame and ironic disparity and discomfort. Haydon accused Fuseli of negligence and impatient abuse of the literary works on which he battened; but Haydon's journal admits his own indifference to the accomplishments of painterly technique: "I really don't care about the half-tint of a cheek. I really do not. I would rather devour Ælian, or search Strabo, and blaze with Homer, – I really would – and give my imagination the reins for hours, than paint a cheek like Vandyke." In literature lies freedom, in painting only the belittling necessity of representation. Haydon's lectures worry about the comparative strengths of poetry and painting, and eventually concede the poet the advantage because, although painting can create emotional effects of an intensity beyond the power of language, it is condemned to surfaces and exteriors, whereas poetry can explore mental space: "poets can make their characters speak their thoughts; painters can only make them look; abstracted reflections or subtle conclusions in morality can never be looked to be comprehended, or painted to be comprehended; no painter could make Newton look as if he had discovered the tides, without extraneous help; but a poet could say so at once".

The painter's devaluation of his own art is summed up in an anecdote of Wilkie's. He, Haydon and a musician entered into a dispute about the respective powers of the three arts. Wilkie said that a painter, a poet and a musician had once agreed to resolve the same question by going to a tavern and using their respective arts to order their supper. The first to make himself understood would be the winner. "The musician played most exquisitely for three-quarters of an hour, but the waiter shook his head; the painter dashed out the resemblance of a roast fowl, and the poet at once said he would have a boiled one." The poet, Wilkie said, had of course won, and their fiddling friend rushed from the room and never forgave them.[10] It is revealing that Haydon should tell such an inconclusive story, in which painting is reduced to mean sign-language, against himself, as if determined to wish failure on his efforts and to convince himself that he is working in an unworthy form.

Notes

1. Fuseli gave three lectures as Professor of Painting at the Royal Academy in 1801, on "Ancient Art", "Art of the Moderns" and "Invention", published in Knowles, *The Life and Writings of Henry Fuseli*, op. cit., vol. II. This and subsequent quotations are from "Invention", Lectures III and IV.
2. Translated and introduced by Margaret R. Hale in *Horn of Oberon*, Detroit, 1973. Quotations from Jean Paul on following pages are from the same source.
3. *Lectures on Painting and Design*, 1844, Lecture VII.
4. James Gillray, "Weird Sisters; Ministers of Darkness; Minions of the Moon", 23 December 1791.
5. *Lectures on Painting and Design*, op. cit.
6. Aphorism no. 239 in Knowles, *The Life and Writings of Henry Fuseli*, op. cit., vol. III.
7. Review of *Tristram Shandy*, *Annual Register*, 1760, reprinted in Alan B. Howes (ed.), *Sterne: The Critical Heritage*, 1974.
8. Reprinted in *The Sunset Ship: The Poems of J. M. W. Turner*, commentary by Jack Lindsay, 1965.
9. 1749, published 1788.
10. Told by Haydon in his lecture on Invention, *Lectures on Painting and Design*, op. cit.

8

Romantic Tristrams

Romanticism, reinterpreting Sterne, removes him from the eccentric periphery of literary tradition to the centre. The disarray of his narrative is justified as an image of the self-questioning of ironic intelligence; his antiquarian pedantry becomes an aesthetic philosophy redefining the vexed relations between mind and body and, a corollary of this uneasy self-division, between the intellectual or sentimental contents of literature and its conventions of form. Earlier chapters have represented aspects of this romantic redemption of Tristram Shandy. His embarrassed collisions between tragedy and comedy, as the first showed, constitute in romantic terms an intimate, ironic collusion. Tragedy and comedy are now ambiguous, unstable moods, and the double plot dramatises their inextricability. Tristram's cabinet of virtuoso oddities and archaisms turns, as the second chapter argued, into a vertiginous palace of thought. His libertinism changes from sensual truancy to intellectual conjecture, and from the pursuit of victims to chaste exploration of the self: these inversions were described in the third and fourth chapters. Tristram's arabesques, the subject of the fifth chapter, are not idle doodling but the signature of a mind whose paradoxical complication is a replica in miniature of the jagged heights and depths of romantic sublimity. The sixth and seventh chapters followed the extension of Shandyean involution to painting, describing Fuseli's attempt to turn his art from mimicry of nature to suggestion of the invisible, metaphoric life of mental conjecture. These various developments have a single purpose: to remake Tristram the freak and exhibitionistic sport as an introvert, and Tristram the wayward sentimentalist as a mysteriously reticent ironist.

The romantic transformation of Tristram from an incompetent novelist into a visionary poet continues throughout the nineteenth century and is, as this chapter will demonstrate, largely the work of German critical philosophers, Lichtenberg, Jean Paul Richter, Friedrich Schlegel, Heine and Schopenhauer, with contributions from the composers Mendelssohn and Mahler. This version of Tristram is inaccurate but nevertheless authentic – more so than the grudging English evaluation which isolates him outside literary tradition or, at best, patronises him as an impudent anti-novelist before his time. The extravagances of the German re-creation of Tristram are countenanced by two peculiar romantic aesthetic notions: one is translation, the other the world-literature which is convened or constructed by translation.

Translation promotes misunderstanding and blurs exact meanings, but in the romantic view this can be revelatory: deformations of the letter of a work may serve to liberate its spirit. A translated writer loses everything but his genius. Yet, for the romantics, genius is the essential thing, and it is in any case detachable from a writer's words. Shakespeare's plays could not be satisfactorily translated, but the idea of Shakespeare could. Like Wilde at the customs barrier in New York, Shakespeare travelled easily because he travelled light, having nothing to declare but his genius. In romantic criticism, genius is the indwelling spirit of the artist, the meaning which lies behind, rather than in, the works he produces: the figure in his carpet, the jewel in his casket. In romantic literary theology, it belongs to the teasingly absent artist rather than to his art. Shakespeare's plays abide affably enough the questions Bradley puts to them; it is Shakespeare himself who, as Arnold acknowledged, does not.

From Coleridge to Arnold, romantic artists inevitably turn into critics because in criticism the mystery of artistic creation is made intelligible. Romantic criticism is theological, for it attempts to reason about the motions of a creative impulse as inscrutable and as primitively impulsive as the god who simply decided to make the world in seven days or the Shakespeare who simply turned out three dozen plays in a short working lifetime, without needing to reflect on his purpose in doing so. The translator is also a theologian, a disciple whose rendering of the inexpressible truth may obscure or distort, but who trusts that, if the letter is tarnished, the spirit remains intact. Viewed romantically, all criticism is translation: hesitant articulation of an imageless deep truth. Therefore translation to a foreign language is not a special case but an extension of the norm. Obliteration of the letter may even guard the integrity of the spirit since, translated, a writer triumphantly discards the lesser truths which adhere to locality and linguistic accident. He becomes universal, the god not only of one tribe but of all literate mankind. This is why Carlyle, in the preface to his translation of *Wilhelm Meister*, insists on the duty of internationalism: "Minds such as Goethe's are the common property of all nations and, for many reasons, all should have correct impressions of them."[1] Notably, it is Goethe's mind which is to be translated into a common property, and, as this happens, that mind or genius is detached from his words, which are its mere and temporary expression. In the course of the nineteenth century, world-literature becomes another wall-less museum in which Homer, Shakespeare and Goethe are happily contiguous, like a Greek vase and a Renaissance altar-piece in the art museum, because all geniuses are contemporary with one another. The modern destiny of art is that literature should be known in translation, music in gramophone recordings, and paintings in reproductions (often black-and-white). Our implicit faith is that art can survive refractions through other media and other languages because these are the vicissitudes of its victorious progress through the world. The damage done to art in this way is the most moving tribute which could be paid to it: like the wearing away of the foot of St Peter's statue in Rome by the kisses of generations of pilgrims.

Georg Christoph Lichtenberg's commentaries on the engravings of Hogarth, published in the literary journal *Göttinger Taschenkalender* between 1784 and 1796,[2] are an early instance of the translation of an artist from one culture to another, and from a visual to a verbal medium; and as an influence on Jean Paul Richter, they are a model for the later critical metamorphoses of Sterne. The degree of creative misunderstanding involved is as great as with Sterne. Hogarth's art is glumly emblematic, weighting each detail with significance, and the progress of decoding the litter of bric-à-brac in his scenes is one of prurient detection and moral appraisal.

Like a visiting social worker, the interpreter notes down the grubby insanitariness, the broken crockery, squabbling pet dogs and overturned furniture as symptoms and prognostications. The scenes are legalistic: each detail starts up as evidence. Thoughts drearily materialise as things, and the very complexity of the imagery is a form of booby-trapping. Even the pictures Hogarth's wretched characters hang on their walls turn sardonically against them, while every domestic mishap grimly enforces the burden of original sin. Hogarth is a satirist whose art is static because its aim is to catch people out, to pin them down. Lichtenberg translates him into a visionary sentimentalist whose scenes are images of the volatile excitement of experience. Hogarth's judicial finality gives way to the sentimental narrator's eagerness to spin out, as Tristram does, the scarcely visible threads of each situation. Details in Hogarth are exhibits in court, degraded and stained with complicity; Lichtenberg makes them into metaphysical conceits, pregnant with unsuspected significance. Lichtenberg's sentimentality is a form of superstition, finding omens and oracles everywhere, even (such is his romantic sense of the diminutive infinitude of nature) in the crawling of an insect. He is cursed with a talent for analogy, an affliction which, as Hamlet and Tristram know, can complicate existence and make it impossible to live straightforwardly, with the purposefulness which narrative reveres and depends on, because the networks of ramification which spin themselves around the simplest action or the humblest object are so intriguing and deluding.

Hamlet flourishes this analogical skill and twits Polonius by declaring a cloud, which in the single vision of Polonius is simply that, to be alternately a camel, a weasel and a whale. Polonius is limited to a miserably prosaic definition of an object, whereas Hamlet can translate it into a metaphor at will. It is appropriate that their converstion should be about clouds which, like water, were to become romantic images of the fluidity and changefulness of consciousness: the shapes which loom and disappear in our daydreaming minds resemble camels, weasels, whales, and Hamlet adumbrates in advance this romantic sense of the fluency of images. But the joke ultimately turns against Hamlet. His facility in inventing correspondences becomes a Shandyean folly but also a tragic impediment. He is fated to deal in stratagems, diversions and analogues rather than actions. Lichtenberg possesses a brain of incorrigible complexity like Hamlet's, which he applies to a Sternean reading of Hogarth. His commentaries describe Hogarth's plates as if seen by a Tristram, an observer whose sympathetic inquisitiveness upsets the brutal foreclosure of Hogarth's art, an observer who is never satisfied and asks scores of Bradleyan questions: Why does the harlot come fron Yorkshire? Why is her destination Thames Street? Why does she have a repeater watch? Why has the cat had its tail cut off? The answers are not worked out by a Victorian process of detection (exercised, for instance, by Ruskin in his interrogation of Holman Hunt's guilty couple in "The Awakening Conscience") but imaged intuitively in the discernment of analogies. Victorian readings of pictures complete the plot. Lichtenberg's interpretations, rhapsodic rather than analytical, frustrate Hogarth's plots, which move briskly to retribution, by creating aureoles of spiritual uncertainty around his shabby characters. No longer a caricaturist, Hogarth becomes, as Lichtenberg calls him, "a painter of souls". Only a commonplace vision, uncomprehendingly literal like that of Polonius, could mistake him for a punitive, exemplary satirist.

As read by Lichtenberg, the careers of the harlot or the rake are caught up in the turning cycle of nature and in the life-drama of the soul, which are described both scientifically and in terms of a doctrine of vitalism. Lichtenberg chemically differentiates three stages of fermentation – vinous, acetous, and putrid – and goes on to find analogies to these processes in all organic mater quickened by the life-spirit, in individual existences and in the destinies of states. Analogy discovers in the universe a patterned structure of macro- and microcosm, cycle and epicycle, and Moll Hackabout the harlot is rolled round in its diurnal course. Her history turns into the aborted drama of Keats's blind and instinctual centre of being struggling to become a soul. In her Golden Age in Yorkshire, and during her Silver Age in London as the mistress of a Portuguese Jew, she can enjoy life's first fermentation. Already by the fourth plate it has turned vinegary in the penitentiary, and the next plate records the transition to putrid fermentation as she expires.

Lichtenberg's philosophy of fermentation is a development of the ideology of Falstaff, who also feels the life force to be liquorish, leavening and vinous. Wisdom, for him as for Keats and the symbolist drunkards of the later nineteenth century, is a potion which refines the senses by deranging them. Prince John, in Falstaff's estimation, is sober-blooded and demure because he takes only thin drink, whereas sherris both dries the brain and sharpens it into witty apprehension, while it warms the blood and sends it coursing to the body's extremities. In Shakespeare's Roman plays, the belly is a grave and deliberate politician with some of the humourless guile of the Lancastrians. In *Henry IV*, however, the flesh is not a well-ordered commonwealth in which the belly distributes welfare payments to its tributary limbs, but a militaristic state whose bellicosity is the result not of self-division but (like volcanoes as romantically analysed by Sir William Hamilton)[3] of the need to discharge energy. Bodily, the pusillanimous Falstaff is the most valiant character in the play, for he has the exhilarating courage of his physical presence and a brave determination to save his life whatever the risk. Sherris, he says, "illumineth the face, which as a beacon gives warning to all the rest of this little kingdom, man, to arm, and then the vital commoners and inland petty spirits muster me all to their captain, the heart, who, great and puffed up with this retinue, doth any deed of courage, and this valour comes of sherris". Falstaff even possesses the disarming modesty of the extremely brave, since he takes no personal credit for his valour but attributes it to drink. Hotspur, on the other hand, is a coward because he is so negligent in the defence of the citadel of his own body.

The Falstaff of the second part of *Henry IV* may be moving from wine fermentation to acetous fermentation: the doctor has divined countless illnesses in his water. But in Falstaff the process is only physical, whereas Lichtenberg's sense of it is metaphysical: the degeneration through three stages hints at someting vaster and sadder, the working of a nature which is eternal because it is mutable, which must constantly destroy in order to create. It is interesting therefore, and an additional connection with the third and fourth chapters of this book, that Lichtenberg should introduce the figure of the libertine to enact some of the ambiguities of the idea. He discusses Rochester as a case of one in whom the three stages did not complete themselves at leisure, but were compressed into a time which normally is hardly sufficient for one. Having been drunk for five years on end, Rochester was old by the age of thirty, underwent a conversion at thirty-one, and died in agonising tedium two years later. He used up a constitution made to last a hundred years in a third of that time. Lichtenberg calculates the rate of dissipation on a biometer which measures the body's durability, and reckons that each year of libertine existence spends the equivalent of three years of placid life. He also wonders if the same acceleration of the cycle might be found in the history of some states.

The libertine's alteration of the physical rhythm of existence endows him with a certain rash heroism (he declares himself for an hour of glorious life rather than an age without a name) and provides as well an alternative explanation of the strange imperviousness to time displayed by Falstaff and Don Giovanni. Lichtenberg has found a biological motive for the episodic nature of these characters. Falstaff prolongs the heady juvenile ecstasy of appetite into later life, indefinitely postponing the inevitable souring and putrefaction. The bibulous Don Giovanni, who rejoices in wine's power to make heads reel and to set his victims whirling in an abandoned dance, is closer to Rochester as registered on Lichtenberg's biometer. As Leporello's catalogue aria reveals, Don Giovanni has contracted into the span of a few years a number of seductions it would take centuries in time and an Ovidian god's ubiquity in space to accomplish; he opens a gap in time, but time abruptly claims him while he is still in the first innocence of appetite, eating, drinking and imbibing delight from everything, before he has had the chance to grow old, stale and putrid. He is as old as the universe in terms of experience, but like Falstaff dazzlingly young in his tirelessness, his refusal to be sickened by excess, and his eternal craving for more.

The arrangement of *Tristram Shandy* is an image of the biometer's panic as time is foreshortened, but in this case as a result of the progress of tuberculosis, not collapse into dissipation. The spaces between the later volumes are accidental, infection-prone stretches of time, and Tristram cannot promise to keep the novel on course because he cannot know what will happen to him in these intervals. As an invalid he is reduced to living from day to day, and working by fits and starts is an artistic method which corresponds to his wise, doomed passiveness. Retiring at the end of Book V, he undertakes to return in a year "unless this vile cough kills me in the mean time". Beginning Book VII he reverts to this guarded contract and points out how pathetically art is at the mercy of life: "I think, I said, I would write two volumes every year, provided the vile cough which then tormented me, and which to this hour I dread worse than the devil, would but give me leave." His unreliability as a narrator is a symptom and an image, like Hamlet's procrastination, of the ills flesh is heir to.

Lichtenberg's image of fermentation recurs in Jean Paul Richter's novel of 1796–7, *Blumen-, Frucht- und Dornenstücke; oder Ehestand, Tod und Hochzeit des Armenadvokaten F. St. Siebenkäs*: flower, fruit and thorn pieces describing, with Shandyean rearrangement of chronology, the wedded life, death and marriage of the parish advocate Firmian Stanislaus Siebenkäs. Jean Paul's hero is a muddled and doting man of feeling in whom a tendency to satirical asperity acts as "a ferment, a leaven or yeast, or, say a kind of irritating engine to that sensitive heart of his of which he was both proud and ashamed at once". He is psychologically double-plotted, compounded of the opposites of flower and thorn, sentiment and satire, levity and moodiness, both bashfully recoiling into himself and merrily exhibiting himself. He is, indeed, Tristram Shandy as conceived by German romanticism.

Sterne's scurrilous physical comedy has become, in this interpretation, nobly mental: he has been allegorised. In his story of the Princess Brambilla, E. T. A. Hoffman contrasts the low buffoonery of Italian comedy with the reflective, self-interrogatory humour of the Germans. Hoffmann calls German humour allegorical, and irony is in fact the romantic mode of allegory, saying one thing but meaning another. The ironist works under cover of the same incognito as the allegorist. The difference is that allegory can be simply decoded, since its meaning lies in a consistent correspondence between letter and spirit, whereas there is no trustworthy technique for deducing the ironist's inverse meanings, which are protected by his constant disavowals and facetious sleights-of-hand, his evasive pretence that what he is says is no more than trivial and occasional. The allegorist's puzzles are the ironist's mysteries. The romantic comedians treated throughout this book are ironists, because they have learned the art of concealing their significance behind a calculated appearance of oddity or idleness: Don Giovanni adopts the mask of the seducer, Faust the monkish posture of the enemy of god, Hamlet that of the incompetent revenger, Tristram that of the retarded child incapable of setting up its top.

The duplicity of the ironist's language replicates the doubleness of his vision. Rhetorically, he dodges between the innocuous letter of what he says and the subversive spirit of what he means. Philosophically, he is caught between literal shackling to a body and to weak, misleading instruments of perception, and the spiritual capacity of imagination, which promises freedom from his physical prison and from time. Describing the damp cold November of 1785, Richter in *Siebenkäs* represents this ironic dualism as a landscape. The low and shrouded sky has deprived Firmian of his happiness. He is a stoic, a latter-day Boethius deriving consolation not from philosophy but from irony, which stimulates him by enforcing his sense of his own littleness. The apprehension of the sublime, in Burke muddied with the cravings for power and achievement, is here miniaturised and purified into an intellectual and ironic experience. Firmian's habit is to run up hills and "seek in the heavens for that which consoles and comforts the anxious and the sorrowful, that which dissipates the clouds which shroud our life, and shows us the guiding nebulae (Magellan's clouds), if nothing else, gleaming through the fog-banks". Atop the Rabenstein, he surmounts earthly life, left behind in the crevices and hollows of the plain, and catches sight of "the aurora of the sun of happiness, though that sun was under his horizon".

Firmian has lifted himself out of his confinement, made himself an Ariel. But Ariel, like his opposite Caliban, is one of those Shakespearean characters whose meaning the romantics renew and extend. As *The Tempest* ends, he and Caliban remain Prospero's victims: Prospero summarily declares Caliban a part of himself, and goes on to nullify the freedom he has granted Ariel by exposing Ariel's element as faded, amateurish scene-painting. Nevertheless, Ariel and Caliban survive Prospero and his vanishing pageant to become terminal gods of romanticism. Their antagonism narrows into ironic similitude. The paradox of this identity between them was referred to in the fourth chapter, when Coleridge confers on Caliban the status of "impersonated abstraction", which would seem to belong to the insubstantial Ariel: the monster is as gross a figure as the libertine, but he is ennobled and rendered abstract, as is the libertine, by the intellectuality of his conception. De Quincey, in his 1842 essay on Shakespeare, also considers Caliban redeemed "by his intellectual power, and by the grandeur of his misanthropy". In the same essay, contributed to the *Encyclopaedia Brittanica*,[4] De Quincey considers Ariel and Caliban as mystical conjectures, "new modes of life, preternatural, yet as far as the poles from the spiritualities of religion", and through the nineteenth century they interact ironically as the inimical yet dependent extremes of the romantic double plot. Ariel represents the mental disembodiment of romanticism, Caliban the grotesque embodiment to which the nimble imagination is condemned: his avatars are Wordsworth's leech-gatherer, Dickens's Quilp, Browning's Caliban on Setebos, and the grimacing Caliban of Wilde who, in the preface to *The Picture of Dorian Gray*, dislikes realism because it shows him how ugly he is and dislikes romanticism because it shows him how beautiful he is not.

Striding along the hills, Firmian is a romantic Ariel who has at last escaped from Prospero and lives "in the free air, close to the ocean of life which stretches on into the invisible distance of infinity". His arms are unfettered, though still bruised by galling iron, and he extends them "as if to soar into the pure bright aether", as if to embrace the peaceful universe and created nature. He is an Ariel who has acquired some of the cosmic benevolence of Faust, flying above the earth and feeling pity for its fog-bound unhappiness. Caliban, however, weighs him down. The ironist knows that he cannot live on the mountain top, that he belongs on the flat plain of necessity not in the open space of freedom, and he moves sadly between the two.

The romantic landscape is an image of this ironic inadequacy, because it is a view from inside a hole, a casement (like Keats's in the "Ode to a Nightingale") opening out into a vastness which we can see but never visit. Landscape is in this sense the consolation for a lost religion: Philipp Otto Runge in 1841 declared that the abstractions of theology had perished, and that religious thought like art was "moving in the direction of the landscape, . . . seeking something definite in this infinity" without knowing where to begin.[5] Landscape painting ironically inverts the theological view of nature. God sees the world from above (like Chaucer's penitent Troilus translated to the eighth sphere), but the landscape painter (like Firmian) sees the heavens, without a god in them, from below. If the landscape painter does discern a god, it is the ambiguous shape of a cloud, like Turner's Polyphemus in "Ulysses deriding Polyphemus". This, as Firmian sees it, is the human lot. Like prisoners or invalids, people are "shut up in their holes, the clouds sail over them, they can only see the mountains far away in the distance, these mountains whence, as from those of the Polar regions in summer midnights, the sun, down below the horizon, can be seen shining with a mild face, as if in slumber". The landscape view is necessarily ironic, since it is that of the infirm, the disabled, the incarcerated. Firmian is oppressed by the louring November weather because it deprives him of the mental space of fantasy, but it sends him back consolingly to the view of the immediate foreground and thus to a domestic contentment which "thrives in the flower-pots of the window-sill".

Tristram Shandy also presents itself as a romantic exploration of landscape. The novelist and reader are companions in a picaresquely digressive journey, and at the beginning of Book VI they make a wayside stop to reflect on the distance they have covered and the perils they have (like Collins's Home in the highlands) escaped: "What a wilderness it has been! and what a mercy that we have not both of us been lost, or devoured by wild beasts in it!" The series of errant lines by which Tristram represents the progress of the composition, mentioned in the fifth chapter as Hogarthian arabesques, can also be read as topography. They are the indentations, furrows, declivities and protuberances of the landscape which stretches behind the travellers, who congratulate themselves on having got safely through the territory of the Jack Asses lurking in one region of this map: "How they viewed and reviewed us as we passed over the rivulet at the bottom of that little valley! – and when we climbed over that hill, and were just getting out of sight – good God! what a braying did they all set up together!" This Shandyean landscape is eminently picturesque, artfully disordered and excavated, a maze of alleys, grottos and sunken lakes.

The end of Book VII bounds hectically ahead from Lunel to Montpellier to Pescnas, Beziers, Narbonne, Carcasson and Castle Naudairy, traversing immensities of space in a sentence in its anxiety to reach Pedrillo's pavilion and pull out "a paper of black lines, that I might go on straight forwards, without digression or parenthesis, in my uncle Toby's amours – ". But Tristram's straight lines never lead anywhere. He sets out with a good will, "I began thus —", but the dash tapers out as an unfulfilled promise into blankness, and the volume ends. When he resumes, revoking his earlier praise for the straight line, he defies the best cabbage planter "to go on coolly, critically, and canonically, planting cabbages one by one, in straight lines and stoical distances". Tristram's vegetables are to have the vagrant, deviant arrangement of the picturesque English garden. The landscape forbids regularity. Straight lines might be possible in frigid and featureless places, Freeze-land or Fog-land, but not in "this clear climate of fantasy and perspiration, where every idea, sensible or insensible, gets vent". This landscape of obliging meanders and wandering paths turns out to be the realm of chivalry and romance (the widow in pursuit of Toby becomes Julia tracking down her Diego) which Hurd had compared in its labyrinthine twistings and interweavings to a William Kent garden, and which for Coleridge constituted mental space. The terrain of Tristram's narrative, in which distances are airily annihilated by mental association and topography whimsically involuted, prefigures the landscape of spiritual possibility which Firmian pines for in his confinement.

The accidental shambles of *Tristram Shandy* grows, as the romantics interpret it, into a metaphysical comedy. The petulantly incompetent Tristram becomes an ironic sage, speculating with extravagant mental freedom on his own imprisoned human condition. Firmian acknowledges two kinds of necessity, which pen in the ironic spirit. One is diurnal, the other seasonal. In the first place, "the daily and everlasting necessity is this – that corn does not ripen in winter – that we have not got wings, though so many lower creatures have them – or that we cannot go and stand upon the craters of the lunar mountains, and looking down into the abysses, which are miles in depth, watch the marvellous and beautiful effects of the sun's rays". The longing for wings is significant. This Icarus-urge is one reason for the romantic fascination with Milton's Satan, who is winged and can enjoy the aerial perspective of craters and abysses described by Richter. Satan is the dangerous, enviable reverse of the grounded landscape painter. On his flight through Chaos to Earth he does see the creation from a god's omniscient point of vantage. The same envy of wings helps to explain the entomological obsession of Fuseli, who reared, studied and painted ants, spiders, wasps and beetles, and must have felt a grudging admiration for these creatures, small, mean and vicious, yet equipped with wings. The romantic ironist's consolation is that, although the body must reconcile itself to trudging along the earth, thoughts may be winged.

The small irritations of diurnal necessity are contained within that larger order of necessity which Firmian calls seasonal. He enumerates our annual afflictions: it rains when the corn is ripening; there are water-meadows which are uncomfortable to walk in; sometimes, because we have corns or don't have shoes, we can't walk anywhere. But Firmian eventually decides that the two orders of necessity are commensurate: "the annual necessity and the daily are of exactly equal magnitude, and it is just as senseless to murmur because we have paralysed limbs as because we have no wings". We rise above the tyranny of nature and the depression of our own mediocrity by embracing them, not by protest. Jean Paul's paradox derives a moral from that collision of formal opposites, tragedy and comedy, poetry and prose, time and space, which August Wilhelm Schlegel, in his lectures on drama, defines as the centre of romantic art: for, as Schlegel puts it, by juxtaposing incompatible forms the artist is freed from the constraints of form and enabled to rise above himself.[6]

Ironic, acquiescent wisdom in morals and ironic havoc in art also coexist in *Tristram Shandy*, where the struggle with shaming or immobilising physical necessity is indistinguishable from the struggle with, and surrender to, the cramping necessities of literary form. For Tristram, the problems of existence are the same as those of composition. The difficulty of keeping pace with the haste of experience, the refractoriness of pen and paper, the strain of communicating a meaning to an imperceptive but quarrelsome reader – Tristram fights all these battles, and gloriously loses them. But in acknowledging the limits of his literary skill he has ironically overcome them: he does justice to the inarticulate complication of his life by the very act of lamenting his inability to do so. The comic calamities of interruption or detour which beleaguer the text demonstrate that the quality of experience can best be suggested in gaps and silences. The meditative blank spaces with which the narrative is aerated are the printer's images for the peace passing understanding, quietening verbal squabbles, which occasionally descends on the family. As well as this punctuation inside the narrative there is the area outside it, the life beyond art to which Tristram at the end of Book V is so eager to return and into which he releases us: part-publication, with variably long intervals between the later volumes, becomes a way of leaving space for reverberation, or for growth between the blocks of narrative.

Tristram's literary achievement in vanquishing disorder by succumbing to it is a model for his reconciliation of himself to his mishap-ridden past, for as Richter says, "all the PAST – and this alone is the subject of our sorrow – is of so iron a necessity that in the eyes of a superior intelligence it is just as senseless of an apothecary to mourn because his shop is burnt to the ground as to sigh because he can't go botanising on the moon, although there may be things in phials there which he has not got in his". Tristram's apparently retrogressive, fractured, feeble intelligence is in fact Jean Paul's superior one, triumphing over its imperfections by gladly admitting them. Even Hegel's rule that freedom lies in the recognition of necessity derives from the self-pitying wisdom of romantic irony.

The romantics rescue irony from its didactic, demonstrative

purpose. Beginning in Socratic philosophy as a curriculum of intellectual instruction, irony is romantically transformed into an art of self-exploration, accomplishing in miniature the sublime task of reconciling the ways of god and nature to man by celebrating human weaknesses and thus surmounting them. One of the literary aphorisms which Friedrich Schlegel contributed to the *Lyceum der schönen Künste*[7] between 1797 and 1800 connects philosophical with aesthetic irony. He declares that novels are the modern version of the Socratic dialogue. Practical wisdom, abandoning the schools, has found a refuge in this liberal form. The definition exactly fits the conversations at cross purpose in Sterne's novels, where mutual incomprehension ironically ushers in sympathetic agreement by confounding the intellect and clearing the way for inarticulate emotional accord. Socrates taught by bemusing his pupils, affecting a guileless simplicity in order to trap them in their inconsistencies. Sterne likewise reveals wisdom to be the product of confusion and misunderstanding. Hence Yorick's preference for not knowing the language of the land he is travelling in: ignorance ensures an open mind and a heart impressionably eager to participate in the Socratic process.

Schlegel's perception of the link between Socratic induction and the novel also illuminates Diderot's encounter with the nephew of Rameau. This is a Socratic dialogue twisted awry, in which the superciliously ironic master confronts a pupil who is impervious and incorrigible. The aphorism even makes the relationship between Johnson and Boswell expand into a complex fiction. The irony of their exchanges is that, while Johnson enjoys a series of temporary victories, it is Boswell who is justified by history, for romanticism dignifies his gauche and eclectic enthusiasms, which Johnson mocks, as portents of cultural change.

As surely as Hal and Falstaff, Quixote and Sancho, or Giovanni and Leporello are paired in illustration of the two-faced complication of human nature, so the alliance of Johnson and Boswell couples opposed attitudes to literature and life, but with altered or inverted values. In the other cases, the heroes dedicate themselves to their missions of politics or chivalry or sexual conquest with a seriousness which is shamed by the inglorious self-seeking of their comic lower halves. The repartee of the prince and Falstaff or Giovanni and Leporello recurs in the conversations of Johnson and Boswell, but now it is the lowly comedian who makes ludicrous pretence at fine feeling and is restrained by his master's philistine contempt for music, mountains, and the Giant's Causeway. Boswell is Johnson's dog, as Falstaff's is Hal's, but the relationship is more entangled. For Boswell is the representative not only (as in his incontinent London journal) of natural man, a recalcitrant Caliban to Johnson's Prospero, but of the new sensibility of Rousseau and Sterne. Superimposed on their tragicomic relationship as master and man is their sibling relationship as representatives, like Jane Austen's Elinor and Marianne, of sense and sensibility. In the former connection, Johnson is loftily tragic, Boswell coarsely or irrelevantly comic; but in the latter the positions are reversed, and Boswell is the heroic adventurer experimenting with new sensations, Johnson the grumbling, uninspired dullard.

According to Schlegel, the novel is the repository not only of the dialectical wisdom of classical culture but also of a visionary harmony which has fled from the scriptures into this liberal form. In another of the aphorisms, he states that novels end as the *Paternoster* begins, with the kingdom of god on earth. Yorick's sentimental journey becomes an apostle's fieldwork, disseminating goodwill, and its end indeed celebrates the establishment of the kingdom of selfless affection in his meal with the Bourbonnais peasant family.

Schlegel devotes another long expository aphorism to Socratic irony, which he considers a form of dissimulation uniquely involuntary and yet at the same time quite self-conscious. Because it is a spiritual attitude rather than a verbal mannerism, it cannot be artificially worked up. As Carlyle argues with regard to Jean Paul Richter, verbal wit is "a poor fraction of humour", the body without the soul, laughter rather than the philosopher's profound and reticent smile.[8] Those who lack the gift of irony will continue to think of it as an enigma, Schlegel says, even when all its pretences and feignings have been exposed. It engages in a Sternean play with the susceptibilities of its listeners or readers, teasing them to recognise how relative and stiff and limited they are as it exults in its own dissolution of these obstructions. It deceives only those who persuade themselves that it is illusory, or are piqued when they feel it trained on themselves. As a form of interrogation it is affectionately solicitous yet ruthless in its intellectual probing. Thus Sterne discomfits his reader by sending him back to re-read a chapter, or by improvising examinations on the text which the reader must pass before he can proceed; however, he does so not punitively but to welcome the reader into the intimacy of collaboration.

Inversely sublime, irony scales down hair-raising thrills of the sublime into what Jean Paul Richter, in describing the physiological effects of comedy, calls a sensuous physical tickling. Irony is the sublime made safe: it enables us to rise above ourselves by witty self-contradiction rather than the violent self-obliteration effected by the sublime. The giddiness of irony – the dullard reels between seriousness and jest, Schlegel says, driven frantic by this vertiginous self-parody – comically miniaturises the overwhelmed dizziness of the sublime. Jean Paul uses a crooked line to symbolise the ridiculous, which for him is indefinable because it has as many forms as there are deformities. The straight line is unitary and single; but deviations from it are multitudinous. The serpentine indentations, backtrackings and elated swoops of the line of irony are a comic diminution of the jagged skyline of the sublime.

Heinrich Heine says that *Tristram Shandy* reveals the landscape of the soul, and despite its minuteness the spectacle is sublime.[9] Heights of elation and depths of gloom appear through the gap Sterne tears in the soul's integument. The view inside the mind is a view of infinity. Sublimity is the realm of enormity, irony of infinite littleness. But Hamlet finds in the cranial nut-shell a kingdom of infinite space, and like tragedy and comedy, or Jean Paul's orders of diurnal and annual necessity, the vast and the minute are opposites which romanticism equates. *Tristram Shandy* is similarly bifocal, sublime and ironic at once. According to Jean Paul's aesthetics, its garrulous vastness makes it a domestic epic, and its prolixity and prevarication are thus mock-sublime qualities. But this idyllic sprawl goes with a minutely riddled and conceited style and an agile technical self-contradiction which belong in the opposite realm of irony.

Here Fuseli's insects recur, for they are ironic images of

vicious littleness opposing and yet resembling the monstrous immensities of the sublime, like Burke's Alps. Fuseli's entomology repeats in miniature the sublime scientific discoveries of seventeenth-century astronomy. In the seventeenth century, the telescope revealed other and incomprehensible worlds beyond and above that inhabited by humans. In the eighteenth century, that discovery was repeated in miniature as the microscope made visible thronging, swarming worlds beneath the human (the Shandyean episode of the fly) as well as within it (Sterne's microscopic scrutiny of the details of motive and response). In various literary reviews, Fuseli uses insects to illustrate the minute deviousness of nature and the clumsiness of human classification of it.

Writing about J. C. Sepp's *Insects of the Netherlands* in the *Analytical Review* in March 1789, Fuseli points to the ichneumon-wasp as an image of the infinity of worlds and the invisibly small scale of nature: "what an idea of evanescent diminutiveness presents the egg of an animal destined to live, to feed, to grow to its full size, to pass through all its changes – within another egg more minute than a common pin's head!" Fuseli's insects belong in the microcosm of ideal smallness, an inversion of the sublime, which Jean Paul identified as the home of the ridiculous. They are humorous creatures because they are reminders of the relativity of our ideas about ourselves, because they mockingly diminish us by being as alert and alive as we are on a much more compact, concentrated scale, and they have an agility in fastening on their prey or in evading enemies which we lack.

The disparaging, belittling plague of insects appears in Fuseli's review of Coxe's *Travels in Switzerland*:[10] "The ant-hunter, the spider and the bee are surely as much nearer to man in the contrivance and instinctive power than the sheep or ass, as they are farther removed from him in organization and size. After the discoveries of the microscope, who can allow expression to a *horse* and refuse it to a *beetle*, or as author calls it, to a *cockchafer*?" Fuseli is claiming for insects the same independence of character Sterne accorded to the ass or Stubbs to the horse. But Stubbs ennobles his equine subjects, making epic protagonists of them; Fuseli's insects are prickly, tormenting satirists. Like the towering mountain peaks of Burke, they humble: "Man, formed for mediocrity, generally judges only from size; but size, whether immensely great or small, is a relative idea, and supposes somewhere an organ capable to judge of it." Human mediocrity is assaulted both from above and below, by giants and dwarfs, by the overwhelming terrors of Burke and the itchy annoyances of Fuseli's insect tribes. The two extremes, mountains and beetles, are linked by Sir William Hamilton in a communication of October 1770 to the Royal Society. Discussing the volcanoes of Etna and Vesuvius, he recommends an alteration of the scale of human study: the progress of natural history has been slow because scientists have "undertaken at once, to write the Natural History of a whole province, or of an entire continent; not reflecting, that the longest life of man scarcely affords him time to give a perfect one of the smallest insect".[11] The Johnsonian survey of mankind from China to Peru has been miniaturised.

Fuseli's satiric insects become, for his romantic successors, harmlessly provocative ironists. Heine uses an entomological image to characterise Jean Paul's jokes which, he says, hop excitably about like fleas battening on his over-heated intellect. Jean Paul himself describes the difference between jest and satire in terms of insect life: the one is a guileless silkworm's cocoon which flies off as a butterfly, the other a cancerous web in wait to catch a fly. The genres resemble the visionary insects with which Blake decorated his songs: the budding chrysalis of innocence, or the fly which as an unthinking fragment of sensuous life is set against the caterpillars of experience. Watching a child's funeral, Firmian Siebenkäs is moved by the sense of a life-cycle so abbreviated as to turn a human fate into that of Blake's fly or Fuseli's wasp. He imagines "the little, obscure, human creature, passing over from the foetal slumber to the slumber of death, from the amnion-membrane in this life to the shroud, that amnion-membrane in the next". But the dead child is granted a Blakean rebirth in vegetative form, like those winged children twining round vines in the songs: "these cut buds of this mould will find a stem on which great destiny will graft them, these flowers which . . . close in sleep while it is still early morning, will yet feel the rays of a morning sun which will open them once more".

Heine even treats Jean Paul's work as an image of the

generative process which Firmian imagines, arguing that Jean Paul's poetic births trail inordinate lengths of umbilical cord in which they eventually strangle themselves. The reason is that Jean Paul dramatises not thoughts but the activity of thinking or, differently put, not thought but brain. His narratives take place in the mental palace or memory-theatre described in the second chapter.[12] The comparison, however sardonically Heine intends it, also fits Sterne, who transforms the novel into an image of the soul's haphazard course from one amnion-membrane to the other. *Tristram Shandy* moves from the moment of conception by way of the fraught emergencies of delivery into a childhood in which difficulties with a top are considered to be spiritual auguries. (The children on Blake's echoing green have kites and bats instead of tops.) Tristram is an ironic counterpart to the Blakean children who grow in nature. Heine suggests some of his innocence by saying that Sterne, whom he casually mentions as the equal of Shakespeare, appears naked in his work, whereas Jean Paul only has holes in his trousers. The novel is about the spirit's zigzagging progress through the obstacle course of experience. It is a metaphysical version of the picaresque, in which the hero's journey ends not, as does Tom Jones's, in the confirmation of social position, but in the acquisition of an identity. This is why an incongruous sanctity surrounds Tristram, as it does the leech-gatherer, or Firmian, whom Liebgeber calls a transfigured being in boots. (The latter detail is subsequently corrected to shoes, because that sounds more sublime.) Tristram is the soul under the aspect of comedy, a "flower-polypus", as Jean Paul calls his Pauline, "stretching out eyeless, palpitating tentacula, from mere *instinct* towards the *light*", a silent soulflower of innocence contrasted with the prickly thorn-bushes of experience.

Tristram's inaction makes him an ironist. His refusal to grow and achieve confers on him that comic wisdom and incongruous sanctity which Heine admires and Jean Paul imitates. The same inaction makes him, later in the romantic century, a tragic character, at least according to Maeterlinck's symbolist redefinition of tragedy. Even the disarray and hasty randomness of his narrative finds a late-romantic justification in the criticism of Schopenhauer, who praises Tristram the incompetent novelist as a metaphysical initiate, a philosopher who perceives that sequential action is a fraud and scatters his novel in space rather than organising it in time as a protest against the illusion of ordered, responsible existence.

Maeterlinck's essay on "The Tragical in Daily Life", collected in the 1897 volume *The Treasure of the Humble*,[13] does not mention Tristram, but is all the same a symbolist apology for his prevarication and his suppression of action and incident. The essay approaches Sterne in its discussion of Hamlet, who has recurred throughout this book as Tristram's original and his protector, an ironist whose inaction makes him tragic. Maeterlinck insists on ridding tragedy of the rhetorical noise and violent action which defame it. Tragedy is to be made still and subdued, as whispered as a lyric, as inquisitively internal as a novel. The only Shakespearean hero to survive this symbolist transformation is Hamlet, for he already shares Maeterlinck's distaste for windy rhetoric and precipitate action. He is tragic because his mode is soliloquy not declamation, meditation not intrigue.

To Maeterlinck, tragedy seems crudely anachronistic. Its plots commemorate an age of feudal disturbance which the nineteenth century has outgrown. Arthur Symons in his essay of 1899 on Mallarmé[14] argues that plot itself is a vestige of intellectual infancy: "we have no longer the mental attitude of those to whom a story was but a story, and all stories good". Defending narrative in *Aspects of the Novel*, E. M. Forster sadly avows its primitivism: the novelist atavistically reassembles the circle of shock-headed savages round the campfire, "fatigued with contending against the mammoth or the woolly rhinoceros, and only kept awake by suspense". The romantic novel confounds narrative, telling stories backwards like Sterne, relaying them from one teller to another like Emily Brontë, endlessly repeating them like Browning, doubling them like Dickens in *Bleak House*. The tragic drama, in contrast, remains brutally primitive, as Maeterlinck says: husbands smother wives, sons avenge fathers, kings poison their rivals, virgins are assaulted.

From this point of view, Hamlet is at least the superior of the insanely jealous Othello, the brawling Lear, or the homicidal Macbeth. Maeterlinck justifies Hamlet's disdain for the revenge play: "I admire Othello, but he does not appear to me to live the august daily life of a Hamlet, who has the time to live, inasmuch as he does not act." Acting and living are now opposites, and acting one leaves to one's servants. The theatre is the province of bluff, hearty resolution and passions torn to tatters, of the rugged hyperbolical Pyrrhus. Living, however, is something more self-absorbed and confidential, which can be done only in the lyrical novel.

The theatre loves movement, but life as Maeterlinck conceives it is motionless. He argues that Aeschylean tragedy excludes movement, the mere temporary agitation of a crisis, in order to represent the slow, discreet, meditative flow of mental life. From this it follows that the beauty and greatness of true tragedies lies not in the actions which make up their plots but in the words. (This is a romantic vindication of the practice of extracting soliloquies from Shakespeare and treating them as arias, and also of Hamlet's cunning: he knows that the soliloquy is a form of interruption and postponement.) Words alone matter; but of those words, only the useless ones really matter, not set-piece soliloquies but asides, intimations, careless rumination. Necessary dialogue is superfluous, while superfluous dialogue is "the only one the soul can listen to profoundly, for here alone it is the soul that is being addressed". Although Maeterlinck finds this exemplified in the relationship between Ibsen's Solness and Hilda, he is in effect describing *Tristram Shandy*, in which the dialogue of people making efforts to engage one another or explain themselves creates merely pain and misunderstanding, and genuine intimacy is established only in casual remarks, ritual gestures and placid silences.

Sterne reappears, perceptively misinterpreted, in another late-romantic critical inversion of the literature of the past, Schopenhauer's essay on the comparative place of interest and beauty in works of art, collected in *Parerga and Paralipomena*.[15] Schopenhauer's category of interest is Maeterlinck's category of mere acting; his beauty approximates to Maeterlinck's living. The essay extends Schopenhauer's metaphysics into literature. Its assumption is that, if the world is no more than representation sustained by the fictionalising timidity of will, if realism is simply our attempt to convince ourselves that our flimsy surroundings have some substance, then literary narrative is exposed as a confidence trick of the chattering, mendacious will. Narrative preys on our interest in events in the hope of persuading us that life in linear, progressive, and reasonable. The subversion of narrative thus becomes a philosophical obligation: to refuse to act or to take part in or tell a story is to release oneself from the importunities and deceptions of the daylight world.

Schopenhauer's mystical objection to narrative provides a formula for rejoining the separate halves of Hamlet's character, his comic truculence and his moody lyricism. Seen in this way, his determination not to be an efficient revenger is an expression of his longing for a quietus, for the Schopenhauerian extinction of an irritatingly wakeful consciousness. Hamlet makes sure that his play is, in Schopenhauer's terms, non-interesting, a collapsed or unsatisfactory narrative, because in doing so he wins his freedom. Schopenhauer makes it a rule that Shakespeare's plays contain scarcely any appeal to the vulgar expectation of interest: "the action does not go forward in one straight line, but falters, as in *Hamlet*, all through the play", which is the serpentine uncoiling of *Tristram Shandy* as well. Otherwise, the action "spreads out in breadth, as in *The Merchant of Venice*, whereas length is the proper dimension of interest; or the scenes hang loosely together, as in *Henry IV*". One play torments its straight line into detours and reversals. The other upsets the most elementary assumptions of literature as a temporal rather than a spatial art, because it opens outwards rather than extending forwards, moving between Belmont and Venice. The third is a miscellany, introducing into art the dangerous, exhilarating principle of randomness. All three, as Schopenhauer interprets them, employ formal self-contradiction as a way towards metaphysical freedom.

From Shakespeare, Schopenhauer passes to Homer, who is also said to lack the instincts of a narrator, because he does not unpick complications of situation but meanders descriptively. The pictorial fixity of his work slows it down. For the romantics, landscape was an alternative to narration: landscape requires the depiction of an instant in space rather than a progress through time, and Schopenhauer ingeniously finds the same retardation in Homer, who "puts one picture after another tranquilly before us, elaborating it with care". Homer excites none of the restless emotion which Schopenhauer calls interest, but calms us into a state of "pure perceptive intelligence". Such knowledge precludes action, which it knows to be useless. Homer "does not arouse our will, but sings it to rest". Schopenhauer might be describing the love duet of Wagner's Tristan and Isolde, which derives from his metaphysics. There, will is inundated by music. Tristan and Isolde do not experience love as a vital principle attaching them to one another and to life, but as lassitude, separateness, a chaste communion of minds, not the urgent friction of bodies. Their story, thanks to Wagner's study of Schopenhauer, is perversely uneventful, non-interesting, a series of anti-climaxes. Isolde meekly agrees to be handed over to Marke moments after her declaration of love for Tristan, and fails to go to his aid when he is wounded. Tedium and repetition are essential to such a work, as they are to the processes of meditation, for in both cases they work to relax all demands on the world, to abandon the narrative sequence of consciousness and to experience thought as eternal repetition.

The man in the joke who went to sleep during the opening bars of *Tristan und Isolde*, then woke several hours later during the final bars only to hear the same themes, and sat up pleased that he hadn't missed a thing, was in this sense a perceptive critic. Nothing, and everything, had happened. The work does not develop, but recurs. Johnson made a similar point when he remarked that if you read Richardson for the story, you would end by hanging yourself. That suicidal end would be a comic parody of the initiation into mystic quiet which Diderot, as explained in the first chapter, felt to be the pastoral effect of Richardson. Johnson is too impatient, too querulously retentive of consciousness, to submit to the hypnosis. He experiences the monotony as a maddening frustration, not as a way towards enlightenment. He hangs himself rather than undergo conversion; he fails the work's initiation test.

Against the illusory continuity of narrative, Schopenhauer sets the alternative of clear-eyed random choice: "it costs no effort to break off in our reading, for we are not in a condition of eager curiosity". The work's spell can be dissolved at will, since its structure is not consecutive, like a narrative, but cyclical. The man sleeping through *Tristan* but missing nothing has as his counterpart the reader of *Tristram Shandy*, who is encouraged by Sterne's fragmentation of the text to read unchronologically. Wherever the book is opened, it will seem to be proceeding in the same inconclusive way, and as it leads nowhere it can also be closed arbitrarily with no sense of abruptness or dissatisfaction. It has created in us a comic anticipation of the uncaring detachment of Tristan and Isolde, who expect nothing of life and go through its motions with a weary, all-perceiving disdain.

Schopenhauer passes from Homer to Dante, whose work is not, he says, an epic but a descriptive poem. He leaves this point unexplained, but it is interestingly subversive. If seen as a narrative, Dante's poem follows the shape of the Christian idea of time, beginning in hell but moving upwards and ahead to the final conquest of paradise. But if it is a landscape, it impartially unfolds the parts of a triptych, which neutrally coexist in space rather than being ordered in time.

Having declared Shakespearean drama and Homeric and Dantesque epic to be forms which refuse to gratify our appetite for happenings, Schopenhauer names four novels which in his view also suppress interest as an offering to beauty. They are *Don Quixote*, *Tristram Shandy*, *La Nouvelle Heloïse*, and *Wilhelm Meister*, and "to arouse our interest is by no means the chief aim of these works; in *Tristram Shandy* the hero, even at the end of the book, is only eight years of age". Hamlet superintends the apprenticeship of Goethe's Wilhelm Meister as much as that of Tristram, and Aurelia, who plays Ophelia in the performance of *Hamlet* described in the novel, describes Wilhelm as a romantic only child, "the first large-born child of the Creation, standing agape", comprehending poetic mysteries yet awkward in ordinary social dealings, wiser and yet more naïve than his fellows, dim-sighted because his gaze is directed inwards. Her account could be transferred to Tristram who, as Schopenhauer's comment reveals, is determined not to grow up but crawls regressively back towards his conception and the complicated family arrangements before his birth.

Tristram's linguistic bewilderment is shared by another of

Goethe's characters, the waif Mignon. She learns slowly and understands little, can write only with extreme difficulty and speaks broken German, but finds release in the nonsensical realm of music, as Tristram does in the abstract area of marginal doodling or by juggling and conjuring with punctuation marks. Only in singing and playing her cithern does Mignon seem "to be employing an organ by which, in some degree, the workings of her mind could be disclosed and communicated". Ophelia also renounces speech for song, drama for lyricism, and the exchange is explained by Wilhelm when Aurelia objects to the lasciviousness of her songs: while Ophelia is a character in drama, she must keep her erotic longings secret, and with Laertes she is prim and reproving; but madness, removing her self-command and unlocking her consciousness, allows her the freedom of song in her lewd ballads.

Schopenhauer transforms *Tristram Shandy* from a narrative into a painting. Interest is a coarse literary quality, but beauty, static and contemplative, is pictorial. While narrative is turning into description, language, as the analogy with Mignon suggests, is turning into music. Like Mignon, Tristram is oppressed by language, and is grateful for the respite of silence or inarticulacy; and, as romanticism proceeds, his baffled intelligence finds a refuge in music. Miming the fluidity and perpetually recurrent inconsequence of consciousness, music offers Tristram a form in which he can think without ever needing to arrive at definite thoughts. His mental space of freedom is a landscape, but also a musical score. Sterne's adoption by German romanticism brings him into immediate contact with music: Mendelssohn mentions *A Sentimental Journey* in a letter to his sisters from Naples in May 1831.[16] He recalls that Goethe had said of the novel that no-one could better "paint what a froward and perverse thing is the human heart".

Sterne's fusion of tragedy and comedy resembles music's capacity to amalgamate opposite emotions: Jean Paul implies as much in calling a movement in his own narrative a modulation into the "remote key" of tender-heartedness. Hence Sterne is an unexpected but apt influence on Mahler, whose symphonies are ironically unstable compounds of tragedy and comedy, and whose musical thinking painfully intensifies the hectic, scrambled, self-questioning procedures of Tristram. The Mahlerian Tristram is the last and most cruelly self-divided of the character's romantic metamorphoses. He is no longer a glib virtuoso but a psychological victim, no longer the gambolling innocent of Jean Paul or Heine but a casualty of experience, wounded in body and mind. In Mahler, Tristram's conceited agility becomes an image of mental unsteadiness, his hobby-horses grim obsessions, his scurrility a symptom of the violent ugliness of the unconscious. Tragedy and comedy, which Tristram ironically equated, develop a mutual scornful distrust. Mahler's tragic despair is mocked by his comic inanity, his childish songs and brass-band fanfares; his beatific comedy, conversely, is interrupted by death and disaster. Tristram's acrobatic fusion of opposites, which hopes to extend human responsiveness and sentimentally reconcile us to ourselves and others, comes to represent in Mahler the schizophrenia of nature and the chaotic impropriety of the mind, in which birth and death, festivity and mourning, are indifferently twined together. Mahler told Freud that he owed this sense of the inextricability of pleasure and pain to an accident of childhood, which might be an incident from *Tristram Shandy*. When still quite young, Mahler rushed from the house during a terrifying quarrel between his parents, and found in the street a hurdy-gurdy churning out a popular song, "Ach, du lieber Augustin". Mahler's music revives the contradictions of that moment whenever a passage of noble suffering is invaded by a jaunty demotic tune. The double plot is in this case a clue to the artist's psychological history.

In his memoir of Mahler, the conductor Bruno Walter mentions the composer's affection for Jean Paul, whose Roquairol lies behind the "self-scourging scorn" of the funeral march in the first symphony.[17] Mahler considered Jean Paul's masterpiece to be *Siebenkäs* and was also drawn, Walter reports, to the nocturnal and demonic humour of Hoffmann. "*Tristram Shandy* was among his favourites, also because of its humour", which Mahler saw as an antidote to the otherwise intolerable tragedy of human existence. Before Tristram can inherit the burden of Mahler's metaphysical gloom he must be purged of his frivolity and indecency. Walter recalls that

Mahler loathed coarseness, and could only excuse that of Shakespeare, Cervantes and Sterne as an unfortunate affliction of their ages, refusing to recognise its essential relevance to their comic meaning. Too much now depends on Tristram to allow him to remain an idle, scabrous comedian: he must be made to grow up into an enlightened ironist.

The idiosyncratic Tristram is redeemed by romantic spirituality. Jean Paul and Heine convert his folly into sanctity, Maeterlinck and Schopenhauer transform his aesthetic irregularities into tokens of metaphysical wisdom, Mahler finds in the comedy of his calamitous life a parable of brave humorous defiance. The discovery of *Tristram Shandy*'s philosophical subtlety, and its translation into a sacred text of world-literature, may seem an elaborate and protracted misunderstanding; but the allegorisation of Sterne is a clue to the romantic sense of the shape of literary history, of the relations, inside that history, between the apparently antagonistic but twin genres of lyrical poetry and the novel, and of criticism's romantic duty to complete literature by making it conscious of itself and of its direction.

The extrapolations from *Tristram Shandy* reviewed in this chapter are important because they discern in Sterne's novel a model for the romantic literary future. According to one of Schlegel's *Lyceum* aphorisms in 1797, that future is to consist in a reconciliation of opposites, and he nominates the novel as the form in which the implications of romantic poetry will work themselves out. Romantic poetry is, he says, progressive and universal. It is imperialism in literature, charged with the mission of reuniting in itself all the hitherto separate genres of poetry, and of dissolving all formal barriers – between art and nature, between prose and poetry and criticism. *Tristram Shandy* accomplishes in advance both of these tasks. Its art is an image of nature: the first two chapters discussed its form as a representation of the mind; in this final chapter it has been treated as a representation of landscape. As well, it is prose, poetry and criticism at once. Tristram is drably prosaic, persecuted by material circumstance, unwound clocks or perilous sash-windows, but at the same time he is an exquisitely sensitive lyrical poet. Prose, in Jean Paul's terms, is his impending physical necessity, poetry his allowance of mental freedom.

Tristram makes no distinction between creation and criticism: his novel is about the difficult process of its own composition, and is preoccupied with the critical problem of self-interpretation.

One impulse of romantic art is, therefore, the desire to absorb and embrace everything: Schlegel's progressive universality. But romantic form always unites opposites, and Schlegel finds in conjunction with this imperial ravenousness another contrary impulse. For, while engulfing experience, romantic art also subdues itself to what it represents. It is egotistically sublime and negatively capable at once. The reason is that, while characterising poetic individuals of every type, the artist is actually doing the opposite and defining himself. Energetic extroversion is his mask for a moody introversion. Again Hamlet is a monitory figure, for Schlegel's paradox reveals the two sides of his character – the chatty, mobile, witty courtier, and the meditative alien – to be the same.

"Artists who only wanted to write a novel", Schlegel says, "have coincidentally described themselves."[18] That comment sums up a number of the identical opposites of this book – the contraction of the tragicomic society of Shakespearean drama into the novel's ironic mental solitude, discussed in the first chapter; the expansion of that narrow mental space into a capacious museum or palace of thought, discussed in the second chapter; Fuseli's transformation of illustrative commentary on the work of others into covert psychological self-portraiture, and of the epic substance of Milton into hazy metaphor. It catches the mystery of the romantic Shakespeare who, like a god in nature, is subjective in his studied objectivity, omnipresent in his enigmatic absence. Shakespeare's plays reveal the artist everywhere because he has so scrupulously eliminated himself from them. It explains the converse case of Sterne, who is everywhere in his work but, because of this officious, meddlesome omnipresence, never manages to compose his own *Life and Opinions*: never, indeed, succeeds in having a life (since, as Schopenhauer points out, he is still only eight years old as the work breaks off) or making up his querulous mind into an opinion.

This fusion of impersonality and subjective intimacy is

doubled by what Schlegel sees as the romantic ambition to join the opposites of epic and lyric. The theories of epic proposed by Jean Paul and Fuseli, discussed in the seventh chapter of this book, have a similar implication. Jean Paul transvalues epic into lyric. For him, epic's vast, leisurely proliferation is an image of lyrical self-immersion and procrastination. Fuseli presupposes an absolute opposition between the generic manner of epic and his own subjective, metaphoric art, but his illustrations to *Paradise Lost* find a subversive, diabolical lyric within the orthodox epic. Schlegel says that only romantic poetry can undertake the epic task of mirroring the entire world which surrounds it, describing the totality of its age. But it does so by becoming lyric: by refracting the world and the age through the medium of a single mind, as Coleridge intended in prescribing a universal education in sciences and humanities as the poet's preparation for the writing of an epic. The epic shield of Achilles has become the lyrical mirror of the Lady of Shalott, plaintively mediating its view of a world in which the poet is forbidden to participate: romanticism exponentiates poetic reflection and multiplies it in an infinite series of mirrors, Schlegel declares. It assembles a general view from a dispersed multitude of partial glimpses. *Tristram Shandy* would seem to be Schlegel's ideal romantic form, for it has the mental amplitude of epic within the concentration and pathetic obstruction of lyric.

Romantic art is massively solid in its epic absorption of the circumambient world, but at the same time weightless and unhampered. It can, as Schlegel says, soar on the wings of poetic reflection; but it lies between Ariel's kingdom of thought and Falstaff's domain of the body, at the ironic midpoint where tragedy and comedy meet. Only romantic art, for Schlegel, can be called free, because the imaginative arbitrariness of the poet will endure subjection to no law. It is, he concludes, the only genre of poetry which is more than a genre, and may be taken for poetry itself: but poetry with an obligation to expand into its opposite, to find its continuation in the novel. Sterne experiences this romantic freedom in advance as irresponsibility, its catastrophes as comic mishaps, its alarms of inspiration as the sudden glory of laughter.

Notes

1. Carlyle's translation of Goethe's *Wilhelm Meister's Lehrjahre* appeared in 1824 and has been reissued, with Carlyle's preface, by Collier Books, 1962.
2. Innes and Gustav Herdan have translated and introduced *Lichtenberg's Commentaries on Hogarth's Engravings*, 1966.
3. Sir William Hamilton's *Campi Phlegraei: Observations on the Volcanos of the Two Sicilies* appeared in 1776.
4. Vol. XX.
5. *Hinterlassene Schriften*, 1841, vol. I, p. 7.
6. See chapter 5, note 9.
7. See chapter 5, note 9.
8. Quoted in Alan B. Howe (ed.), *Sterne: The Critical Heritage*, 1974.
9. Heine's discussion of Sterne, from *Die Romantische Schule*, 1833, is included in Alan B. Howe (ed.), op. cit., pp. 449–50.
10. In *Analytical Review*, December 1789–January 1790.
11. See note 3.
12. Heine on Jean Paul quoted in Alan B. Howe (ed.), op. cit.
13. Trans. Alfred Sutro, 1911.
14. In Arthur Symons, *The Symbolist Movement in Literature*, 1899.
15. Arthur Schopenhauer, "On the Metaphysics of the Beautiful", 1851, chapter XIX of *Parerga and Paralipomena*, trans. E. F. J. Payne, vol. II, 1974.
16. 28 May 1831, *Letters from Italy and Switzerland*, trans. Lady Wallace, 1881.
17. *Gustav Mahler*, 1958.
18. In *Lyceum der schönen Künste*, see chapter 5, note 9.

Index